'*Research Methods for Sports Studies* has been my go-to text since I first started teaching undergraduate research methods to sport and leisure students. While research methods textbooks have burgeoned, I have continued to find this book really useful. The book has helped me to teach my undergraduate classes in a more practical and hands-on way, focusing on research as a process, using the suggested activities. Written in an accessible way, the book covers all of the essentials of both quantitative and qualitative research and demystifies the process of doing research. My students have found the explanations of positivism and the ways ontological and epistemological standpoints influence the methodological decisions they make accessible. Students embarking on their own research projects have also found the book helped to make the process less daunting. Now in its fourth edition, it includes some useful new sections and chapters such as the importance of social media, and its impact on various truth claims. It also comes with useful resources for time-pressed teachers.'

Belinda Wheaton, *Professor, School of Health, University of Waikato, Aotearoa New Zealand*

Research Methods for Sports Studies

Research Methods for Sports Studies is a comprehensive, engaging and practical textbook that provides a grounding in qualitative and quantitative research for students studying programmes related to sport and physical activity.

Leading the reader step-by-step through the entire research process, from identifying a research question and collecting and analysing data to writing and presenting the research report, the book is richly illustrated throughout with sport-related case studies and examples from around the world. *Research Methods for Sports Studies* is designed to be a complete and self-contained companion to any research methods course and contains a wealth of useful features, such as highlighted definitions of key terms, all-new case studies from active researchers and practical research exercises. Now in a revised and updated fourth edition, and in full colour for the first time, the book features expanded coverage of key topics such as online research, data visualisation, image analysis, source evaluation, mixed methods and the philosophical foundations of research. It also includes new material on the challenges of researching during a pandemic and reflects on the importance of diversity and inclusion, from feminist and indigenous methodologies to increased diversity of cases and researcher voices.

This is an essential read for any student undertaking a dissertation or research project as part of their studies in sport, exercise and related fields, including sport management, sport development, the sociology of sport, sport marketing, sport-related tourism, sport coaching, physical education and other similar degrees.

Additional online material is available for students and instructors, including web links, multiple-choice revision questions, PowerPoint slides and additional learning activities for use in and out of class.

Ian Jones is Associate Professor in Sport at Bournemouth University, UK.

Research Methods for Sports Studies

Fourth Edition

Ian Jones

Routledge
Taylor & Francis Group

LONDON AND NEW YORK

Cover image: Stanislaw Pytel / Getty Images

Fourth edition published 2022
by Routledge
2 Park Square, Milton Park, Abingdon, Oxon, OX14 4RN

and by Routledge
605 Third Avenue, New York, NY 10158

Routledge is an imprint of the Taylor & Francis Group, an informa business

First edition published by Routledge 2004
Third edition published by Routledge 2015

British Library Cataloguing-in-Publication Data
A catalogue record for this book is available from the British Library

Library of Congress Cataloging-in-Publication Data
Names: Jones, Ian, 1970- author.
Title: Research methods for sports studies / Ian Jones.
Description: Fourth edition. | Abingdon, Oxon ; New York, NY : Routledge, 2022. | Includes bibliographical references and index.
Identifiers: LCCN 2021042139 | ISBN 9781032049847 (hardback) | ISBN 9781032017525 (paperback) | ISBN 9781003195467 (ebook)
Subjects: LCSH: Sports—Research—Methodology. | Leisure—Research—Methodology. | Qualitative research.
Classification: LCC GV706.8 .G726 2022 | DDC 796.07—dc23
LC record available at https://lccn.loc.gov/2021042139

ISBN: 978-1-032-04984-7 (hbk)
ISBN: 978-1-032-01752-5 (pbk)
ISBN: 978-1-003-19546-7 (ebk)

DOI: 10.4324/9781003195467

Typeset in Sabon
by Apex CoVantage, LLC

Access the Support Material: www.routledge.com/9781032017525

Contents

CONTENTS

CONTENTS

Figures

Tables

Expert case studies

Preface

When the first edition of this book was published almost 20 years ago, its intention was very simple: To provide those new to research in sport with an accessible guide to undertaking the research process, from developing a question, to collecting data, to the final write-up of the research itself. Over time, that intention has remained unchanged, and this is reflected in the structure and content of the book, which is designed to be informative without being complex. Both teaching and learning about research methods can be challenging, and it can be all too easy to discourage those wanting to develop their research knowledge by over-complicating key ideas, identifying issues and putting up barriers to understanding. Hence the aims of the book are as follows:

1   To stimulate interest in sport research, to inform the student as to the importance of research in developing knowledge, and to encourage the student to both read further research and, more importantly, to carry out their own research into their own areas of sporting interest.
2   To act as a practical handbook for researchers. Rather than to be read in one go, the text acts as a resource that the researcher can refer to at different times during the research process.
3   To relate elements of the research process to actual examples of sport research, so that the theory introduced can be related to actual practice.

The intended audience for this edition also remains the same. Its primary audience will be students undertaking courses in sport-related studies, including sport management, sport development, the sociology of sport,

sport marketing, sport-related tourism, sport coaching, physical education and other similar degrees. The text may also be of interest to sport scientists looking to undertake research more focused in the social, rather than natural sciences. Finally, it may be of interest those working in the sport and leisure industries, where research may be a requirement of the position.

It isn't possible to separate a research-methods text from the field for which it is written, and there have been a number of developments in sport studies research since 2004. One key message that has always been central to the text is that there is no 'best' way of doing research, and it is pleasing to note that, since the first edition was published, there has been a clear (though not complete) trend towards acceptance, rather than derogation of alternative methods and approaches. (It seems hard to believe that at the time of the first edition there were still some questioning the role and quality of qualitative research, for example.) On the other hand, there have also been the negative impacts of research assessment exercises (such as the UK's *Research Excellence Framework*) and the rise of the 'portfolio' researcher, where we see greater number of academics publishing in varying, unrelated areas, resulting in a focus towards quantity rather than quality of research, and an emphasis upon superficial measures of 'success' (such as altmetrics). My advice to the reader of this book is to always aim for quality over quantity. This will always give you a better overall final product, whether it be a single dissertation or a more sustained research career.

Even if you are not looking to undertake future research yourself, there has never been a greater need for a more widespread understanding of 'research'. Another significant change within broader society since the first edition has been the growth of social media and its impact upon people's understandings of 'truth', perfectly illustrated by the plethora of COVID-19 related information, some of which was well argued, well supported and accurate, and much of which was inaccurate, poorly argued and often deliberately misleading. The pandemic has been a perfect example of why we all need an understanding of research, whether we are researchers or not. Only through developing such understandings will we be able to critically evaluate the vast amounts of information with which we are becoming increasingly subjected to on a daily basis, to evaluate its validity, and to understand its meaning.

The structure of the book

This book is based upon the concept of the 'research process'. While it could be argued that the conceptualisation of the research process presented here is perhaps too neat and tidy, and that 'real life' research rarely follows such a structured approach, it is nevertheless a useful framework upon which to develop an understanding of sport research. The first chapters introduce the concepts and traditions of research and are concerned with the underlying theory and philosophy of sport research. Chapter 1 introduces the concept of research and its role within sport studies. Chapter 2 outlines some of the differing approaches to the nature and acquisition of knowledge. Chapter 3 then introduces the concept of the research process, around which the remainder of the book is based.

The first stage of the research process is that of selecting an appropriate topic for investigation, and Chapter 4 outlines some of the strategies that can be used to identify and assess suitable research questions, aims and objectives. Chapter 5 introduces the concept of the literature review, the actual processes of finding and reviewing the literature, and writing this review in an appropriate format. Chapter 6 then introduces the importance of identifying the appropriate theories, concepts and variables within a research project. Chapter 7 describes some of the different designs you can use to carry out your research. Together, these first seven chapters provide you with the 'background' information essential to understanding the nature of research itself and the issues specific to the development of your own research project. The second part of the text is concerned with the issues related to actually undertaking a research project. Chapters 8–12 look at some of the data collection methods that you can use. I examine the use of questionnaires, interviews and unobtrusive methods in these chapters, and I introduce a particular methodological approach – that of sports ethnography – in Chapter 11 and the nature of online research in Chapter 12.

The third part of the book is concerned with the analysis of the data that you will collect and the reporting of the research. Chapter 13 outlines some of the techniques of analysing quantitative data and introduces a relatively new tool for data analysis – JASP – as a tool for the analysis of quantitative data. Chapter 14 describes how to analyse and make sense of the qualitative data that you may collect. Chapter 15 discusses putting it all together, in terms of writing up your research report. Chapter 16 is of interest for those undertaking research as part of a taught course, for example those undertaking a final-year dissertation as part of a degree course in sports studies, where some of the specific issues of student research are covered.

Using the book

It is likely that you will be using this book in one of two ways. First, you may be undertaking a research methods course as part of a wider programme in a sport-related subject. If so, the content of the book is designed to be roughly consistent with a typical teaching schedule (schedules will vary considerably; however, the content tends to remain relatively constant). In this case, you may well find yourself reading the book sequentially. Second, you may be using it as a handbook to assist you with an actual research project, in which case you may be more selective in your approach. For example, you may wish to read the chapter on student issues (Chapter 16) at an early stage.

Whatever your situation, I have provided a number of activities at the end of each chapter. The general activities will be suitable for those learning about research and will provide valuable experience of some of the elements of the research process. Other activities will be more appropriate to help you while you are actually carrying out the research, and these will help you in assessing your own research.

Finally, it is important that you view research as an opportunity, whether it is an opportunity to engage with an area that attracts you, an opportunity to develop your own interests, an opportunity for personal development, or even as a personal challenge that will test your abilities to the full. Whichever it is, I hope that you will enjoy the research process and be successful in your research career.

Ian Jones
Bournemouth University
June 2021

Acknowledgements

It's almost impossible to write acknowledgements without missing people out, so I apologise in advance to anyone I may inadvertently omit, or for the rather generic approach I have adopted to try and avoid this. Even though I was trying to avoid naming names, I would like to acknowledge the role of Simon Whitmore at Routledge, who has, since our first discussions about the text in 2002, been a constant source of guidance and enthusiasm for the project, and who has been central throughout its lifespan. Without Simon's support, there would never have been a first, let alone a fourth, edition.

I would also like to thank the reviewers who gave up valuable time to suggest improvements to this edition. I am sorry if I wasn't able to incorporate them all. One I did manage to make was to include a number of case studies from various authors worldwide, each of whom has really added value to the content, and I'm delighted that they were able to contribute in areas where their knowledge far outweighed my own.

The first edition emerged very much from a Leisure Studies Association conference, and I would like to thank the LSA for being such a positive association to be part of. The mix of scholarship and collegiality I have experienced there is a model for all academic associations.

Finally, I would like to thank colleagues and students at Bournemouth University, especially (but not only) those in the erstwhile School of Tourism, from whom I learned a great deal.

Chapter 1
What is research?

What is research?

This chapter will:

- Introduce the concept of 'research'.
- Discuss some of the reasons why we undertake research.
- Outline the different types of research.
- Describe how to approach the reading of research articles.

Introduction

Sport is an incredibly complex social institution. 'Few activities in the lives of ordinary people around the world bring together physicality, emotions, politics, money, and morality as dramatically as sport' (Besnier *et al.* 2018, p. 1). Forms of sport are played in every country in the world. Participants may range from multiple medal-winning 'super-elite' athletes performing in front of global audiences to one-off casual participants lacking any real competence. It may bring people together through shared sporting identities, but it can also be divisive, leading to violence and abuse, both on and off the field. It can be a force for social inclusion, as well as leading to social exclusion. The experiences of those involved may be overwhelmingly positive; yet for others, negative experiences may be the dominant outcome. The health benefits of sport are widely discussed, but less is made of the harmful consequences of participation. These are just some of the many complexities within the field, complexities that make it an incredibly rich and rewarding thing to understand more fully, whether as a coach, manager, educator, marketer, or any other sport-related professional.

DOI: 10.4324/9781003195467-1

We already know a lot about sport. The fact that you are reading this book suggests that you have an understanding of its varied nature, impacts and experiences, whether focusing upon factors that influence performance at an individual level, the relationship between sport and well-being, or the broader impacts of sport at a global level. Yet there is still more to find out. As with any social science, the study of sport involves the examination of constantly changing behaviours that take place within a largely unpredictable, complex and dynamic social environment. It is within this context that research becomes, as Daniel Wann (1997, p. 17) suggests, 'the lifeblood of any scientific discipline. Without it, disciplines would stagnate, failing to advance past their current limits and understanding'. Our understanding of sport is therefore never complete. The social context within which sport takes place is always changing, whether as a result of long-term trends related to race, gender, or ethnicity, or more seismic occurrences, such as the COVID-19 pandemic. Thus, our knowledge is never absolute, and it is only through continual research that our understanding of sport continues. This understanding, in turn, informs future teaching and practice.

Research is not only for academia, however, and the skills associated with research are important not only for those wishing to publish in academic journals or to write a dissertation. There are countless professions where a knowledge and understanding of research methods is important. Those employed in the sport marketing industry, for example, may need to be able to assess the effectiveness of a particular promotional strategy or understand the process by which sport consumers adopt a new product. Sport development officers may need to assess the reasons for non-participation in physical activity by members of a particular community. Coaches may wish to identify the impact of a change in leadership style upon team cohesion. Governments may wish to measure the impacts of a pandemic upon the physical health of the population, and so on.

Finally, undertaking research also helps you develop more generic skills such as critical thinking, the ability to understand the importance of data to draw conclusions and the ability to communicate ideas to a wider audience, skills that are increasingly important in any context, but particularly so in contemporary society. A crucial skill you can develop is the ability to assess concepts such as 'truth' or 'facts'. On a daily basis, we are fed such 'facts' through social media. An understanding of research is crucial in being able to assess the validity of the claims that are made and to be able to critically evaluate the information we receive on a continual basis is something that is essential within the post-truth era.

The characteristics of research

Leedy (1985) and Walliman (2001) note a number of characteristics of research. These include the following:

- Research is generated by a specific research question, hypothesis, or problem.
- Research follows a specific plan or procedure – the research process.
- Research is empirical – it aims at increasing understanding by interpreting evidence and reaching conclusions based on that evidence.
- Research requires reasoned argument to support conclusions.
- Research is reiterative – it is based on previous knowledge, which it aims to advance, but it may also develop further research questions, which in turn are answered by further research.

Research is therefore more than just searching for facts. Many people associate research simply with methods of data collection such as interviews and questionnaire surveys. Such data collection is just one part of a wider process, however, and other parts of this process are equally important. Six general stages can be identified:

1   Developing the idea, where you need to decide upon the research question, the aim of your research, the research objectives and, in most cases, the theoretical framework that underpins the research.
2   Planning the study, identifying what data are needed to answer the question, choosing a research design, identifying which methods will provide such data and where the data is obtained.
3   The actual data collection stage, where your data are collected by one or more research methods.
4   The analysis of the data – organising and explaining the findings with reference to previous work, and the theoretical framework adopted, or the generation of new theory.
5   Drawing appropriate conclusions, acknowledging both the strengths and limitations of the research and identifying further questions that emerge.
6   The reporting of the research to communicate the findings to others.

These are all part of what can be termed the *research process*. The research process refers to the various parts of the overall process that guides a research project. This will be dealt with in more depth in Chapter 3.

Why undertake research?

As I have already suggested, much of our knowledge about sport is based upon research carried out by others. By undertaking systematic investigation into certain areas, we have increased our knowledge about sport dramatically in recent years and can also maintain such understanding in a rapidly changing environment. The ways in which knowledge can be advanced by research are outlined by Hussey and Hussey (1997), who summarise the different purposes of research as follows:

- To investigate some existing situation or problem.
- To provide solutions to a problem.
- To explore and analyse more general issues.
- To construct or create a new procedure or system.
- To explain a new phenomenon.
- To generate new knowledge.
- A combination of two or more of any of these.

Each of these can be fruitfully applied to many different aspects of sport. A further – and equally valid – purpose of research is to allow you to engage with an aspect of sport that interests you, so that you can add to existing knowledge as a personal achievement. Carrying out research into a specific area is one of the best ways to develop your own understanding of a particular area of interest. Finally, you may also wish to enhance your employment prospects in a particular area of sport. Undertaking a detailed piece of research, for example in the form of a dissertation, is often a good way to convince an employer that you have the interest, competence and ability to undertake sustained independent study in a certain area.

 KEY TERM

ACADEMIC JOURNAL

Reading journal articles is a good way to develop a broader understanding of what research actually is. Although the term *journal* may describe a number of different types of publication, I will generally be referring to academic peer-reviewed journals within this text. Academic journals are generally published several times a year and report the most up-to-date research on a particular discipline or area of interest, such as the economics of sport or sport marketing. Most academic journal articles have undergone some form of peer review process, whereby the quality and rigour of each article is assessed by a number of reviewers, each of whom will be an expert in their field. This ensures that the articles within such a journal are of an appropriate standard. Some relevant sport-related journals include:

- *Sociology of Sport Journal.*
- *Journal of Sport Management.*

- *Journal of Sport Behavior.*
- *Journal of Sport and Social Issues.*
- *Journal of Sport and Tourism.*
- *International Review for the Sociology of Sport.*
- *European Journal of Sport Management.*
- *European Sport Management Quarterly.*
- *Sport Management Review.*
- *Sport in Society.*
- *Qualitative Research in Sport, Exercise and Health.*

This is not an exhaustive list, and there are also a number of non-sport-specific journals that publish sport-related articles, so you shouldn't focus entirely on the ones listed here. In addition, you should not restrict yourself to journals published in your home country, but remember that there are high-quality sport journals based all over the world, all sources of high-quality research.

The different types of research

There are a number of different ways of classifying research, depending upon the purpose of the research, the data that are collected and how such data are analysed. You don't need to get too concerned with this typology when developing your research question, but it's useful to have a broad understanding of the different types.

Exploratory research

Exploratory research takes place where there is little or no prior knowledge of a phenomenon. Thus, there is a need for an initial exploration before more specific research can be undertaken. This type of research looks for clues about the phenomenon, attempts to gain some familiarity with the appropriate concepts and looks for patterns or ideas emerging from the data without any preconceived ideas or explanation. An example of this would be the study of Hing *et al.* (2014), who investigated the impact of gambling promotions during televised sports events upon subsequent gambling intentions of young people, an area where there had been little prior research, or the exploratory study of Guicciardi and Pazzona (2020) to examine how people responded to the new norms of physical activity post-COVID-19 in Italy. The nature of exploratory research means that overly rigid research questions or hypotheses are inappropriate, and often the direction of the research will emerge as the study progresses. Exploratory research is often followed up by further research that tests any initial conclusions that are generated.

Descriptive research

Descriptive research describes a particular phenomenon, focusing upon the issue of what is happening, or how much of it has happened, rather than why it is happening. The study of Martinent *et al.* (2012), for example, which described the differences in the frequency, direction, duration and co-occurrence of emotions among table-tennis players, was a good example of this, as was Hanni *et al.*'s (2020) study to determine how many Swedish soccer players had experienced a soccer related concussion in their playing careers. With descriptive research, there is generally less focus on explaining the results obtained. Descriptive research is often used quantitatively to track changing patterns of sport, such as monitoring participation over time, or to assess or evaluate the outcome of something, such as an economic impact study of a mega event, or as is often the case with qualitative research, to present a 'rich' evocative picture of an aspect of sport to the reader, such as Gwartz and Spence's (2020) rich description of how sport employees espoused their organisation's 'higher purpose'.

Explanatory research

This type of research is involved in explaining why something happens, often assessing causal relationships between variables or the impacts and effects of a phenomenon. Thus, a researcher interested in why sport advertising might lead to body image concerns in adults would be undertaking explanatory research. The study of Scelles *et al.* (2013), which developed an explanation of the factors affecting attendance in French Ligue 1 football, is an example in that it sought to explain *why* people attended matches. Explanatory research requires some sort of theoretical framework so that explanation may be deduced from the data (theoretical and conceptual frameworks are discussed in more depth in Chapter 6). Explanatory research allows us also to forecast future phenomena, based on the explanations we generate.

Pure and applied research

Each of the types of research I have identified thus far can also be placed on a continuum between pure and applied research, depending upon its context. At one end of the continuum, pure research takes place to explore a particular concept or issue, without regard for a specific problem, and may be carried out to simply gain a better understanding of the overall concepts, for example the development of a general model of coaching behaviour. Such research in itself has no immediate value beyond contributing to an area of intellectual inquiry. Applied research, on the other hand, is undertaken to solve a specific problem or provide a solution to a practical question. An example of this may be a particular sport organisation that wishes to explore potential markets and commissions research to determine demand for a sport-related service or product, or research to explain why individuals drop out from a particular fitness programme after a short period of time. Closely related to the idea of applied research is the concept of action research, which uses a cycle of 'action', research into the effects of the action, critical reflection and refinement to understand the impacts of the initial action, for example Hoskyn *et al.*'s (2018) study of the 'action' of hosting tennis tournaments upon leveraging subsequent participation.

Primary and secondary research

There is also a distinction that can be made between primary and secondary research. *Primary research* refers to research that has involved the collection of original data specific to that particular project, for example through using research methods such as questionnaires or interviews. *Secondary research* refers to research where no such original data are collected, but the research project uses existing (or secondary) sources of data, for example census or archive data, or data that have been collected for another study but that can be reanalysed to answer a different research question. An example of this can be seen in the study of sport policy impact on the sustainability of community sport programmes by Ikramullah *et al.* (2018), who used monitoring data that had already been collected from 45 different community programmes that was subsequently made available to the public. Often there is confusion between secondary data and the literature review, and students will often say that they used secondary data in the form of a literature review, but they are different things.

Theoretical and empirical research

It is also possible to distinguish between theoretical and empirical research. Theoretical research generally uses the findings from existing works to develop new insight, theory and explanation. These new ideas are not tested through collecting evidence in the form of primary data, but instead they focus on the theory itself. Empirical research, on the other hand, supports the development of new ideas through the collection and analysis of data, and the research is 'data driven' (*empirical* means based upon observation or measurement rather than theoretical reasoning). Thus, a researcher who develops a theory of sport fan violence through visiting a library and developing their own explanation through reading existing work will be undertaking theoretical research. The researcher who takes this one step further and collects data to test their explanation will be undertaking empirical research. Although theoretical research has its merits, I would suggest that you should – if possible – support your findings empirically through the collection of primary data.

Disciplinary approaches to sport research

It is also worth introducing the idea of disciplines at this stage, and the range of disciplines within which sport research is undertaken (I discuss this in

Chapter 6 as well). A discipline focuses upon a particular way of looking at a subject using its own distinctive theories and explanations, such as the disciplines of history, education, geography and economics. Sociology, for example, focuses upon our behaviour as social beings, and the impact of social forces upon the way we behave, whereas psychology focuses upon the mind, its associated mental functions and their impact upon behaviour and performance. 'Sport' itself is not a discipline as such (calling it a 'field' would be more accurate), but it is studied within a range of disciplines, for example sport psychology, or the sociology of sport. It is a good idea to identify your disciplinary approach, as it will help guide you through the various approaches associated with that discipline and also help you with finding relevant literature in your area. Sometimes this will be clear. If you are reading this book while undertaking a sport psychology degree, for example, then your discipline will be psychology. Sport management students will generally study a variety of clearly defined disciplines, such as economics, marketing or strategic management. If you are undertaking a programme in 'sport studies' or 'sport coaching', however, then your chosen research discipline may be less clear.

You may also come across terms such as *multidisciplinary* (approaching your research from two or more disciplines), *cross-disciplinary* (using approaches from other disciplines to inform your own approach) and *interdisciplinary* (where your approach does not fit into a specific discipline but generally takes elements, theories and approaches from varied disciplines to create an approach that crosses traditional disciplinary boundaries). If you are considering such an approach, you may want to read, for example, Doherty's (2013) paper exploring the possibilities and challenges of this approach. There is often the assumption that these three approaches are stronger than research from a single discipline, which somehow makes them always preferable; but in reality multi/cross/interdisciplinary work can be done poorly, and research from a single discipline can also be excellent. As always (and a key message that runs throughout this book), the approach should relate to the research itself, and different research projects may suit different approaches, rather than there being a single 'best' approach.

 KEY TERM

DISCIPLINE

A discipline refers to a particular approach to the study of an aspect of sport, and the approaches, techniques and theories used to study and explain that particular aspect. Thus, sociologists are interested in the relationship between sport and society, and they have developed particular sociological theories to explain sport behaviour. The discipline of psychology, however, is more interested in intrinsic influences upon sports behaviour. Each discipline will have a number of sub-disciplines, so sociology, for example, would encompass feminist sociology, cultural studies and so on. Understanding your 'home' discipline is helpful in guiding your approach, finding literature and understanding the methods associated with that discipline.

Some misconceptions about research

As well as being able to define what is meant by research, it is also useful to describe some of the misconceptions often associated with the term. For example:

1   Research in the way that I have conceptualised it is not simply the gathering of existing information. Reading an article on the economic impacts of major sporting events and making notes is not research. Neither is collecting existing information to write an essay or paper on the economic impacts of the Summer Olympics. Gathering existing information is simply one part of the wider research process.

2   Nor is research simply the collection of new data. You may be interested in the reasons why individuals take up competitive tennis. Simply going to a tennis club and asking them is not research. Again, this is simply one part of a broader process.

3   Research is not setting out to prove an opinion, based on personal experience. For example, if you do not attend major sporting events because of ticket prices and decide to set out to prove that ticket prices are the most important deterrent to attendance, you are not carrying out research.

4   Research is not the production of something completely original. Often students are daunted by the suggestion that they are required to produce some original findings, and they often overestimate what is meant by 'original'. Even at the highest academic level, there are very few 'breakthrough' pieces of research within the social sciences, and even in peer reviewed journals, there are many examples of what I would call 'rearranging knowledge'. Most research involves adding to existing knowledge, rather than creating new knowledge, for example the testing of existing theories on new situations, which would still produce original findings. Hence even much of the work that has recently been done on the impacts of COVID-19 on sport has built upon existing theories and ideas about sport participation. The production of a significant level of original knowledge is generally a requirement only of postgraduate degrees such as MPhil or PhD.

5   Research does not always involve a problem. Many textbooks – including this one – do use the term *research problem*. Although research often involves the solving of a problem, it can, as is often the case in theoretical research, simply be done to advance the scope of human knowledge or to explore an issue where the researcher has a personal interest.

Understanding sport research

By far the best way to begin to develop your initial understanding is to read a variety of actual research located in sport-related journals. While research textbooks will provide the necessary theoretical grounding, Worsley (1992, p. 79) notes that they do tend to 'present an unreal and idealised account of research'. He goes on to suggest that:

> The best way to learn about research methods, apart from conducting research under supervision, is also, alas, the one requiring most effort. Most students . . . reading a book or article pay most attention to the theories or concepts used and the overall argument, some attention to the actual substantive findings, and very little heed to the methods used. This is particularly so if the results are statistical or presented in tabular form. Yet simply paying more attention to how a study was done, what the substantive results were, and assessing whether they support the conclusions, will teach more than reading a dozen texts.

The suggested activity at the end of this chapter involves you reading and assessing some sport research. This is an activity that should not just be done once you have read this chapter, but you should ensure that reading and evaluating research is done on a continual basis. You will find that, as your research knowledge increases, you will be able to evaluate the research more confidently, assess the methodologies and methods adopted, and be able to identify the strengths and weaknesses within a piece of research. At first, this may seem a difficult and daunting task, especially if you are reading research undertaken by experts in a particular field. You should persevere, however, as the benefits will be worthwhile. Try not to be put off by barriers such as complex statistical analyses, or by the seemingly impenetrable academic writing that is often used (especially in some of the more sociologically based pieces of research). You should try initially to find some less complex articles, especially if the research is in an area with which you are not overly familiar, and focus on the points outlined in the following text.

How to read research

As I suggested earlier, you may find reading research articles a difficult task at the beginning of your research career. Thomas and Nelson (2010) and

Baker (1994) provide a few useful pointers to bear in mind while you are reading a piece of research:

1 Locate and read articles from an area you are comfortable with. By doing this, the concepts involved and the technical language often used may not be as big a stumbling block as otherwise may be the case. It is also more likely that you will be able to understand the overall aims of the research.

2 Read studies that are of interest to you. Do not feel obliged to read through every article at first. Neither should you be afraid to stop reading after you have started if the article is not of interest – do not attempt to plough through it! Think of the areas that you enjoy, and focus on them at the beginning. If you have decided to focus on sociological research, and you have an interest in the Olympics, for example, then search for articles related to the sociology of the Olympic Games. If you play a particular sport, then search for articles on an aspect of that sport. Use your personal experiences and interests to guide you.

3 Read the abstract first. The abstract will help you decide whether the article is relevant without having to read the entire paper. If the article doesn't seem of interest after you have read the abstract, then move on to another article.

4 Identify the research question and objectives. Is the research question a clearly defined hypothesis or a more open area for investigation? What is the overall aim of the research? What about the objectives? Why is it important that this topic is researched?

5 Consider the setting of the research or the sample chosen. Where were the data collected? Who from? If a particular sample was chosen, such as children, or the elderly, then can you relate that choice to the overall research question? What were the strengths and/or limitations of this choice?

6 Evaluate the methods chosen to collect data. Were, for example, people interviewed, given a questionnaire or observed online? Why was this method (or methods) chosen?

7 Identify the most important findings made by the author and the contribution to knowledge or understanding that the research has made. Who are the findings important to, and why? Do the findings suggest any further research that should be undertaken?

8 Try to identify the impact of the research. Who would benefit from the findings, and why?

9 Do not be over-concerned with how the data were analysed at this stage. If you have a paper with statistical analysis, for example, do not pay too much attention to what tests were used and the level of significance at first. This can come later as your understanding progresses. Try simply to determine the general meaning of the results.

10 Finally, be critical but objective. You may find it difficult to evaluate the research critically, especially considering that it is likely that the reviewing process adopted by most journals would screen out most examples of questionable research. Try to assess, however, the strengths and limitations of the research. What would you have done differently, if anything?

KEY TERM

ABSTRACT

Research reports often commence with an abstract. The abstract is a short section, generally of about 150–250 words, outlining the aims of the research, the background to the study, the methods employed to collect data, the sample from which the data were collected and a summary of the main conclusions and the contribution of the research to knowledge or understanding. Abstracts allow researchers to identify whether a piece of research will be valuable in their own studies without having to read the entire article.

The second way of learning about research is to undertake it yourself. This is especially useful if, for example, you are to undertake a one-off piece of important research, such as a final-year undergraduate or postgraduate dissertation. Try to undertake a small research project beforehand, ideally during your training in research methods, so that you do not approach your research 'cold', but with some awareness of the research process, its potential pitfalls and the time and effort required to undertake a research project.

Summary
- There are a number of definitions of research. Defining research is perhaps less important than understanding its nature.
- Research is important for the advancement of any academic field or discipline.
- Research can be classified as exploratory, descriptive or explanatory, depending upon its purpose. It can also be classified as either theoretical or applied, depending upon the level of application of the findings to 'real-life' situations.
- Research may involve the collection of new data (primary research) or the use of existing data (secondary research).

- The best way to begin to develop your understanding of research, its role and the types of research is to undertake some reading. Choose some appropriate articles, and begin to read!

Activity

You should familiarise yourself with the key academic journals in your area of interest. If you are interested in sport management, for example, ensure that you locate and read at least one article from the *European Sport Management Quarterly*, *Sport Management Review*, *Qualitative Research in Sport, Exercise and Health* or any other appropriate journal. When you have located an article that you are comfortable with, read it bearing in mind the questions outlined under 'How to read research'.

You should also begin a research diary. In this diary you should be recording everything of importance to your own research, from your initial ideas to contact details of potential informants. Such a diary can be an extremely useful resource, and you should ensure that it is as detailed as possible. Some of the things you may include in such a diary are:

- Summaries of your meetings with tutors/supervisors.
- Ideas relevant to the research, for example in terms of potential information sources or possible directions for the research.
- Problems that have arisen and ideas as to how to deal with such problems.
- Short- and long-term objectives.
- General thoughts about the research process.

Further reading

Rather than suggest any particular reading for this chapter, the activity should be sufficient. At this stage, however, you should also be reading around your own subject area and beginning to develop a few ideas about your own research. Make sure you record these in your research diary!

Chapter 2
Research traditions in sport

Research traditions in sport

This chapter will:

- Outline the general philosophical approaches underlying the research process, explaining what is meant by ontology and epistemology, and the various standpoints that exist when considering the nature of knowledge and understanding.
- Describe the characteristics of (and relationships between) qualitative, quantitative, mixed methods, and deductive and inductive research.

Introduction

In Chapter 1, I suggested that one of the aims of sport-related research is to advance our knowledge of the field. This raises a question of what we mean by 'knowledge' and helps the reader understand that the nature of any knowledge gained is inextricably tied to the beliefs and actions of the researcher and the audience rather than being a single concrete 'truth'. This can be illustrated with a question continually asked amongst sport fans: Who is the greatest athlete of all time? Could we compare, for example, Muhammed Ali, Tiger Woods, Michael Schumacher, Serena Williams and Usain Bolt? There are several ways we could do this. One way might be to measure achievements such as career earnings and titles won, and develop a statistical model to give a single objective (some might say 'scientific') answer. Another way might be to interview sport fans for their opinions and explore their various subjective viewpoints, giving a wide range of responses,

DOI: 10.4324/9781003195467-2

reflecting the feelings of each fan. Each of these approaches takes a different view of what 'knowledge' is, and how to gain such knowledge, and hence gives us different answers to our original question, none of which we can say are right or wrong. How we think about knowledge is the branch of philosophy called *ontology*, which is the study of what knowledge actually is, and this is closely related to *epistemology*, which is the philosophical study of how such knowledge is acquired. So ontology would explore the nature of greatness in sport, and the extent to which it is 'real', objective and measurable, and epistemology would explore how we find out who is the greatest athlete. Hence, ontology and epistemology are strongly linked to each other and to how we understand any knowledge gained through research. Although you may think that such philosophical debates may lack immediate relevance to your own research project, an awareness of ontology and epistemology is important for three key reasons:

Firstly, the issues related to the differing philosophical approaches are important to some extent in all research that you will encounter, even if they are not explicitly referred to. Thus, a broad ontological and epistemological awareness is important so that you have a framework within which you can understand the assumptions inherent in the different research that you will read, the position of the researcher, their key decisions during the research process and how they analyse, interpret and discuss their findings.

Secondly, your research will be influenced by your own prior beliefs as a researcher, and by understanding this (as well as making these beliefs clear in your research), your research is strengthened. A researcher with a realist ontology, who would believe in a single reality, for example, may see the sporting world as rational, objective and independent of those who inhabit it, and seek a single 'truth'. Another researcher who favours a relativist ontology may see it as a social construction of individuals who create and make meaning of that world, and that the 'truth' is relative to whoever is experiencing that world at a particular time. By acknowledging ontological and epistemological concerns, the researcher in each case can ensure coherence between how the research is carried out in terms of questions asked, approaches to and methods of data collection and analysis, and the drawing of conclusions. Such coherence is a key characteristic of high-quality research.

Thirdly, if you do not have any prior beliefs about the nature of knowledge, an understanding of ontology and epistemology may help you to determine the most appropriate design to answer your research question. Thus, if you are interested in understanding the subjective experiences of individuals, then this might lead you to an appropriate approach. If, however, you are interested in describing, comparing or measuring, or researching a well-established concept, then an alternative approach may be more appropriate. Hence ontology and epistemology do not always have to precede the research question; instead they can equally be explored once the research question has been identified.

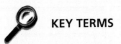

KEY TERMS

ONTOLOGY AND EPISTEMOLOGY

Ontology refers to the philosophy of the existence and nature of phenomena. Is knowledge a 'thing' that can be observed, or is it something that is experienced? You might, for example, be thinking about doing a study on coach effectiveness. What is the study actually about? Is it about the observable, measurable performance of the team or the experiences of those being coached, experiences that are constructed at the individual, subjective level? Each concept will have a different ontology, and your answers to these types of question will form your ontological position.

Epistemology ('the study of knowledge') is the branch of philosophy that deals with how knowledge of such phenomena is acquired and what counts as knowledge. Thus, are the perceptions of the players actually evidence that can be used to answer the question? Or would some form of objective measurement be more appropriate? These are issues of epistemology.

The nature of knowledge

By looking at ontology and epistemology together, we can see a number of ways to approach our research. Firstly, we can examine the idea of ontology. There are two basic positions: realism and relativism. A realist would see the social world as something ordered, logical and objective that can be explored through observation and measurement to find a single reality, for example the idea that we can define the greatest athlete of all time by how successful they were during their career. This can be contrasted with a relativist approach, which would argue that what is 'real' is subjective, depending upon who experiences it, with no single 'truth', and that fans would each conceptualise and experience greatness differently.

Secondly, we can look at things from an epistemological perspective. Again, I will put forward two contrasting positions. The first is objectivism. This suggests we can make observations about our area of interest, collect objective data and answer the question accordingly to give a single 'truth'. Hence, we can measure the number of career titles to give a single, incontrovertible answer to our question. A subjective approach, on the other hand, would argue that individuals create their own reality, and that rather than seek a single truth, researchers have to construct an impression of the social world as seen by each individual. Thus each fan would construct their own view of greatness, as the emphasis is to present the reality of the individual, not of the broader aggregated social world. This approach tends not to give a single answer; indeed, it may well produce divergent findings.

Table 2.1 Approaches to research

	Ontology	
Epistemology	Realist	Relativist
Objective	Positivism	
Subjective	Post-positivism	Interpretivism
	Critical realism	

When we look at these together, we get a number of broad philosophical standpoints as outlined in Table 2.1 (note that a relativist/objective combination is a contradiction, and hence doesn't exist): Each has differing epistemological and ontological assumptions, and each has differing implications for the types of research questions that are asked, the subsequent methodology adopted, the nature of the data that are collected, and the analysis and interpretation of such data.

Positivism

Positivism is a realist, objective approach that suggests that the only 'true' or valid form of knowledge is that which is 'scientific', that is where the principles and methods of the natural sciences (such as chemistry or physics) are used to study human behaviour, which in itself is objective and tangible in nature. In the same way that a chemist can observe the effect of adding one chemical compound to another, make precise observations or measurements and develop laws of nature, the social researcher can observe human behaviour and measure 'facts', and 'laws' or theories of behaviour can be developed. These 'laws' could then be applied to other contexts to explain or predict future behaviour. (One of the early goals of sociologists was to be able to develop a number of such laws that would one day be able to predict all aspects of human behaviour.) Positivists would assume that the sport environment is relatively stable across different times or settings. Within such a stable context, the precise measurement and analysis of observable, concrete and real 'facts' allows the development of theories, which can then be tested through further measurement. Measurements themselves should be objective and not subject to the influence of the researcher's values or interpretation; others could see the same evidence and reach the same conclusions based on that evidence. This approach to obtaining knowledge involves precise measurements, which can be controlled or manipulated by the researcher. Such exact measurement allows statistical analysis that provides an impartial and precise answer. Finally, the whole process of investigation is objective: The researcher has no influence on the findings. Concepts such as feelings, emotions or beliefs have a limited place in research as they cannot be directly observed or measured, and they are not constant over time. Such an approach has a number of characteristics, including:

- *Control.* The researcher is able to control one variable and assess the influence that it has on another variable, for example the presence of a crowd upon shooting performance in a particular sport. The researcher can control the size of the crowd, measure both the crowd size and performance, and draw inferences from the data.
- *Replication.* To explain a phenomenon, the same results would need to occur if the experiment were to be repeated – that is, an increase in crowd size would always lead to a decrease in performance.
- *Hypothesis testing.* Positivistic research generally involves the creation of a hypothesis, which can then be systematically tested.

The positivist approach has its undoubted strengths, notably in terms of precision, control and objectivity. Through precise control and measurement, objective information is created, which can then be subject to statistical analysis, removing the need for intuitive interpretation. As a result, 'scientific' conclusions can be drawn.

 KEY TERM

HYPOTHESIS

Generally associated with quantitative research, a hypothesis is essentially a predicted result based on existing knowledge that can be tested through the collection of data. For example, a hypothesis may be that 'Higher income is positively related to higher participation levels in outdoor sports'.

As well as a hypothesis, research projects will also present a null hypothesis. A null hypothesis suggests that there is no relationship between the variables under investigation. It is the null hypothesis that is tested by statistical analysis. (Chapter 13 will examine this issue in more depth.)

Post-positivism

Post-positivism is an approach closely aligned to, and generally not considered completely distinct from, positivism (Brustad 2002). Indeed in Table 2.1, it probably straddles the line between objectivism and subjectivism. The first of the general tenets of post-positivism is that it is, in reality, not possible to gain a truly objective understanding through measurement and observation, such as advocated by a totally positivist stance, and that there are limitations inherent within an approach that attempts complete objectivity that need to be recognised, such as the influence of the researcher and their own values and biases. Second, there is a rejection of dualistic thinking in terms of things being either subjective or objective, or correct or incorrect, and acknowledging the complexity of the subject under investigation. Third, post-positivism is characterised by the researcher adopting a 'learner role', learning with and about participants, rather than adopting a 'tester role', as is the case with hypothesis-driven research. Finally, post-positivist approaches are characterised by a much greater openness to different methodological approaches and will often include qualitative as well as quantitative methods, with a greater emphasis upon the use of multiple methods to look at a single phenomenon using a variety of means.

Critical realism

Emerging from post-positivism and becoming increasingly used within sport research, critical realism refers to approaches that take elements from positivism and interpretivism whilst attempting to overcome the weaknesses of each. It acknowledges that there are objective realities that can be observed but accepts that a positivist approach may not be suitable to understand such realities. Equally, it argues that the focus of interpretivist research upon subjective experience and multiple realities lacks usefulness in, for example, firstly acknowledging that things exist outside our experiences of them, and secondly defining why things happen, thus suggesting that there is, in fact, a social reality to be examined that is external to and independent of the individual. With a focus upon four levels of 'reality' (material, ideal, artefactual and social) critical realists gain knowledge through the use of theories, which can then be used to identify casual mechanisms and explanations, rather than subjective description and interpretation. Once this explanation is determined, by understanding why something happens, critical realists would suggest, it makes it easier to suggest solutions, and hence has potential to address as well as describe issues. As such, critical realism is becoming increasingly prominent in research that seeks out to address issues in sport (such as those described by Andy Adams in his description of his use of critical realism in this chapter).

CASE STUDY

USING CRITICAL REALISM IN SPORT RESEARCH

BY DR ANDY ADAMS, BOURNEMOUTH UNIVERSITY

Some of my research has looked at social capital and voluntary sport clubs; human rights and elite sport participants and more recently sport and leisure volunteering pre- and post-COVID-19. In each of these instances critical realism (CR) has provided me with the key organising principles for making sense of the research questions and how I will develop research to effectively meet particular aims and objectives.

I tend to agree with Denscombe (2002) that borrowing from 'other perspectives', when necessary, can help to achieve 'robust and valuable findings that are possible under the circumstances'. In this regard a sound methodology is critical to ensure research questions are answered precisely, accurately and with some efficiency, but pragmatically takes on what Locke refers to as 'underlabourer' role (Dunn 2003) to legitimise answers for one's research questions. For me when examining issues of how humans interpret or understand the implementation of ideas that will affect their lives, often policy and/or ideologically inspired ideas, then a CR position often feels appropriate. This position, which whilst accepting that social reality exists, also accepts that knowledge is a social construct (Baert 2005), and is therefore not necessarily considered an 'entity' or a fixed coordinate outside of its socio-historical and political setting. In this respect for most of my research critical realism has provided a means and a rationale for asserting that legitimate knowledge is inseparable from its context. This contextual predominance has tended to ensure that I do not treat knowledge as being ideologically and politically neutral. CR enables me (or any researcher) to see that knowledge is charged with identifying power relationships both apparent and hidden and is both reflective and morally charged.

Interpretivism

Although the positivist approach is clearly well suited for research into aspects of sport such as biomechanics, anatomy or other disciplines more aligned with the natural sciences, sport is, for many, a social phenomenon. That is those who participate in, watch or manage sport are acted upon by a number of external social forces, but they also have free will to respond to such forces in an active way and are not inanimate objects whose behaviour can be understood in terms of causal relationships. When examining sport we cannot predict whether X will always cause Y, as – unlike the subject matter of the natural sciences – we all have, to differing extents, freedom to act in and experience sport in different, subjective ways. This subjectivity forms the basis of the interpretative approach. We do not measure this subjectivity numerically – such an approach would argue that these concepts are too complex to be reduced to numbers. Rather, they are 'measured' using words, statements and other non-numerical measures, collecting data from the viewpoint of the participant. The data are then interpreted by the researcher, who attempts to uncover meanings, values, explanations and so on. It is the study of processes rather than the outcomes that is generally of importance to the interpretative researcher. This approach also avoids any search for a single 'truth', instead seeking understanding and acknowledging that there are multiple truths. The interpretative approach allows the researcher to gain an insider's perspective, to try to understand the subjects 'from within' and to explore and uncover explanations, rather than deduce them from measurements. Thus, whereas a positivist approach may statistically identify a relationship between X and Y, an interpretative approach may be able to describe and explain that relationship from the viewpoint of those being investigated.

You may also come across alternative interpretivist paradigms. Thus, you may see approaches labelled *critical theory*, *phenomenology*, *constructivism* and *critical interpretivism*, to name just some. Critical theory emphasises the existence of social 'realities' within historically situated social structures. Within critical theory, there is focus upon approaches such as feminist and indigenous methodologies (see the pieces by Dr Jayne Caudwell within this chapter that discuss these ideas) and critical race theory (CRT), which explores how racism is systematically embedded within society (do read Hylton 2009 for an introduction to CRT).

CASE STUDY

FEMINIST EPISTEMOLOGY AND METHODOLOGY

BY DR JAYNE CAUDWELL, BOURNEMOUTH UNIVERSITY, UK

Feminist researchers seek to critically analyse how gender operates in societies and cultures. Epistemology and methodology are not gender neutral; and feminists argue that we need to think about how knowledge is produced and how it is made legitimate. For example, I (Caudwell 2002) wrote about women's experiences of football as a 'particular and located footballing epistemology'. I did this because knowledge of football, at the time, could be described as male-centric, largely ignoring women and girls' experiences of the game.

However, feminist epistemology and methodology are not just about adding on women or adopting a specific standpoint (from the perspective of women/feminism); they challenge what we know, how we know it, what counts as knowledge and how this knowledge will be used. For example, Barbour's (2018) work on dance critiques white Western epistemology. She focuses on the body, movement and embodied ways of knowing, and she argues that the everyday lived experiences of the body connect with the feminist slogan 'the personal is political'. She shows how an understanding of women's moving bodies can challenge and transform dominant modes of femininity.

In our edited book about feminism and sport, leisure and physical education (PE) (Mansfield *et al.* 2018), we have a section on feminist epistemologies, methodologies and method. We introduce the chapters in the section as providing 'case studies of a particular method and how a feminist sensibility can inform methodology to ensure women's knowledges and experiences are centre' (p. 204). For example, Beal (2018) writes about feminist ethnographies and how they can be used to create more opportunities for women and girls in sport.

Within the edited collection, we discuss concepts such as reflexivity and positionality to explore the researcher's role in the process of knowledge production and to address ethical aspects such as the relationship between the researcher and the research participants. Feminist researchers are keen to avoid 'hit and run'/'smash and grab' research, which simply takes 'data' from research participants. Intersectionality is another important concept, and Watson's (2018) chapter is a call for feminist researchers in sport, leisure and PE to see women's differences and inequalities.

Constructivist and phenomenological approaches suggest that multiple realities exist, formed within a particular context. The researcher studies how reality is 'constructed' by the individual within this context. Critical interpretivism is a blend of several overlapping elements: historiography, ethnography, comparison, investigation, critical sociology and 'gonzo' ('gonzo' refers to a particular type of approach that involves the researcher taking a position that is as close as possible to the subject without becoming part of it, and using that position to present a vivid and personalised account).

CASE STUDY

INDIGENOUS APPROACHES TO SOCIAL RESEARCH

BY DR JAYNE CAUDWELL, BOURNEMOUTH UNIVERSITY, UK

Research traditions in sport tend to reflect what we can refer to as Western approaches to the nature of knowledge. It is stated at the start of this chapter that how we approach the production of knowledge is inextricably tied to the beliefs and actions of the researcher and audience. Western knowledge production has a history that is linked to, and follows shifts in: religion and secularisation, rationalism and reason, democracy and capitalism. For example, the approaches that are often viewed as 'legitimate' are framed by Western philosophy, science and medicine.

Indigenous approaches to knowledge represent a system of beliefs and actions with a long history that connects people with the land, the physical environment, the spiritual and experiential; they are considered holistic and evolving. However, indigenous peoples have often been studied and represented by Western research approaches. Groups such as First Peoples, Aboriginal Peoples, Native Peoples – including Māori, Native Americans, Inuit and Sámi – have been the 'object' of the researcher's gaze. This means that indigenous cultures and lives have been conceived and interpreted by non-indigenous researchers. This type of research occurs within the broader social, political and economic spheres of colonization.

Sport researchers are becoming more aware of colonization, anti-colonization and decolonization as well as the need to privilege indigenous voices and worldviews (McGuire-Adams 2020). Indigenous approaches start from a focus on indigenous knowledge and ways of being. Research methods involve stories or narratives, sharing circles and art-based methods. In their research on a group of teenage girls from the Cherbourg Aboriginal Settlement in Queensland who competed in marching in the 1950s and 1960s, Osmond and Phillips (2019) use storytelling (yarning) as a research method. They argue it is also methodology because of the traditions of 'talking circles', 'peacemaking circles' and 'healing circles'. Sharing circles have been, for a long time, and remain communication, ceremony and ritual within indigenous cultures and lives.

Pragmatist approaches

A final approach is that of pragmatism. This views the research question itself as the key driver of the approach to be taken, which (depending upon the question) can use elements of both positivist and interpretivism, mixing different data and different methods depending on what is seen as the 'best way' to get an answer. The research question itself, therefore, drives the key decisions made, rather than a philosophical standpoint. Often this is used to justify a mixed methods approach, an approach that seems to mix incompatible assumptions about the sporting world. What this doesn't mean (although often the case in sport-related research) is that we can ignore questions of ontology and epistemology when taking a pragmatic approach. Instead we should still be aware of them and how our findings reflect the nature of 'reality', and for who.

Quantitative and qualitative research

In the preceding discussion, it was noted how differing assumptions could be made about the nature of knowledge and how such knowledge is to be obtained. These differing assumptions are translated into the use of different types of data. As outlined earlier, positivists assume that behaviours can be observed and objectively measured and analysed. Such objective measures are generally, although not always, numerical in nature. The use of numerical measurement and analysis is referred to as a quantitative approach, that is research that involves measurable 'quantities'. Thus, you may be interested in the relationship between economic investment in sport and subsequent success. You may approach this by measuring how much money has been invested into a particular sport and measuring performance in that sport in terms of medal counts at major events such as the Olympics. This would give you a set of numerical data, which could be analysed to determine any relationship. This is quantitative research. Both variables are directly measurable and easily converted into numerical form, which can then be statistically analysed. Quantitative data are thus closely aligned to the positivist approach.

A POSITIVIST QUANTITATIVE STUDY: THE RELATIONSHIP BETWEEN SPORT ACTIVITY AND EXPERIENCE IN WINTER SPORT TOURISM

Hallmann *et al.* (2012) were interested in the relationship between sporting activities and behaviour, and how these influenced the overall winter sport tourist experience. They noted that, as objectivity was important, and cause and effect were to be studied, the study was positivist in nature. To determine the relationship, elements of the experience such as hedonism, novelty, interaction, local culture, comfort, safety and stimulation were all measured quantitatively on a five-point rating scale (from 1 = strongly disagree to 5 = strongly agree). Through statistical analysis, the researchers were able to determine that only two single winter sport activities (alpine skiing and sledge) influenced the winter sport experience, and a combination of activities (such as alpine skiing and sledging) seemed to be particularly important in increasing the sport tourist experience.

Qualitative research, on the other hand, aims to capture meanings or qualities that are not quantifiable, such as feelings, thoughts and experiences, that is those concepts associated with interpretative approaches. Qualitative research uses non-numerical data – often collected over an extended time period – to describe and understand concepts. Such concepts are difficult to meaningfully convert into numbers, and thus it is data in the form of words that have to be interpreted by the researcher that are relevant. Unlike quantitative research, the issue of 'how many' is not relevant, as Krane *et al.* (1997, p. 214) suggest:

Placing a frequency count after a category of experiences is tantamount to saying how important it is; thus value is derived by number. In many cases, rare experiences are no less meaningful, useful, or important than common ones. In some cases, the rare experience may be the most enlightening one.

The characteristics of quantitative and qualitative research are summarised in Table 2.2.

In certain areas, for example sport psychology, early research was dominated by positivist, quantitative approaches. Controlled experiments were undertaken in laboratory settings to measure behaviour and develop 'laws' of human activity. Much of this research did provide useful information; however, the need to understand the underlying experiences, feelings and emotions related to such behaviour has been acknowledged in recent years, and as a consequence qualitative research has become increasingly important. Previous arguments as to the relative merits of each approach have largely diminished, to the extent that qualitative research is now no longer seen as 'inferior' to quantitative research.

Table 2.2 Characteristics of quantitative and qualitative research

Quantitative	Qualitative
Uses numerical analysis to measure social phenomena to provide 'facts'	Relies on non-numerical analysis to provide understanding
Assumes a single, objective social reality	Assumes social reality is a subjective experience
Assumes social reality is constant across different times and settings	Assumes social reality is continuously constructed and related to the immediate social context
Uses statistical analysis to determine causal relationships	Objectives are description, understanding and meaning
Studies samples with the intention of generalising to populations	Uses smaller samples, or 'cases'
Researcher is objective and 'detached' from the subjects under investigation	Data are rich and subjective
The setting is often contrived	The location of the research is often natural
Data are collected using inanimate objects, for example pen and paper, smartphone or laptop	The researcher is the data collection instrument; flexible approach to data collection
Associated with the positivist approach	Associated with the interpretative approach
Generally deductive	Generally inductive

AN INTERPRETATIVE, QUALITATIVE STUDY: FACTORS AFFECTING MOTIVATION IN ELITE ATHLETES

To achieve success, elite athletes need to be highly motivated over a long period of time. Keegan *et al.* (2014) were interested in the question of how key social agents – coaches, team-mates and parents – influence such motivation. To understand this, they collected qualitative data that explored the subjective beliefs of 28 elite athletes in the athletes' own words through interviews and focus groups. This data suggested that, by exploring the athletes' own perspective rather than simple casual relationships, there were 'complex contextual interactions between the immediate behaviours of social agents and the impact on the athlete's motivation' (p. 97), with coaches and peers being focal influences. Only the coach-athlete and peer-athlete relationships appeared to be important in influencing motivation towards sport, with parents being more limited to emotional and moral support.

Choosing quantitative or qualitative approaches

The decision to collect either quantitative or qualitative data depends upon your philosophical standpoint, the nature of the research question and the objectives of your research. Obviously if you are a realist who is interested in the measurement of a particular phenomenon then you will need to collect quantitative data. If you are more interested in the thoughts or feelings of people from an interpretivist standpoint, qualitative data will be more appropriate. There is no one 'better' approach; rather the approach should be linked to, and appropriate for, the research question. Do not, for example, decide to collect qualitative data simply because you are uncomfortable with statistical analysis. It is also important, as Buckley (2007) notes, not to view a 'softer' qualitative route as an easy option, as qualitative research is often extremely complex and can be less straightforward than some quantitative options. For many students, especially those whose initial exposure to sport has been through more 'conventional' report writing, qualitative research is very much a learning process. He adds that 'making mistakes and learning through problem solving are a natural feature of most people's first experiences with qualitative research' (p. 91).

Mixing quantitative and qualitative data

You may also decide to mix quantitative and qualitative data through a mixed method (MM) approach (for example when taking a critical realist approach). While some academics suggest that the two forms are incompatible, relying on differing epistemological assumptions, and others suggest that time constraints, the need to limit the scope of a study and the difficulty of publishing such findings are also factors against mixing qualitative and quantitative data (Creswell 1994), mixed approaches are becoming increasingly influential within social sciences as a whole. Their use within sport, however, is more limited, with Van der Roest *et al.* (2013) suggesting that they are still underused, poorly legitimised and often weakly designed in sport research. If well designed, however, mixed approaches can lead to strong research. As Nau (1995, p. 1) suggests, 'blending qualitative and quantitative methods of research can produce a final product which can highlight the significant contributions of both'. For example, qualitative data can be used to 'support and explicate the meaning of quantitative research' (Jayaratne 1993, p. 117) in terms of providing some explanation to quantitative measurements. You can mix quantitative and qualitative methods in the following ways:

1   One may facilitate the other (sequential mixed methods). Thus a piece of quantitative research may identify the existence of a particular occurrence that could then be explained through the collection of qualitative data.
2   Both approaches investigate the same phenomenon concurrently. Quantitative methods may be used to collect numerical data from a large sample, whereas qualitative methods may collect 'rich' data from a smaller sample.

Greene *et al.* (1989) have identified five purposes of mixed method studies:

1   Triangulation (seeking convergence and corroboration of results from different methods studying the same phenomenon).
2   Complementarity (seeking elaboration or clarification of the results from one method with results from another).
3   Development (using the results from one method to inform another method).
4   Initiation (discovering paradoxes and contradictions that lead to a reframing of the research question).
5   Expansion (i.e. seeking to expand the breadth and range of inquiry).

One thing you should consider at the outset is whether you have the time and resources to carry out multiple methods (the use of different methods to address different research questions regarding the same phenomenon) or mixed methods (where two methods are used to address the same research question) study. Often, such approaches require more in the way of time and money, so this can be an important consideration, especially if you have constraints related to time and resources. A final aspect to consider is that many mixed methods studies result in two separate studies lacking a clear link, and you need to ensure that a mixed methods approach answers a single, rather than multiple, research question in almost all cases.

A MIXED METHODS STUDY: COMBINING QUANTITATIVE AND QUALITATIVE DATA TO EXPLORE THE EXPERIENCES OF OLDER ADULTS USING THE Wii VIDEO GAME SYSTEM

Keogh *et al.* (2014) examined whether the use of a Nintendo Wii video game could have any impact upon the functional ability, physical activity levels and quality of life for older adults. They were able to determine through quantitative analysis that there were actual benefits, such as increases in muscular endurance, physical activity levels and psychological quality of life. In addition, however, qualitative data collected through a focus group allowed them to determine how participants actually experienced such changes, finding out that the experiences revolved around three main themes (feeling silly, feeling good; having fun; and something to look forward to), suggesting that participants developed a sense of empowerment and achievement after some initial reluctance and anxiousness, feeling that using the Wii was fun and an opportunity for greater socialisation.

Deductive and inductive research

There is one final distinction that can be made between different approaches to research in terms of deductive and inductive research. Deductive research is more generally associated with positivist and quantitative research. It involves the development of an idea, or hypothesis, from existing theory, which can then be tested through the collection of data. A hypothesis is a statement of the relationship between two variables that can be tested empirically; for example, a hypothesis could be that 'Children with parents who participate regularly in sport are more likely to have positive attitudes towards sport participation themselves'.

Deductive research progresses through the following stages:

1 A statement regarding the theory used to underpin the research.
2 A statement deduced from that theory that would suggest, if the theory is true, the relationship between two or more variables – your hypothesis.
3 Collecting data to test this hypothesis.
4 Using the results to confirm, modify or refute the theory used to develop the hypothesis.

Inductive research is more often associated with interpretative or post-positivist studies. Here, the pattern is to collect data and analyse that data to develop a theory, model or explanation. For example, you may be interested as to the usage of social media by sport fans during COVID-19. You may find that there is not enough existing evidence to develop a hypothesis. You could undertake a content analysis (see Chapter 10) of social media usage, analyse how social media is being used and subsequently develop an explanation. This theory can then be tested and refined if necessary through further data collection.

What approaches are suitable for my research?

Although it is important to have an awareness of the research traditions and approaches described here, it is also important not to be too constrained by them when undertaking your research. First of all, you should not consider any approach as necessarily better than any other, but you should choose the approach that best suits the objectives of the research. For example, if you are interested in measuring a clearly observable phenomenon in an area where there is a considerable amount of existing theory, then a positivist deductive approach may be appropriate. If you are interested in explaining why something is happening and the area is relatively new or under-researched, then an interpretive inductive approach may be better. It is relatively easy to become immersed within the complex issues of ontology and epistemology without linking these issues to the key question: What approach will best suit my research?

Second, time and resources can be a major issue. Inductive research tends to take longer and may take more resources than deductive research, as theories have to emerge from the data rather than be tested by data collected in one go. A third consideration is that deductive research is often lower risk than inductive research, where it can be possible for many hours of data collection to prove fruitless.

A final – and often overlooked – consideration is that of your own stance. You may – as many experienced researchers do – develop your own preferences towards a particular approach. Some of the questions that you may want to consider are:

- What are my own ontological and epistemological preferences?
- Can I measure the phenomenon I am interested in numerically? Or is this inappropriate?
- Am I concerned only with measurable 'facts'?
- Am I concerned with the individual's views or explanations of what is happening?
- Do I think that the 'truth' is different for each individual, that I cannot develop scientific 'laws' of behaviour?
- What would I be happier doing in terms of positivist or interpretative research?
- Am I seeking to identify why things happen in the social world with a view to recommending change?

Summary

- A number of broad approaches to the nature of knowledge exist – such as positivism, post-positivism, interpretivism and critical realism.
- Positivists adhere to the tenets of the natural sciences and view behaviour as directly measurable and explainable via laws.

- Post-positivism, although often aligned with positivist approaches, has a more flexible view to the nature of knowledge and how such knowledge is developed.
- Interpretivists suggest that individuals have freedom to act in particular ways and that they experience things differently. Thus, the researcher has to interpret 'reality' from each individual's experiences.
- Critical realists acknowledge that there is an objective 'truth' to be found within the social world to understand the nature of why things are the way they are.
- Distinctions can also be made between quantitative and qualitative research. Quantitative research is based upon numerical measurement and analysis. Qualitative research is based upon non-numerical analysis of words, feelings, emotions and so on.
- Research may follow a deductive or an inductive process. Deductive research involves the testing of a pre-determined theory, explanation or hypothesis. Inductive research generates the explanation from the data collected.

Activity

Reread some of the research articles that you used at the end of Chapter 1. For each article, try to identify:

- Is the research positivist, post-positivist, interpretative or critical in nature? What are the key factors that lead you to this decision?
- To what extent has the author acknowledged issues of ontology and epistemology?
- What type of data are collected? Quantitative, qualitative or a combination of both?
- Does the research follow an inductive or a deductive approach? If the research is deductive in nature, try to identify: (a) what is the underlying theory used by the researcher(s) and (b) what is the hypothesis?
- Is there a coherence between the ontological and epistemological stance of the research, the data collected and the conclusions drawn?

Locate a journal that publishes a range of positivist research, such as *Sport Management Review*, for example, and compare and contrast those studies with those published in a journal such as *Qualitative Research in Sport, Exercise and Health*, which focuses upon alternative approaches. Look at the different types of questions asked in each, the type of data collected and the methods used.

Identify a study that uses mixed methods. Is the rationale for mixing methods clear? What has the mixed methods approach added to this study above that of the use of a single method?

ABOUT YOUR RESEARCH PROJECT

- Is your own research positivist, post-positivist, critically realist or interpretative in nature? Have you considered alternative approaches, such as indigenous or feminist methodologies?
- Is there coherence between your ontological and epistemological stance, and how you intend to carry out the research?
- Are you collecting quantitative or qualitative data? Can this be reconciled with your choice of approach?
- Are you following a deductive or an inductive design? Can this be reconciled with your answers to the previous questions?

Further reading

There are a number of books that discuss the ideas in this chapter, but initially I would recommend one of the following as a good start to cover some of the issues that are raised in this chapter.

Baranov, D. (2013) *Conceptual Foundations of Social Research Methods*, London: Routledge.
Bryman, A. (2016) *Social Research Methods*, Oxon: Oxford University Press.
Crotty, M. (1998) *The Foundations of Social Research*, London: Sage.

Chapter 3
The research process

The research process

This chapter will:

- Introduce the concept of the 'research process'.
- Outline the different stages of this process.
- Describe how the different stages interrelate as part of one overall process.

Introduction

When we initially consider the idea of research, our first thought is often to think of the collection of quantitative or qualitative data through interviewing, questionnaires or other methods. While such primary data collection is an important part of many research projects, research is much more than simply collecting data, and it is essential to consider data collection as part of a wider process involving important stages both before and after. This chapter introduces this concept of the 'research process', describes the elements within the process and explores the relationships between the elements. It is important that you have an understanding of all elements of the research process before commencing your research project so that you have an idea of the 'big picture'. At this stage I would strongly recommend reading the excellent text by Neil *et al.* (2014), which, through reference to a number of varied examples from a varied range of disciplines, shows how different sport researchers have navigated this process through reference to real-life accounts of research and the key decisions that were made. This book is well worth a read before you start your own research process.

The research process
The research process described in the following section is a particularly sanitised model of carrying out research. In reality, the process is much less neat, and you will find that you will not usually follow the process stage by stage but will often move continually back and forth between the elements or carry out two or more of the elements concurrently, especially if you are undertaking a more interpretative or qualitative study (see Chapter 2). It's more important to realise that this is *what* you will do, rather than *when*. Although different models of the research process exist, each containing different numbers of stages, most include the same general elements. The research process that is outlined here consists of nine elements (Figure 3.1).

Figure 3.1 The research process

It is important to remember that these are not isolated, discrete stages, but actually part of one overall process. It may also be the case that for certain approaches the order of the stages may be somewhat different; for example, a qualitative research project may involve a continual integration of reviewing the literature and data collection, and the development of a conceptual framework after data collection. Thus, you should be prepared to be flexible, depending upon the nature of the research being undertaken. Whatever approach you take, however, it is important that you maintain a sense of coherence within the overall research project, or what some refer to as a 'golden thread' or 'vertical thread'. This thread should be the research question, and everything within the research process should be related to answering that question. This chapter will briefly outline the stages of the research process. Each of the areas will be covered in more depth in later chapters of the book.

Stage 1: Selection of topic

The stage that will take up most (if not all) of your time at the beginning of your research is that of actually selecting a topic and developing a preliminary research question and set of objectives. The selection of your research question is a crucial stage, as an inappropriate topic or question will often lead to irretrievable difficulties later in the research, so it is worth dealing with this stage carefully. It is unlikely that you will develop a final question and set of objectives at this stage of the research process, and further work, as outlined in stages 2 and 3, are important in developing and assessing your question more fully. I will discuss some of the issues related to coming up with a research question in more depth in Chapter 4.

Stage 2: Reviewing the literature

This stage is covered in more depth in Chapter 5. A literature review essentially consists of identifying, critically reading and evaluating existing literature on the topic to assess the state of knowledge and understanding in the area, and identifying how your proposed question relates to that state of knowledge and how it fills any gaps within that knowledge. During this stage you should aim to become an 'expert' in your field of research. The literature review is generally done alongside the development of the theoretical and conceptual frameworks (stage 3 of the research process). Reading widely may also alert you to other helpful factors, such as whether similar research has already been carried out, the findings that you could expect, or provide descriptions of the theoretical frameworks and previous methodologies adopted by others doing similar research.

Stage 3: Development of theoretical and conceptual frameworks

As you read the literature, you should be continually developing and refining your theoretical and conceptual frameworks. This is a stage that can often be overlooked in the haste to collect data. It is, however, a vital part of the research process, and it is important in alerting you to potential problems before they occur. Your theoretical framework refers to the underlying theoretical approach that you adopt to underpin your study, for example social learning theory or self-determination theory. The conceptual framework defines and organises the concepts important within your study. These issues are covered in more depth in Chapter 6.

Stage 4: Clarification of the research question/hypothesis

Stages 1, 2 and 3 of the research process will initially, in many cases, become a circular process, whereby initial research questions are chosen, investigated and amended or rejected for a number of reasons. For example:

● The question lacks sufficient focus.
● The conceptual framework has identified problems in either defining and/or measuring the appropriate concepts.
● There are too many moderating or intervening variables.
● The project lacks feasibility in terms of complexity, access, facilities or resources.

Stages 1–3 can take longer than initially anticipated, and you may well become discouraged by a lack of success in identifying a good research question. There are no easy methods to come up with an appropriate question, and it can be very much a case of perseverance. Once you have developed a good, focused research question, then the rest of the research process is based upon answering that question. A common fault is the lack of clarity over the overall aim of the research, and the importance of developing a clearly focused question and set of research objectives at this stage cannot be overstated.

Stage 5: Research design

Once the focused research question has been ascertained, the next stage is to consider two questions:

● What data do I need to collect to answer this question?
● What is the best way to collect the data?

This stage considers more than just the practical methods of collecting data, such as choosing questionnaires or interviews, but also a number of broader issues. The typical issues considered by the researcher might include:

- What is my ontological and epistemological standpoint? How does this influence the key decisions I make?
- What overall research design should I use? Will I, for example, use a cross-sectional, experimental or longitudinal design?
- Will I need to collect primary data, or will there be suitable secondary data to use?
- What methods – for example interviews, questionnaire surveys and so on – will be the best ones to collect the primary data?
- Who should participate in the research, and how will I gain access to them?
- What are the exact procedures that I should adopt in my data collection to ensure I obtain quality data?
- Are there any ethical issues associated with the research?

These issues are covered in depth in Chapter 7, as well as throughout much of the rest of the book.

Stage 6: Data collection

Once the issues identified in stages 4 and 5 of the research process have been addressed, then you should have a clear idea of what data to collect and how to collect them. The background to this is dealt with in more depth in the next chapter, and the actual practical issues of collecting data are dealt with in Chapters 8–12.

Stage 7: Data analysis

The data you collect in stage 6 need to be analysed to provide answers to your research question. Methods of data analysis should always be related to the objectives of the research, that is, your analysis should answer the research question or hypothesis. In your discussion of the results, reference should also be made back to the literature reviewed in stage 2; for example, how do the findings add to this literature? Do they support the literature? If not, what are the possible reasons why? A common fault is to discuss the findings with no reference back to the literature reviewed as part of stage 2 of the development of the conceptual framework. Chapter 13 deals with issues of quantitative analysis, and Chapter 14 discusses some of the methods of qualitative data analysis that you may use.

Stage 8: Drawing conclusions

This should relate back to the focused research question. Here, the answer to the research question(s) should be clearly stated. You can evaluate how successful you have been in achieving your research objectives, and highlight the strengths and weaknesses of the research. You may also want to make recommendations for further research, given that many projects raise as many questions as they answer.

Stage 9: Dissemination

An essential part of the research process is communicating the findings to a wider audience wherever possible. For some, this audience may be limited to just the examiners of the research, but there are also a number of other options, such as publishing your work in journals, presenting it at conferences and more informally through social media. The various ways in which you can share your research are discussed in more depth in Chapter 16.

Planning the research process

At this stage, it is also worth emphasising that this process will not be a smooth one for much of the time, and it's a good idea to consider some of the things that will make the research process as positive an experience as possible.

- Start the research process early. You may well have a timescale of a number of months (or longer) to complete the research, but remember – it will take you all of this time. Set a number of precise and measurable goals in terms of what you want to achieve, and when, and ensure you monitor your progress continuously. Make sure you build in enough time to allow for contingencies and also for any other assessments that you are required to do during this time. You might be someone who thinks that they work best under pressure by leaving things later than necessary and working to unnecessarily tight deadlines. You don't. Give yourself time to do justice to the research.
- Read as much as you can as soon as you can. Don't restrict your reading too much at first, but be prepared to explore a variety of sources, especially if you are still focusing your research question.
- Start writing as soon as possible. Don't worry about word counts, and don't worry that not everything you write will end up in the final submission. Your writing will improve significantly as you progress through the research process, provided you are writing on a regular basis. Don't try to complete things in the order they will finally appear. (For example, when starting to write your review of literature, don't start with the beginning. Start with writing about what you are most comfortable with.)
- Make sure you make the most of your supervisor throughout the research process. They are there to work with you and help you produce the best piece of work of which you are capable, but this requires you

to take control of the relationship. It is your responsibility to arrange meetings and set the agenda for discussion. Don't expect your supervisor to tell you what to do; they are there to advise you on the decisions you have made and the ideas that you have developed.

- Do not talk to friends about the progress they are making or the support they are receiving, and do not listen to rumours about what is expected. In reality, there is often very little correlation between what others say they have done and what they have actually achieved. There are also a number of different ways of approaching the research process, so others might well be doing things in a different way. If you have any queries about the requirements, you should only consult sources such as any guidance or handbook that you might have been provided with, or your supervisor.

Summary

- Research is not just about the collection of data. Data collection is important, but it is simply part of a wider process – the research process.
- The research process follows nine steps: Selection of topic, reviewing the literature, developing your theoretical and conceptual frameworks, clarifying your research question, developing a research design, collecting data, analysing data, drawing conclusions and disseminating your findings.
- Relating your project to the research process will allow you to develop and answer your research question in a logical and systematic manner.

Activity

- Locate a copy of Neil *et al.*'s *The Research Process in Sport, Exercise and Health*, and choose one of the chapters most closely related to your own discipline or interests. Try to get an idea of the process that the author went through, from the initial formulation of the research problem to the final dissemination of the research.
- Reread one of the pieces of research from the activity suggested at the end of Chapter 1. Can you relate this research to the research process? Does the research follow this process? Are the steps easily recognisable?

Further reading

Neil, R., Hanton, S., Fleming, S. and Wilson, K. (2014) *The Research Process in Sport, Exercise and Health: Case Studies of Active Researchers*, London: Routledge.

Do try and read this text. It illustrates the research process through a number of different cases, including those related to sport management, sport ethics, coaching, sport development and the sociology of sport, each relating the research to the wider research process, explaining the key elements of the research process and how they were addressed by the author.

At this stage, it can also be a good idea to catch up on your reading to get you thinking about the different ways in which the study of sport has been approached and the various, diverse aspects of sport within society. Try to locate some of the key textbooks and journals in your particular field, and try to get a feel for the range of topics that are covered and some of the key theories and ideas that exist within those topics. The following are texts that you may want to browse:

Coakley, J. (2016) *Sport in Society: Issues and Controversies*, Boston, MA: McGraw-Hill.
Coakley, J. and Dunning, E. (eds) (2002) *Handbook of Sports Studies*, London: Sage.
Houlihan, B. and Malcolm, D. (2015) *Sport and Society: A Student Introduction*, London: Sage.
Jarvie, G. (2018) *Sport, Culture and Society*, London: Routledge.

Alternatively, you may want to browse through some peer-reviewed journals. Try journals such as *Sociology of Sport* or the *Sport Management Review*, for example, or any journals published in your particular areas of interest. Start thinking about the areas of sport that really interest you, and try to get a feel for some of the research that has been undertaken in those areas.

Chapter 4
Research questions, aims and objectives

Research questions, aims and objectives

This chapter will:

- Describe some of the ways by which you can identify and develop a potential research area or research problem into a research question.
- Outline some ways by which you can focus your research question.
- Discuss some of the means by which you can assess the strengths and weaknesses of your research question.
- Describe the content of a research proposal, and identify some of the common weaknesses in such proposals.

Introduction

Coming up with a research question can be a difficult and frustrating time, yet it is immensely important, and decisions made at this stage will impact the entire research process. Hence it is worth investing time now, as getting things right at the start will save you huge amounts of time later. In this chapter I will describe some of the strategies that you can use to identify and develop a research question, focus the aims and objectives of your research, and also outline some of the means by which you can assess your proposed research question.

Before you start considering your research question, it is worth revisiting the concept of research outlined in Chapter 1. As noted there, a feature of research is that it adds to knowledge. Often, however, students over-estimate the extent of originality required in a research project and feel that they have

DOI: 10.4324/9781003195467-4

to produce something completely new. In reality, this is unrealistic. You are far better thinking in terms of how you can do something that adds to what we already know. It should have some degree of originality, but often this can be achieved in a number of ways, as I will discuss later in the chapter.

Coming up with a research question

You may be lucky enough to have a clearly defined, focused research question from the very start. Alternatively, you might be struggling even to determine a broad area to explore. If you fall into the second group, Veal and Darcy (2014) and Saunders *et al.* (2000) provide a number of possible sources to help you:

- *Existing sport literature.* Past research projects are a useful source of ideas. By looking at recent research, for example reading journal articles, you may develop an idea of the questions currently being researched in your field of interest and assess the types of subjects that are at the forefront of research. Alternatively your institution may have an archive of past dissertations or theses. From such reading you may encounter a certain idea, argument or theory that interests you, and that you would be interested in developing further. Even if the work seems to have been done, you can still make an original contribution, and the various ways to do this are outlined later.
- *Literature from other disciplines.* Alternatively, you could look at journals from outside sport and see whether there is research that could be applied to a sporting context. Journals from your 'home' discipline (such as sociology, psychology and so on) can be useful here; for example, you might browse through the *Journal of Management* and come across Malhotra's (2021) editorial about the challenges of post-pandemic work to both individuals and organisations, and this might get you thinking about how these challenges might be enacted within the sport context. Alternatively, you might encounter the work of Biermeier-Hanson *et al.* (2021) in the *Journal of Psychology* that focuses upon leader-follower authenticity and think about how this might be applied within the coach-athlete relationship. Going outside the confines of sport research and sport-related journals can be incredibly valuable, yet it is often overlooked as a strategy.
- *Social concerns.* Do not just think about sport as being in a 'bubble', separate from the wider society, but instead as inextricably linked with that society with its broader contemporary concerns and issues. These concerns and issues provide a wealth of areas for the sport researcher. The obvious one at this time is that of the impact of COVID-19, for example its impact on sport participation, provision or spectating. There are also many other concerns that provide the basis for valuable

research questions. You may be interested in the sport experiences of migrants, the online abuse of athletes or the impact of terrorism, for example. Concerns such as climate change, poverty, civil rights and gender inequality (to name just four) are all important areas to explore with reference to sport.

- *Popular issues.* As well as broader social concerns, there may be certain popular issues that are worthy of investigation. Choose a media source and identify the relevant sporting issues of the moment. As an example of this, an examination of *The Guardian* newspaper of 12 April 2021 identifies issues of gamesmanship in football, the impact of head injuries in the NFL on behaviour, billionaire acquisitions of NBA teams, social media abuse of cricketers, gender equity and horse-racing, and athlete transgressions in golf – all potential research areas.

- *Your own history and personal characteristics.* What are your own strengths and interests? In what subjects are you both knowledgeable and interested? What about your own career aspirations? If you are interested in a career in sport marketing, then it would be a logical idea to undertake research in this area. If you would like to become a coach or teacher, then undertaking a related piece of research will not only give you valuable experience but will also be beneficial for your CV. In terms of your own history, do you have an in-depth knowledge of a particular sport, for example? Maybe you have acted as a sport volunteer and would like to use that knowledge. Think about your own sporting experiences, positive and negative, and explore those as potential starting points.

- *Brainstorming.* Brainstorming is a good way to develop topics. Discuss potential ideas with others, and use this interaction to develop, critique and refine possible questions. Write down as many words as you can think of related to the areas of sport that interest you. Then write words such as *why* and *how*, and see whether any questions emerge. Do not critique or judge ideas while going through the process; the aim is simply to generate as many areas as you can. Do not rule out any ideas at an early stage.

- *Your tutors.* Your tutors will have their own research areas and areas of expertise, and they will generally be extremely happy to supervise in these areas. Talk to your tutors and see whether they can guide you in the right direction (although it is not necessarily their role to provide you with a question). Read some of their publications, and think about whether you could make your own contribution to their research. This approach has the advantage that your tutor will have an extensive knowledge of the subject area, and working with them in their specialist area can be a particularly rewarding experience. If you put together an excellent piece of research, you may also be able to publish that research with them in a peer-reviewed journal.

When you have identified a topic and have undertaken some preliminary investigation, it may well seem that your topic has already been explored in some depth, and there may be little scope for original research. If this is the case – and it is very likely that it is – you should not be discouraged. As I noted earlier, almost all research builds upon and uses existing theories and ideas. Often, your originality comes not from generating new ideas and theories, but in using existing ones in an original way. Veal (2006) provides a number of examples of how you could do this:

- *Geographically*. Certain theories may have been developed and empirically tested in one area but have not received the same attention elsewhere. Thus, you may find research focused on sport in China or Africa. Undertaking similar research in the UK would provide you with the basis for an original study. Alternatively, existing research may have examined sport provision in an urban context. You may wish to carry out similar research in a rural setting, which again would form the basis for an original study.
- *Socially*. You may find that certain social groups have not received as much attention as others. Existing work may focus exclusively upon men and exclude women, or you may find a certain theory that has not been applied to the elderly or to the physically disabled, for example. Certain groups, such as trans athletes, may be under-researched in nearly all aspects of sport, and existing studies could be developed to research with this population to provide some novel findings.
- *Temporally*. A theory may have been developed a number of years ago, thus its relevance in contemporary society could be investigated. Comparing the findings would be an original study in itself. You may also come across a study that took place some years ago. Collecting more up-to-date data may also form the basis for an original project.
- *Methodologically*. You could collect different data to explore a phenomenon. An example may be if you find a theory that has been tested quantitatively, and you apply a qualitative research design, or if you collect data using in-depth interviews rather than questionnaire surveys.

Once you have the initial research area, you need to be thinking about developing your research question. The crucial point here is to ensure that the question is sufficiently focused. One of the continual complaints of examiners of research projects is that the research question chosen is too broad. Stating that 'I would like to research the growth of Western sport in China', for example, is too broad and lacks direction. Which sport are you interested in? All sports, or just one of them? What exactly is it about the growth that you are interested in? Are you interested in the whole of China, or a particular region? What is the timescale of the research? The research question is vital for a good piece of research. Without a good, focused question, it is almost impossible to carry out research successfully. De Vaus (2001) suggests some guidelines to focus your question that can be applied to sport research, and these are outlined in the following section.

DEVELOPING A RESEARCH QUESTION: ALCOHOL USE BY SPORT STARS AND THEIR STATUS AS ROLE MODELS

Jones (2014) provides an interesting account of how his research question about the relationship between alcohol use by sport stars and their status as role models emerged from both his academic and personal interests. He explains how he initially found questions related to ethics and morals to be the most interesting he encountered during his early studies, leading him to specialise in the ethics of sport. He then became interested in negative and sensationalised newspaper coverage of sport stars within the press. Through being able to apply his own academic background to a current issue that was receiving a lot of media attention, he was able to identify first a broad research problem – that of the effect of vices on sport stars' ability to be role models – and second a number of specific research questions, such as the extent to which individuals were morally responsible for their actions.

Focusing your research question

1   Define all of your concepts (or 'building blocks' of the research question). If you are discussing participation in sport, what exactly do you mean by the concepts of 'participation' and 'sport'? Do you mean participation in all sport? Or just organised sport? Does it mean regular or sporadic participation? The term *regular* itself is problematic: For example, participation once a year or once a day could both be termed 'regular'. Unless you can clearly define or specify your core concepts, you cannot develop your research question. Any ambiguity over your key concepts needs to be removed.

2   What is your timeframe? Are you interested in the contemporary picture, an historical analysis or do you want to measure changes? If so, over what time period?

3   What is the geographical location? One community, facility or sport team? Are you going to compare one or more locations?

4   What aspect of the topic are you interested in? If you are researching the commercialisation of the Olympics, for example, are you interested in the economic aspects, the experiences of the athletes or the impact of commercialisation upon spectators?

5   What is your unit of analysis (i.e. the 'thing' that you collect data about and from which you draw conclusions)? Is this a person (e.g. sport participant or fan), an organisation (e.g. a sport team) or an event?

The following is an alternative process that you may find useful in helping to focus your research question:

1   Write out your provisional research question. For example, you may be interested in leadership styles and whether different types of coaches demonstrate different leadership styles in a particular coaching situation. This leads you to a provisional question, such as 'Do coaches have different leadership styles depending upon whether they are coaching team or individual sport?' While the area is appropriate, it is, as it stands, far too broad as a question. There are, for example, many different types of coach, and the term 'sport' is so broad as to be essentially meaningless in this case. The question clearly needs more focus.

2   Identify the key terms (or 'concepts' – more about them in Chapter 6) in the research question, for example *coaches*, *leadership styles* and *sport*.

3   Try to identify whether you can break down each of your key terms into more focused categories or make them more specific through a clear definition. The first thing to do is to focus the subject of your research, in this case the concept of a coach. Either through exploring the literature or developing your own thoughts and ideas, you may break down coaches into 'male' and 'female' (see Figure 4.1). Knowing that there may well be gender differences in leadership styles (Eagly and Johnson 1990), you could make the decision to focus on male coaches to remove this variable. This still leaves a very broad concept, so you may then decide to focus through making the decision to concentrate on amateur coaches, as you may well have greater access. Finally, you could focus on experienced rather than novice coaches, as measured by their total number of coaching hours.

4   The next stage is to do the same with any other key terms. As noted earlier, the concept of 'sport' needs much more clarification. There are several ways to do this, one of which may be to identify which sports you are focusing on, for example golf and squash as individual sports, and soccer and hockey as team sports; or, you may simply decide to take a broad sample from a range of sports. More focus can then be achieved by following the process just described, for example deciding to focus on non-elite sport (again due to access issues). As before, gender issues lead you to focus on one area (female sport), and a further variable might occur – that of the level of the team being coached; so to remove that, the decision is made to focus on junior (i.e. under 18) sport. You can then identify a number of alternative research questions.

Thus, by identifying alternative categories, and making choices between categories, the question has been focused from:

Do coaches have different leadership styles depending upon whether they are coaching team or individual sports?

N

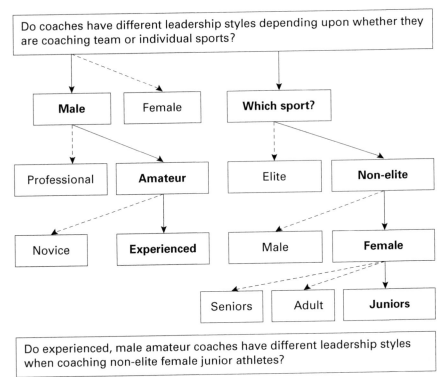

Figure 4.1 Focusing a research question

to

> *Do experienced male amateur coaches have different leadership styles depending upon whether they are coaching team or individual non-elite female junior sport?*

The new question is considerably more focused, and it will lead to a much greater chance of success in terms of the overall research project. It's very tempting when developing your research question to look at the expected word count of the submission (for example 10,000 words) and to worry about how you are ever going to write that many words about a focused topic. Don't worry. Your problem is more likely to focus upon keeping it *within* the word count.

Even when you have decided upon a research question that you think is appropriate, it is not always possible to undertake the research to answer that question. You will also need to consider the 'CAFE' acronym (Clarke *et al.* 1998) to ensure that it is feasible. CAFE refers to four considerations, these being complexity, access, facilities and resources, and expertise:

Complexity

A particular topic may involve several competing theories, or just one complex theory. Could you do the topic justice within your research if this is the case? This may be the case if you are limited by time or resources, or in terms of your own personal background. Do you have the ability to undertake a research project in the chosen area? A good research question involves writing a lot about very little, rather than the other way round, and an overly complex question will make this difficult. A simple, focused question is often better, as it allows you much greater depth.

Access

How easy will it be for you to collect the data? How realistic is it, for example, to send questionnaires to professional sport club owners or elite athletes and expect a response? What will happen if the pandemic continues? There is often a tendency to be over-optimistic in terms of response rates and so on, and you need to consider this carefully. Generally you are better advised to use more accessible samples. There is no correlation between the level of sport and the quality of research at all, so a study on casual amateur basketball players is just as worthy as a study on Olympic athletes. Simply having access to an elite sample doesn't necessarily make it a good area to research.

Facilities and resources

Consider the demands of your research. Will you, for example, require extensive travel to carry out interviews? Will you require any specialist video or IT equipment? You need to identify any specialist resources at this stage.

Expertise

Consider your expertise. Would you be happy undertaking a research project that necessitated the use of complex multivariate analysis? If you are undertaking a sport management programme, then do you have the relevant sociological or psychological expertise to examine group behaviour in sport? If you are undertaking a dissertation as part of a taught programme, it may well also be wise to consider the expertise of your tutors, especially if they are particularly renowned in a certain field.

Gill and Johnson (1997) note that your topic should also have, if possible, a symmetry of potential outcomes. What this means is that your research will have value no matter what your findings are. You may be interested to find out whether there is a relationship between the anxiety of umpires before a game and how many years they have been umpiring. If there is no such relationship, then the findings may have little interest or relevance. One solution is to amend the research question, for example to investigate the causes of stress among umpires. In this way, the findings will have relevance and interest whatever they are. In this instance, you need also to confirm any assumptions; for example, you are assuming that umpires actually experience stress! You should also avoid research questions that can be answered with a simple 'yes' or 'no'.

CHOOSING YOUR RESEARCH QUESTION

When you are developing your research question, you should continually refer to the following list:

- You must have a focused research question. Vague statements of intent such as 'I would like to investigate violence in sport' are inappropriate. If you cannot clearly state your research question, then you will need to revisit your intended research.
- The research question must be of interest to you. Research projects take a considerable amount of time and effort, and you should ensure that you have sufficient interest in the research to be able to read extensively around the topic; spend time, effort and resources collecting data; and write a substantial research report at the end. If you lack sufficient interest, then your chances of completing the research project are correspondingly reduced.
- The research question must be feasible – especially in terms of time and resources. Most projects have a limited time allocation, and you should ensure that yours is achievable within the time.
- There should be an appropriate theoretical underpinning for the question.
- The data must be obtainable – you should not assume that by sending questionnaires you will get a response. Sport governing bodies, for example, are often inundated with requests from researchers and may be unlikely to respond.
- You must have the appropriate skills to undertake the research.

You will also need to develop a number of research objectives. These are the objectives that you will need to achieve in order to answer the overall research question. They are essential in guiding your approach. As an example of this, Stewart *et al.* (2020) carried out a study to explore transsexual women's experiences of their communication and voice use in sporting environments. To do this, they determined the following objectives:

1   How aware were trans women of their vocal communication and voice use within a sporting setting?
2   Did trans women perceive their voices as impacting on their wellbeing and/or participation in sport?

3   What aspects of sporting environments did trans women perceive as impacting on their vocal communication and voice use?

4   What strategies did trans women think would facilitate their voice use and vocal health during sport training, competition and social functions?

These objectives guided the research throughout, from identifying relevant literature to developing an appropriate methodology, guiding the data analysis and drawing conclusions. Hence, the researchers were able to identify that voice was the significant factor towards acceptance in sport, and also the need for strategies such as the appropriate use of voice and voice training to enhance integration.

Note that these objectives are about what will be achieved, rather than the processes that you follow, so something like 'to distribute a questionnaire' is not an objective. When setting your objectives, remember the 'SMART' acronym. Thus, your objectives need to be:

- Specific. You must be clear about what is to be achieved.
- Measurable. You must be able to identify when such objectives have been achieved.
- Achievable. You must have a likelihood of success in achieving your objectives.
- Realistic. The objectives must be realistic in light of any constraints that you may face, such as time, money or access.
- Time bound. You should be able to set specific targets for when each objective is to be accomplished.

Thus, if you are interested in the cultural impacts of professional sport, you may set yourself an objective 'to review the literature on the cultural impacts of hosting a mega-event'. While the review of literature is a necessary process, by relating it to the earlier list, we can see that it is not an objective. The outcome needs to be clear with any of your objectives, rather than the process, so in this case 'to review the literature to identify an appropriate theoretical framework within which to measure cultural impacts' would be preferable.

Writing a research proposal

An important part of many research projects, and a key element for anyone wishing to secure funding for research, is that of writing a research proposal, or a plan of the intended research programme. Even if it is not a formal requirement, it is still a useful exercise to undertake during the early stages of your research. You should try to produce your own research proposal as soon as you have determined your research question even if one isn't needed. This proposal can be very effective in clarifying in your own mind the overall aim of the project and how you intend to achieve that aim, as well as to identify potential problems with the study. Requirements for a research proposal will depend upon its purpose. However, there is certain information that will generally be required:

1 A clear statement of the overall aim and associated objectives of the research.
2 A statement outlining the originality, relevance and importance of the research.
3 A brief description of existing work in the area.
4 A clear link to be demonstrated between the aim of your research and that existing work highlighted previously.
5 How the research is to be conducted, the research design to be adopted, anticipated methods and an indication of the likely sample group, sample size and recruitment methods.
6 How the data collected are to be analysed.
7 The anticipated timescale for the research.
8 Any specific requirements in terms of access, financial requirements, etc.
9 The potential impact of the research.
10 Any ethical issues that may be relevant to the study.

Weaknesses in research proposals

In many cases, your research proposal will be assessed by either your institution or funding body. If it is not, then you need to assess it yourself, which can be a difficult task. One way to do this is to compare your proposal against a set of criteria or headings. Leedy (1985) has listed the weaknesses commonly found in research proposals, and by comparing your proposal with his list, you may be able to identify weaknesses in your own proposal. The most relevant weaknesses identified are listed below.

The research problem:

- The problem is of insufficient importance or unlikely to produce any new or useful information.
- The hypothesis upon which the research is based is unsound, or it is not based on any existing evidence.
- The problem is more complex than the investigator appears to realise.
- The research is overly complex, with too many elements.

The approach:

- The proposed methods are not suitable to achieve the research objectives.
- The description of the approach lacks specificity and clarity.
- The research design has not been carefully considered.

- The statistical aspects/details of the means by which qualitative data are to be analysed have not received sufficient attention.

Personal characteristics:

- The researcher does not have adequate experience or ability to undertake such a project.
- The researcher seems unfamiliar with recent or important work in the area.

Even if you are not required to produce a research proposal for assessment, it is essential that you consider the points raised here and critically assess your own research proposal. Even better, get a colleague to play 'devil's advocate' and critically question your proposal. It is much better that problems are identified at this stage, when you can change your approach, than after you have begun to carry out the research.

Summary

- The first stage of the research process is to identify a research topic for investigation. This can be a difficult task, but it is important to the success of the subsequent research project.
- There are a number of sources of ideas for research topics, the main ones being existing literature, social concerns and popular issues, personal characteristics and preferences, brainstorming, and debate with your tutor.
- Although some degree of originality is desirable, the extent of this originality is often overestimated. There are a number of ways by which research can be seen to be original; for example, through applying existing theory to new situations or using different approaches.
- The topic should lead to a focused question, which forms the 'vertical thread' of the research.
- Answering the research question must be achievable, in terms of the personal abilities of the researcher, access to an appropriate sample and the availability of any specialist resources or equipment.

Activity

You should come up with two or three possible research questions. Assess each question, and for each:

- Identify whether you feel that it is a good research question. Try to identify the limitations of each of the questions and rewrite accordingly if necessary. Apply the principles of Figure 4.1 to your own questions to see how they could be focused.

● Identify a series of objectives that would need to be met to answer each question.

● Assess those objectives in terms of SMART; that is, are they specific, measurable, achievable, realistic and time bound? Again, rewrite if necessary.

ABOUT YOUR RESEARCH PROJECT

The activities in this chapter are all important to your research project, and you should carry them out with reference to your proposed question. You should also undertake the following tasks:

■ Refer to the criteria mentioned earlier in the chapter (see the box 'Choosing your research question') and assess whether your research question fulfils these criteria.

■ Can you relate your question to the four elements of CAFE outlined in this chapter?

■ Is your question sufficiently focused, or can you focus your question further in any way?

Further reading

The book suggested at the end of Chapter 3 (Neil, R., Hanton, S., Fleming, S. and Wilson, K. (2014) *The Research Process in Sport, Exercise and Health: Case Studies of Active Researchers*, London: Routledge) also has some good relevant material in terms of this chapter, as does Armour, K. and MacDonald, D. (2011) *Research Methods in Physical Education and Youth Sport*, London: Routledge.

Chapter 5
Reviewing the literature

Reviewing the literature

This chapter will:
- Introduce the role of the literature review and outline why it is an important part of any research project.
- Describe some of the sources of literature available to you.
- Describe some guidance for assessing the quality of the literature that you identify.
- Provide guidance on writing and presenting the literature review.

Introduction

Before commencing data collection, and before you have even considered your research design, it is important that you become knowledgeable in your chosen subject, understanding not only the appropriate concepts but also the work that has previously been done on the subject and the key findings that have emerged. As Jankowicz (1995, pp. 128–9) notes:

> Knowledge does not exist in a vacuum, and your work only has value in relation to other people's. Your work and your findings will be significant only to the extent that they are the same as, or different from, other people's work.

Reviewing the literature is an essential task in all research. No matter how original you think the research question may be, it is almost certain that

DOI: 10.4324/9781003195467-5

your work will be building on the work of others, often from outside the field of sport. It is here that your review of such work is important. A literature review is the background to your research, where you demonstrate a clear understanding of the relevant theories and concepts, the results of past research into the area, the types of methodologies and research designs employed in such research and areas where the literature is deficient. This reading will then form the basis for a significant element of your research report, where your understanding of this literature is presented in a written form. Thus, the literature review can be seen to consist of two different aspects:

1   The actual process of locating, reading and organising the appropriate academic literature.
2   The presentation of the information collected as part of the research report.

Thus, you will need to read and report the literature critically, demonstrating an awareness of the state of knowledge on the subject, both in terms of the strengths of existing literature and any weaknesses or omissions. You also need to place your own research question within this context. The reader of your research needs to understand and appreciate your research in the light of existing work. This understanding will come from your definitions and explanations of key terms and concepts, your review of the research that has been undertaken and the key findings emerging from that review.

Purposes of the literature review

You should consider the purposes of the review of the literature before you start, as this will make it easier for you to identify the things that you should be looking to do. These are as follows:

- To demonstrate your familiarity with, and knowledge of, the subject.
- To determine the extent of past research into the subject matter. It is important to determine at an early stage whether you have identified an original research question (as discussed in Chapter 4) or whether you are simply repeating past research. The review of literature will enable you to identify gaps in existing research, which can be addressed through your research.
- To provide an outline of the relevant theories and concepts important within your research project. Using an appropriate theory is important to allow you to have a framework within which to explain your findings. Concepts are important so that others may share and understand your findings in the knowledge that the often rather abstract phenomena under investigation are clearly outlined. The literature will be able

to help you gain a clear understanding and definition of appropriate concepts, as well as provide an indication of how they have been used in past studies.

- To focus the research question. As I noted in the previous chapter, one of the biggest problems faced by researchers is that they struggle with the research because they have not sufficiently focused or delimited their research question. By reading how others have focused their research and gaining an understanding of the types of questions that have been tackled in the past, you will be able to gain ideas on focusing your own research question and get an indication of the type of research questions that have been successfully answered in the past.

- To develop a hypothesis and null hypothesis, if appropriate. Your hypothesis is the predicted outcome of the research based upon logical reason or existing evidence. The literature will help you to develop this hypothesis. Otherwise your hypothesis is likely to be no more than educated guesswork! Hypotheses are generally associated with positivist, deductive and quantitative research, and they are normally not a feature of qualitative research.

- To help ensure all relevant variables are identified. A thorough search of the literature should identify all the moderating variables that may have an influence upon the research programme. Identifying such variables allows you to ensure that they can be addressed within your methodology.

- To identify methodologies and methods that have been successfully utilised in the past. You may be able to gain valuable insights into how others have approached similar questions, for example in terms of sampling methods, data collection instruments, methods of analysis and so on (although you should avoid simply replicating existing methodologies without careful consideration).

- To allow comparison of your findings with the findings of others. You will normally compare your findings with the findings of other researchers, thus you will need to identify these. You will also need to identify how your work builds on the work and adds to knowledge.

Quantitative and qualitative studies – the differing nature of the literature review

One of the differences between a quantitative and qualitative study is in their use of the literature. Generally (although not always), this is in terms of the scope of literature presented within the review itself. Quantitative studies tend to have a more extensive review that covers the full range of relevant literature and are guided very much by the content of the review in terms of what is measured, the formation of hypotheses and the subsequent analysis of data. It is rare for new literature to be brought into any discussion. It is perfectly acceptable, however, for a qualitative study to present a briefer 'overview' of the literature and to allow the relevant literature to emerge from the themes developed from the data (see Chapter 14 on qualitative analysis), demonstrating an 'ongoing dialogue with the literature' (Jones *et al.* 2013, p. 32) and allowing new literature to be presented within the discussion. Indeed some qualitative researchers see the inclusion of too much literature at the start of a project as bad practice, potentially biasing the subsequent research or pushing it in a certain direction before the data is collected. Thus a qualitative literature review is more of a guiding framework rather than the more rigid framework that supports a quantitative study.

Sources of literature

One worry that researchers beginning a project often have is that there will be insufficient literature available, especially if the question is tightly focused. In practice, this is rarely (if ever) the case. A search through library databases and search engines will soon demonstrate the large, indeed overwhelming amounts of information available to you. The problem tends to lie in where to find the appropriate information and what to do with the information when you have found it. There are a number of varied information sources, of which the main ones available to you are as follows.

Books

These are an obvious source of information and often are the first information resource to be utilised. Books are good for providing a broad overview of the topic and describing the key research that has been undertaken. However, they are unlikely to be sufficient, as they will often lack depth or focus upon the topic being researched, especially if they are general textbooks. Another potential problem is that books may become outdated, especially in a rapidly developing field such as sport. Thus you should ensure that you are looking at the most recent texts available. Books will often provide you with a list of further useful sources in their reference section or bibliography. I would strongly recommend using books to develop your initial understanding of the topic before focusing on more specialist journals as your understanding develops.

Peer-reviewed journals

These will be the most important sources of information to you. You should be using contemporary articles from peer-reviewed journals wherever possible. Peer reviewing is a process whereby the work submitted for such journals is assessed by independent, expert reviewers who ensure that the publication is of the appropriate standard. Such journals will show the up-to-date research being carried out in your area. Most journals will now publish their latest articles online before the print copy, and it's always worth having a look through these to see what is 'cutting edge' in your area.

Conference papers

These are often more difficult to obtain, and the quality may not always be as high as with journal articles, as they might not have gone through any peer review process. However, they do often provide useful insights into the type of research being carried out in the field, especially in terms of work in progress, or developing fields of study. If you can attend conferences in your subject area, then this is an excellent method of identifying the most up-to-date research being carried out.

Past theses

These can provide large quantities of detailed information, with more extensive literature reviews and methodologies than would be the case for peer reviewed articles. You can search relevant indexes, such as the Index to Theses (www.theses.com). Once you have identified relevant theses, they can be obtained using interlibrary loans; or they are becoming increasingly available to download from university digital repositories, or EThOS (Electronic Theses Online System).

Newspapers/magazines

These can provide useful and up-to-date factual data. Back issues of quality newspapers are also widely accessible. Care needs to be taken with such sources, however, as reports may be distorted in some way, and such sources generally do not provide a bias-free perspective in their analysis of sporting issues.

Trade journals

Trade journals will provide useful data on current trends and developments in the area; however they are not aimed at an academic audience. They may not be available as widely as academic journals in libraries, and you may need to contact the relevant association directly if you require particular issues.

Social media

Although you shouldn't be using social media as a source of literature in itself (although it does, as we shall see later in the book, provide an excellent source of data), it can be a useful resource. Once you've identified the key authors in your field, follow them on social media if possible. This can be an excellent way of finding out what they are currently working on, as well as other information related to their research area.

Finding the literature

Much of the relevant literature will be indexed within various databases or search engines, which can then be searched using one or more keywords. The search will provide information about articles containing that keyword so you can decide whether the article is relevant to your research, and enough detail will be given for you either to locate the article in your library or to obtain it from other sources. You may also be able to use a citation index; for example, *Google Scholar* has an extremely useful "cited by" function, which will identify other works that have cited a particular article themselves. Searching electronic sources is not a guarantee of being able to find all of the relevant literature. It requires careful planning. You should, beforehand, write down all the key terms that may be appropriate to your research project, including variations. Identify alternative words for each key term (for example *coach* and *instructor*, *fan* and *spectator*) and note variations in spelling (for example *behaviour* and *behavior*, *organisation* and *organization*).

There are a number of databases and search engines that you can use to search for relevant literature. This is not an exhaustive list, so check with your librarian for any other sources of information. Some of the databases will be freely accessible; others will require you to log on using a username and password. If this is the case, see your librarian to find out how to get these details.

- Google Scholar. This provides a straightforward way to search for literature across many disciplines and sources, including journal articles, books, abstracts and theses, from academic publishers, professional societies, online repositories, universities and other web sites. This is an excellent starting point for your literature search. Google Scholar also ranks results based on factors such as where they were published and how often and how recently they were cited. There is the option to see who has used the articles you find as well, using the 'cited by' function, which provides both further relevant literature for you, as well as also providing some clues about the worth of the research (although remember that more recent articles will be cited less than those that are older).
- SportDiscus. This contains references to journal articles, books and conference papers from a variety of disciplinary approaches, such as sociology, psychology, physical education and so on, from 1975 onwards.
- ASSIA. This is a general database focusing on health, psychology, sociology, economics, politics, race relations and education; however it does contain a number of useful sport-related articles.

- PsychInfo. If you are undertaking research into the psychological aspects of sport, then you should access this database. It contains psychological abstracts from key journals from as early as 1887.
- Sociological abstracts. This will help you locate articles that have approached sport research from a sociological perspective.
- Pro Quest. This will enable you to locate articles in the areas of business, management, economics and finance.
- British Humanities Index. This is a general index covering a variety of newspapers and journals. It will be of interest to those studying sport from a humanities perspective, such as those researching sport history.
- Zetoc. This grants access to the British Library's Electronic Table of Contents (ETOC) and provides details of a range of journal articles and conference proceedings.

You can also search:

- Library catalogues. You can search for items on library catalogues. However, such searches are less detailed. They are a good means to locate appropriate books but are generally less useful to locate journal articles.
- Internet searches. There is a wealth of information on the internet. However, searching the internet can be a difficult and time-consuming task. As I suggested earlier, there is also less 'quality control' of sources, and you need to be extremely cautious in your use of the internet.
- Publishers' web pages. These can be a valuable resource and will often list journal contents pages as well as relevant books. For example, *www. routledge.com/sport* will provide up-to-date information on the sport-related books produced by Routledge.
- Reference lists. One method to quickly develop your bibliography is to locate a relevant, up-to-date book or article. Read the list of references at the end of the work, and identify important sources from the references. Obtain those references, and repeat the process looking for new sources. Using this method, you can build up a substantial bibliography in a relatively short period of time. Be aware, however, that this is unlikely to identify very recently published sources.

Faced with this wide range of sources in a number of different formats, beginning the literature review will seem a daunting task. Unfortunately there is no one best way of finding the literature to begin with. The important advice to be aware of before you start is as follows:

- Start as soon as you possibly can. If, for example, you are undertaking a final-year dissertation, then you should be looking to begin your literature search towards the end of the preceding year if at all possible. Be systematic as far as possible, but always be on the lookout for relevant literature that you may uncover by accident.

- Have a search strategy – don't randomly enter search terms in an ad hoc manner.
- Don't restrict your search to sport related sources. Use the wider discipline or other fields to help you, for example explore the wider literature from management if you are researching leadership in sport, or some of the more generic literature on consumer behaviour if you are interested in peoples' decision-making processes when buying sport equipment.
- Keep careful records of your searches and of any literature that you uncover from the beginning of the search. Do not imagine that you will be able to locate relevant details later.
- Try to locate the 'classic' sources early in your search. Use the 'cited by' function of Google Scholar to explore how these sources have been subsequently used. If you were doing, for example, a study on barriers to participation, then you may identify Crawford *et al.*'s (1991) highly influential paper on constraints to leisure participation. Google Scholar shows that this paper has been cited over 2,000 times and allows us to see which authors have used their ideas. Given the paper is now 30 years old, we can also refine the timescale to find citations since 2020. This gives us, after probably one minute's work, a list of approximately 200 papers, many of which are highly relevant.

Focusing your literature search

A common error, especially in student research, is to focus too early in the initial review of literature and become discouraged at the apparent lack of available sources. Thus, the student who is interested in why women begin to play rugby union, may – quite correctly – identify theories of socialisation as a possible theoretical framework. The student may then carry out a search for literature on women's socialisation into rugby, find relatively little of it and become discouraged by the apparent lack of material. An alternative, and more appropriate, approach would be to avoid becoming too focused in the initial search for related literature, for example by undertaking a search using the following general strategy:

- Theories of socialisation in general. You may find research into the socialisation of women into many social groups seemingly unrelated to sport, such as into education, medicine and business. You must remember, however, that both the underlying theoretical frameworks used by these authors and the methodologies that have been used in such research may provide important background information to you, so do explore alternative fields of study.

- Socialisation into sport. There is a wide range of literature based upon socialisation into sport, such as Richard *et al.*'s (2021) study of the socialisation into sport of French Paralympians. Again, although not directly related to the research question, the study provides valuable and up-to-date material about sport socialisation.
- Socialisation of women into sport. You may now focus further by investigating the research carried out on the socialisation of women into sport, to identify any particular gender issues that may be appropriate, again even if not seemingly directly related, for example M'mbaha's and Chepyator-Thomson's (2019) study of the socialisation of women into leadership positions in sport.

By the end of this search, even if no literature has been found specifically on the socialisation of women into rugby, you should have achieved the following:

- To have gained a clear understanding of the theoretical concept of socialisation.
- To have an overview of the nature of existing research into the socialisation of women into various social groups, research into the area of socialisation into sport and the socialisation of women into sport.
- To have identified gaps in the research, which can be used to help you develop your research question. You will then attempt to fill a gap in the literature with your own research.
- To have developed ideas about the possible findings of your own research.
- To have developed ideas on possible methodologies that could be used based on past research.

CASE STUDY

SEARCHING FOR THE 'TRICKLE-DOWN EFFECT': CONDUCTING THE LITERATURE REVIEW WHEN THERE ISN'T A GREAT DEAL OF LITERATURE!

BY DR STEPHEN FRAWLEY, AUSTRALIAN CENTRE FOR OLYMPIC STUDIES, UNIVERSITY OF TECHNOLOGY SYDNEY, AUSTRALIA

There are various ways the literature review can begin. The researcher can start by exploring what has been written specifically about the topic and published in the leading peer-reviewed journals for that field of study. Another possibility is starting wide, by looking at what has been studied across various fields and within various types of publications, not only peer-reviewed journals. Sometimes researchers who are exploring a topic that has not been widely studied have little choice but to deploy this second option. This approach applied to research I was involved with at the *Australian Centre for Olympic Studies* (ACOS) not long after the completion of the Sydney 2000 Olympic Games (Veal *et al*. 2012, 2019).

A group of us from ACOS wanted to understand what impact the hosting of the Olympics had on sport participation in Australia. When we started to explore what had been written about this general area, often termed 'the trickle-down effect', we were somewhat surprised to learn little research had been conducted and essentially nothing of relevance had been published in the leading sport management/policy journals. So, what literature did we find that helped us develop our research? In the very beginning we found an academic monograph, a small study by the Australian Bureau of Statistics (ABS) and two journal articles, both located outside the area of sport management and sport policy. The monograph we found was a collection of chapters written by mainly Spanish academics that explored the social and economic impact of the Barcelona 1992 Olympics (De Moragas and Botela 1995). Within the book there were a couple of chapters that explored the sport impact to emerge from the hosting of the Games (Sust 1995; Truno 1995). While both chapters were based on very small samples and contained a number of limitations, they provided many worthwhile ideas for the ACOS team. The study by the ABS (2001) was also limited by the fact that it had only been published a few months after the completion of the Sydney Games and that any extensive sport legacy would need to explore a much longer timeframe. This aside, the study provided a small amount of evidence that we needed to take into account.

The first journal article we found was published in an Australian-based leisure studies journal (the *Australian Journal of Leisure and Recreation*). The research was conducted in New Zealand and explored the impact of media coverage of the Barcelona 1992 Olympic Games on sport participation in New Zealand (Hindson *et al*. 1994). This paper was very useful in that it collected empirical data from New Zealand sporting organisations and was conducted with a solid methodology.

The second journal article we uncovered was probably the most important piece of research that helped set up our series of ACOS studies (Veal *et al*. 2012, 2019). The paper was titled "The Price of Gold", and it was published by two sport scientists (Hogan and Norton 2000) in a sport science journal. The work of Hogan and Norton, while not looking specifically at the sport participation legacy of the Sydney 2000 Olympic Games, explored the previous 20 years of sport funding in Australia and the impact that funding had on the number of medals won, whilst also comparing the change in physical activity across Australia for the same period of time. The work also demonstrated that, despite the Australian government spending billions of dollars on elite sport, there was no evidence of a 'trickle-down effect' in Australia for the period 1980–2000.

While only small in number, this literature was very important in shaping our research – that being the attempt to understand whether hosting the Sydney 2000 Olympic Games had a positive impact on sport participation in Australia, and therefore providing evidence of a 'trickle-down effect'.

Assessing the literature

Once you have identified the literature, then the next stage is to read, digest and fully record the literature that you have found. While you read each article, you should consider both the content of the article and the implications for your own research project. You should make notes while you are reading each article with this in mind. You should also carefully record the full reference for your bibliography. Once you have read and made notes on several articles, then you should consider organising them into a structured form, placing together articles that take a similar approach.

MAINTAINING YOUR REFERENCES – USING ENDNOTE

You are going to collect a lot of literature throughout the research process, and it is crucial to maintain accurate records of the literature you find on an ongoing basis and not to rely on being able to construct your reference list at the end of the project. I would strongly recommend using EndNote. This service allows you to collect, store and manage your references, either through an internet-based service (EndNote Online) or as downloadable software (EndNote Desktop). You can insert your references automatically into Word documents and create reference lists in the required format. You can also download references from many databases straight into EndNote.

It is important that you don't assume that each piece of literature you find is of the same standard. Not every source you locate will be appropriate, for example it may lack relevance or quality. You will need to critically assess the quality of the literature that you obtain and ensure that you pay more attention to works that are more relevant or of higher quality than to works that are only partially related or of lower quality. There are a number of criteria that you can use to assess these factors, including:

- What is the source of the literature? Is it from an international, peer-reviewed journal or a trade magazine, for example? A peer-reviewed article should carry more weight than the trade journal, yet the trade journal may be more useful in identifying areas of study that are of immediate relevance and practical interest. A trade journal will, however, generally lack any sort of academic or theoretical framework. When you use peer-reviewed journals, don't fall into the trap of focusing too much on journal rankings, however, as excellent work will be published in lower-ranked journals (and indeed weaker work will find its way into more highly ranked journals). Look at each piece of work on its own merits.

- Who are the authors? Are they recognised experts in the field? What other work have they published in this area? Do they have a coherent body of work in the area, or are they publishing in a wide range of areas with a limited focus on one aspect of sport?
- Is that piece of literature referenced elsewhere in other articles on the subject area? If so, are such references positive or critical? How many citations has the work received, and in what type of publication? (Remember, however, that recently published work will not have had time to build up high citations.)
- When was the article published? Is it a recent article, or has it been superseded by other research?
- Using your own knowledge, how good do *you* think the article is?

Be prepared to be critical of the research both in your reading and the write-up of the literature review if you can support your criticisms. This may especially be the case if the work is several years old, and theories and methods have since developed, or if your source has not been subject to an academic review process.

Reading the literature

It's often useful to have a checklist to guide you through the reading. Some or all of the following are helpful to think about:

1 What is the paper trying to find out? What is the central research question or hypothesis?
2 What is this paper trying to do that is new or original?
3 What theory underpins the research?
4 How strong do you think the methodology is? Has it used the right methods, with an appropriate sample? What are the strengths and weaknesses of the methodology?
5 What are the key findings of the paper?
6 How does the paper relate to existing work in the field? Does it support or contradict it?
7 What are the implications for your research? How does it inform your study?

Assessing internet and social media sites

If you are going to use internet or social media sources in your literature review, you need to assess them in terms of their quality and usefulness. Anyone with the correct equipment can put a web page on the internet or edit existing pages (such as Wikipedia), and being available on the internet is no guarantee of accuracy or quality. Do not, however, rule out the use of such sites as some will contain valuable and high-quality information. Many will, however, be inaccurate or misleading. Therefore, it is your responsibility to assess each site. There is no fool-proof way of doing this; however, there are a number of questions that should be asked:

- Who produced it? Was it:
  - An academic with expertise in the area?
  - An academic institution or publisher?
  - An official company or organisational web page?
  - A personal web page?
- What are their qualifications or credentials for producing such material?
- What was their purpose in producing the page? Might this impact upon the content in some way?
- Who was their intended audience?
- Have any claims been supported by evidence (for example, links to peer-reviewed sources)?
- Has the content undergone any form of refereeing process?
- When was the page last updated?

The COVID-19 pandemic demonstrated clearly, however, that even material produced by seemingly credible individuals is subject to bias, selectivity and simple disinformation. So be very careful in your use of any such site.

How do I know when I have collected enough literature?

The question of when you have sufficient literature is a difficult one to answer. There is no set amount of literature that you should include, and some research projects will contain much more literature than others. You should aim to reach what could be referred to as 'saturation', that is when reading new articles, you are coming across the same references again and again. If you have all of these references, then this suggests that you have covered the main literature sufficiently. Do make sure, however, that you keep an eye on the key journals in your field throughout the remainder of the research programme to ensure you don't miss anything relevant that is published after you have completed your literature search (although you would not be penalised for not including an article that was published close to your submission date). The number of sources you cite is also not always an indication of the quality of the literature review, and it is how you use the sources that is more important. A well-constructed review with fewer references is far preferable to a poorly written review with many references, and thus the question of 'How many?' should be less important to you than 'How have I used them?' (the PhD thesis of the academic John Nash, portrayed in the film *A Beautiful Mind*, had a total of two references).

Writing up the literature review

You will need to communicate your review to readers of the research report, so that they also can judge how your research fits in with existing work. A common error is to produce an annotated bibliography rather than a review of the literature. An annotated bibliography is a list of sources, each of which is followed by a brief note or 'annotation', stating and evaluating the content of the research and its usefulness to your own research project. Instead, your review should demonstrate to the reader the underlying state of knowledge in the area, highlight the gaps in existing research and demonstrate how your research fits in to the state of existing knowledge. This will involve much more of a synthesis of the literature into a coherent review rather than a list of sources.

The literature review should start with an introduction, identifying the topic under investigation and providing a context for the review. This should be followed by the main body, where the literature is reviewed. Often it is useful to begin the review with a broad overview of the relevant ideas, concepts and definitions before narrowing down to more relevant works. Note that a literature review is not simply a list of relevant literature but an organisation of past work into a logical structure under common themes or ideas. A literature review where each paragraph focuses upon the work of a single author is usually a sign that the researcher has produced an annotated bibliography rather than a literature review. Whereas an annotated bibliography is ordered by author, a literature review should be ordered by idea, and past research should be grouped together under appropriate categories, for example:

- Studies involving similar research problems.
- Studies involving similar methodologies.
- Studies coming to similar conclusions.

Those studies that are seen as more significant to your research should be dealt with in more depth than those that are less relevant; for example, you should give information about the aim of such studies, the methodology that was employed – including details of the sample – and a clear outline of the findings. For less important works, a brief summary of the findings may suffice. It is important that the literature review is not just a generic review of the subject matter. It should, instead, be a review of the state of knowledge of the subject area of your research project and the implications of such knowledge for your own programme of research. At the end of each section, you should summarise such implications for your research project. Finally, you should conclude the literature review with an evaluation of the current state of knowledge in the area and summarise the relationship of your study to the literature, suggesting your anticipated findings – if appropriate – in the form of a hypothesis. You should ensure when you write up your literature review that you make it clear how the work of others is related to your study. It is also important to assess where the literature may be deficient. If your study is filling a gap in existing literature, for example, you should aim to clearly demonstrate that such a gap exists in your review and relate your research question to this gap. I recommend that you select a highly regarded journal publishing sport-related research, such as the *Sociology of Sport Journal* or the *Journal of Sport Management*, and read as many literature reviews as possible to get a 'feel' for what a well-written review is like.

Structuring your literature review

Effectively, in most cases, the literature review needs to tell the reader three things:

1   What is known about the subject under investigation.
2   What isn't known.
3   What the research question is, and how it relates to Points 1 and 2 (listed here).

There are two broad ways to structure the review. The first is a 'funnel' approach, which is shown in Figure 5.1 (based on a study exploring how

Figure 5.1 A funnel approach to writing a literature review

women became socialised into combat sport). Here, the review starts with broader concepts and ideas before becoming increasingly focused towards the research question.

This approach works quite well when there is a single theoretical idea; for example, here the focus upon socialisation allows this structure to move from general ideas at the start to become increasingly focused towards the research question by the end. You may, however, decide to include a broader range of ideas into the review. You may decide to examine older women's socialisation into combat sports and decide that a review that simply explores socialisation theory fails to address all of the key issues. Hence, you might want to include material on aspects such as older people's experiences of sport and gender ideologies surrounding women's participation in combat sport. Here, a thematic literature review would be more appropriate. As can be seen in Figure 5.2, rather than a single theme (socialisation) that becomes increasingly focused towards the question, a variety of themes are presented. These are then 'tied together' at the end, where the overall implications of the various ideas within the review are summarised.

When you write a literature review, you should follow the same guidelines as with any piece of academic writing. Always begin the review with an introduction and complete it with a summary – you should also introduce and summarise any major subsections of the review. If you feel that it is appropriate, you don't have to have just one literature review chapter – break it up into two if necessary. Remember to cite all sources, and make sure that they are all included in your bibliography or reference list. Avoid statements such as 'It is a well-known fact that. . . ' or 'It is widely believed that. . . ' unless

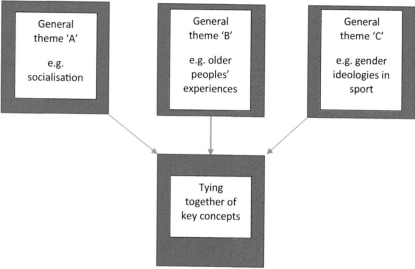

Figure 5.2 A thematic literature review

you can provide evidence to support such claims. You should also avoid the use of jargon or technical terms and attempt to make the review as readable as possible. As with any piece of work, ensure that you check your grammar and spelling carefully, as mistakes will detract from the quality of the review.

A further point concerns the inclusion of direct quotations. It is all too easy to insert large numbers of direct quotations into a review, and this can seem a quick and easy method to boost word counts. However, it can be a debatable practice. I would recommend that you keep the use of direct quotes to a minimum and only use them when the original author has stated a point in such a clear and concise manner that you are unlikely to be able to state the point as well yourself. Otherwise, use your own words as far as is possible. A literature review should demonstrate your ability to understand the broad state of knowledge in your area, not your ability to cut and paste from varied sources. In terms of the actual structure, it is often a good idea to follow the same sort of approach that I suggested with finding the literature. Start with a broad perspective and introduce your key concepts and theories. Gradually focus your review so that it becomes more specific to your particular research question.

THINGS TO CONSIDER WHEN WRITING THE LITERATURE REVIEW

- Gain familiarity with the subject before writing, but start writing as soon as you can.
- Construct your bibliography as quickly as possible – identify and access the key sources that you will need at the earliest possible stage.
- Allow yourself much more time than you initially think you need to write the review. It is rare to complete the review in one go, and generally a number of rewrites are necessary. You should be prepared for this.
- Work from an initial plan, but be prepared to continually refine and develop your structure as your understanding progresses.
- Include subheadings where necessary to guide the reader.
- Summarise your key findings regularly in longer literature reviews. Don't force the reader do the work in terms of understanding the point that you are trying to make; make it clear to them.
- Be selective – include literature that is relevant to your research, and spend more time on higher-quality or more important articles.
- Extract the relevant information from each study you use. Do not spend an inordinate amount of time describing each study in depth.
- Be up-to-date. Look at the dates from your bibliography. Are the key works recent, or are they several years old? If the latter, are they still 'cutting edge', or have they been superseded by more recent works? Do include, however, 'classic' works in your field wherever appropriate. Simply because a piece of work may be ten or more years old doesn't mean that it doesn't have value. Use your judgement!

Referencing other authors

You will need to reference the work of others throughout your literature review (as well as the rest of the report). A reference consists of three elements:

1   The text or idea that has come from the original author, whether quoted directly, paraphrased or summarised. For example, the following extract from Hutchins and Rowe's (2012) book *Sport Beyond Television* discussing the image associated with the typical sport journalist may be included within a literature review (inside quotation marks, as it is a direct quote):

    'The stereotypical image of a print sports journalist, though, has proven resilient. Crudely exaggerated for the purposes of argument, it is that of a star-struck, sports-loving newspaperman who "got lucky" by being paid to do what other people who aren't celebrities or dignitaries have to pay for – watch sports events from the best seat in the house.'

2   The abbreviated reference within the text to show where the statement originated. Normally (although not always) this is placed at the end of the statement, for example: ' . . . from the best seat in the house' (Hutchins and Rowe 2012, p. 125). This shows that the authors of the quote were Hutchins and Rowe, the source was their text published in 2012, and the quotation was taken from page 125. If you had simply taken their ideas and rewritten them in your own words, then the page number is not necessary. If you had referred to two different works by the same authors, both published in the same year, then you should differentiate between them using 2012a and 2012b.

3   The full reference in the reference list or bibliography at the end of the research report. The in-text reference allows the reader to identify the full source of the quotation or idea here, for example: Hutchins, B. and Rowe, D. (2012) *Sport Beyond Television*. New York: Routledge.

The full references are then placed in alphabetical order in either a reference or bibliography section at the end of the research report. Thus, the reader can, simply by looking at the reference within the text, locate the full details of the source material.

There are a number of purposes for referencing. Jankowicz (2000) provides a useful list to outline the key purposes:

● To attribute a quotation. If you use the words of other authors, you must enclose them using inverted commas and provide a reference, rather than claim them as your own. As I noted earlier, for such direct quotations you should also provide the page number, as is shown in the following example: '*Until fairly recently, most sociologists, and social historians, and many anthropologists have neglected sport as a potentially fruitful object of study' (MacClancy 1996, p. 1).*

- To justify an important statement. If you are making an important claim, then you should support your claim with a reference. An example of this may be that you want to make the point that sport has, for a long period of time, been overlooked by many as an area of academic study, and therefore you write a statement to this effect. At the end of the statement you should support your claim through providing a reference to other authors who agree: *Sport has been overlooked for many years as a legitimate area of academic study (MacClancy 1996)*. This shows that you have not simply made up the statement, but that it is a statement based on a source. This source can then be checked by the reader. Note that a page number is not required, as you are not directly quoting the author.

- To justify your approach. You may wish to justify your approach to your research by referring to similar authors who have taken the same approach or used similar theories or models with successful results.

- To demonstrate breadth of reading. A further advantage of consistently referencing your sources is that you can demonstrate the breadth of your reading (although you should resist the temptation to throw in references at every available opportunity). It is tempting to include references that you have not actually read or used as a strategy to boost your bibliography and demonstrate more reading than you have actually done. This practice should be avoided.

Wherever possible, you should use the original text or article rather than use what is referred to as 'secondary referencing'. If in your reading of Hutchins and Rowe (2012) you find a reference to the work of Marshall and colleagues (2010) on the rise of lunchtime audiences for internet sport, for example, then it's important that you don't give the impression that you've directly accessed and read the text by Marshall *et al.* yourself, which would be misleading. To avoid such potential problems, you should acknowledge in the text that what you are citing or quoting has come from another source (that you have actually read). Thus, rather than write: 'As Marshall *et al.* (2010) note, the growth of the lunchtime audience for internet sport content is a prominent example of change in the way sport is consumed', which would suggest that you have read their work yourself, you should acknowledge the true source of your information. For example: 'As Marshall *et al.* (2010, cited in Hutchins and Rowe 2012) note, the growth of the lunchtime audience for internet sport content is a prominent example of change in the way sport is consumed'. Thus it is clear that you have gotten your information from Hutchins and Rowe, rather than the study of Marshall *et al.* You should then only include Hutchins and Rowe (2012) in your list of references or bibliography.

Mistakes often made in the literature review

Many inexperienced (as well as more experienced) researchers find writing the literature review a difficult part of the research process. Unfortunately there are no easy answers, and it is the case in most instances that you will have to rewrite and restructure the literature review a number of times. Even well-known authors publishing in top journals will have rewritten their literature reviews a number of times. For this reason, I recommend that you commence the writing of the review as soon as possible, rather than leaving it to the last minute. Common mistakes include:

- Making the review simply a list of past studies, or producing an annotated bibliography.
- Not relating the literature review to the study, and making it simply a general review of the subject matter rather than providing background to your study.
- Not taking time to identify the best sources and give such sources due emphasis, while at the same time overemphasising weaker or less important sources.
- Failing to appreciate the relevant wider (i.e. beyond just that which is sport-related) literature.
- Relying on secondary rather than primary sources of literature (textbooks rather than journal articles, for example).
- Uncritically accepting the findings of existing literature rather than critically evaluating it.

One of the most common errors with the literature review is that it reads as a stand-alone piece of work about the broader topic, without relating to your research question; that is, it should not be just a review of the literature per se, but rather it should be a review of the literature in terms of how it relates to what you are doing. By reading the literature review, the reader should get a sense of how your research question has 'emerged' from the literature. By the end of the literature review, there should be a clear indication of what you are doing, how it is adding to existing literature and, if appropriate, what you could expect to find.

Identifying secondary data

Using existing literature can help you not only in terms of providing the background to your own data collection, but it can sometimes provide you with the actual data to answer your research question. Data can be separated into two forms: Primary data – data that you have collected yourself, through your own questionnaires, interviews, observations and so on – and secondary data, which have already been collected by others. Secondary data come in a wide range of forms, such as research articles, annual reports, government publications and so on. When searching through the literature you may find secondary data that will help you answer your research question. This may be either raw data or data that have been previously analysed. Using secondary data can save a significant amount of time and effort, and it may even produce higher quality data than if you had collected it yourself. Both quantitative and qualitative data can be reanalysed, although its more common to reanalyse quantitative data. Don't overlook the possibilities of reanalysing qualitative data, however; it's worth a read of research such as Oman's (2020) reanalysis of data from the UK Office for National Statistics (ONS), which allowed her a much better understanding of the role of leisure activities such as sport to national well-being than was created by the initial analysis.

There are potential problems with using secondary data, however. First, you need to ensure that the data collected was valid and reliable, and not subject to any serious methodological errors. Second, you need to be aware of when the data was collected and whether it is still appropriate or is dated. Remember that secondary data were collected with a different purpose from the one that you are to put them to, and you should always be aware that the original author of the data may have been subject to particular constraints, had a particular agenda and so on. Finally there may well be ethical issues with certain forms of data (especially qualitative data). You need to be aware of any issues and state them clearly in the final written report (it is no good being aware of the limitations if you don't make this awareness clear to whomever will assess your report). When using secondary data you may wish to consider:

- Who collected the data? What were their qualifications for doing so?
- What was the purpose of the data collection? Were there any factors that may have influenced the collection and presentation of the data? Was the data collection sponsored by an outside organisation, for example?
- How were the data used or analysed by the original author?
- Have the data been used as secondary data in any other research project of which you are aware?

USING SECONDARY DATA TO EXPLORE PROFESSIONAL ATHLETES' INVOLVEMENT IN CHARITABLE FOUNDATIONS

Tainsky and Babiak (2011) wanted to explore and profile professional athletes participating in philanthropic activity within the NBA. To do this, the authors were able to use existing data on the athletes, including their salaries, ages and other relevant information on NBA players gained from a number of reliable sources such as ESPN.com, often using more than one source to corroborate the data. They then used Google, the Foundations

Directory and the NBA Players Association web page to identify which players had established foundations, and they followed relevant hits to decipher the name of the foundation, its mission and the existence of a link to the player's team foundation. Information on which players established foundations was verified by the Sports Philanthropy project. They then examined tax forms to identify the amount of support player foundations were giving and to whom. The data allowed them to determine that older, higher-paid athletes were more likely to create foundations and that association with a charitable team also predicted athlete philanthropy.

How do I know when I have completed my literature review?

You will reach a stage where you think you are approaching the end of your literature review. If so, you need to ask yourself the following questions:

- Have I covered the key literature? If I have read recent journal articles in the field, are there any sources used by the authors of those journals that I should have used?
- Is the literature review up to date? Have I covered recent sources? Have I included any outdated material?
- Do I relate that literature to my research question?
- Have I included literature that contradicts, as well as supports, my viewpoint?
- Have I produced a critical assessment rather than a descriptive review?
- Have I organised the review into a logical and coherent structure rather than simply producing a list of literature?
- Have I identified the gaps/weaknesses in existing literature?
- Does my research question emerge clearly from the literature?

Summary

- It is important that you develop your own expertise in the subject matter at an early stage in the research process. This is done through locating, reading and reviewing relevant literature.
- The written review of this literature also forms an important part of your written report.
- In your search for literature, you should not restrict yourself. Broaden your search at the beginning, and be prepared to seek out different sources. You should then gradually focus your review towards your particular research objectives.
- Always relate your review to your own research question, rather than simply making it a review of the state of knowledge in the area per se.
- Literature may, in certain cases, provide you with existing data with which you can achieve your research objectives.

Activity

The best way to get a 'feel' for what a literature review involves is to read as many reviews as possible. Choose a subject area of interest to you. Locate a number of sources pertaining to the topic using each of the search methods discussed in this chapter, such as Google Scholar. Ensure that at least two articles that you locate are recent pieces of research from peer-reviewed journals. Read the articles, and pay special attention to the literature reviews. You should note how the author has structured the review, what has been included and how the review is focused towards the overall research question.

ABOUT YOUR RESEARCH PROJECT

Once the first draft has been completed, you should critically assess your own literature review. Consider the following points:

- Have you included all the key works, or are there any omissions that you are aware of?
- Have you used a range of sources, including journal articles, or have you relied upon a few textbooks?
- Have you synthesised your reading into a comprehensive review of the literature, or have you just listed descriptions of past research?
- Have you chosen an appropriate structure for the review?
- Have you related the review to your research question and considered the implications of the literature review for your research question?
- Have you correctly referenced all of your sources, paying particular attention to secondary referencing?

Further reading

There are a variety of resources (including online) to help you with your literature review. Some good starting points are:

Efron, S. and Ravid, R. (2018) *Writing the Literature Review: A Practical Guide*, New York: Guilford.
Hart, C. (2009) *Doing a Literature Review: Releasing the Social Science Research Imagination*, London: Sage.
Ridley, D. (2012) *The Literature Review: A Step-by-Step Guide for Students*, London: Sage.

Chapter 6
Theories, concepts and variables

Theories, concepts and variables

This chapter will:

- Introduce the role and importance of theory within your research project.
- Describe how you should be able to relate your question to existing disciplines in sport.
- Describe how to develop a conceptual framework for your study.
- Introduce and define the concepts of reliability and validity, describe the relationship between the two, and outline their importance within a quantitative research project.
- Discuss the terms *reliability*, *credibility*, *trustworthiness* and *rigour*, and discuss their importance within a qualitative research project.

Introduction

In Chapter 5, I talked a lot about the role of the literature in identifying past theories and concepts that could be relevant for your study. For many students, the importance of theory within a research project can be a difficult issue, yet it is one of the most important considerations and in many cases underpins the entire research project, especially if you are taking a deductive approach to your research. While it might be tempting to go into the data collection stage of the research as soon as possible, you do need to spend some time thinking about the theories and concepts involved, and developing an appropriate theoretical framework within which your data can be analysed, interpreted and explained. This chapter introduces some of the issues related to choosing your theoretical framework and relating this framework to your study. Theories themselves are constructed from concepts, and a key process here is to identify exactly what concepts are involved, their relationships to each other, and how they are to be investigated, so that your data can be related to your choice of theoretical framework. This is the process of developing your conceptual framework, and this idea will also be outlined. Finally, the issues related to how you measure your concepts, and the quality of such measurement, whether quantitative or qualitative, will be discussed.

Theories and theoretical frameworks

Theories are, simply, explanations of why things occur. If you drop a football, it will fall to the ground at a particular speed. If you repeat the experiment, the result will be the same. All your results show is that a football will fall to the ground at the same rate each time, and no more. This is, therefore, an example of very basic descriptive research. To explain why this is the case, an appropriate theory is required. In this instance, the theory of gravity can explain your findings, that is to say *why* the football always dropped at the same rate. The same theory could also be used to predict that any further footballs dropped would also fall at the same rate. We can either identify the theory of gravity beforehand and test it by dropping the football in a deductive manner, or we could follow Sir Isaac Newton – who collected his data beforehand, according to tradition, by observing an apple fall – and then develop his theory of gravity in an inductive manner, which could then be applied to other contexts (for example applying the theory of gravity to sports where it has a major impact, such as archery or gymnastics). Whichever way we choose, the data itself is of limited value. Only when it is related to theory can we explain the findings and take our understanding beyond the basic descriptive level. It is therefore important that your research has a theoretical grounding if you want your research to be more than simply descriptive, and this will come from the theory that you choose to underpin your research project. At an early stage, you should be thinking carefully about your theoretical underpinning.

Social theories, dealing with the behaviour of individuals who have free will, individual choice and who are subject to unpredictable events or occurrences, will clearly have less predictive power than those of the natural sciences. This notwithstanding, theory is still significant to your research in being able to draw connections between concepts and developing explanation. Its role can be demonstrated using a relatively simple example. Imagine that you have come up with the following research question: 'Do sport fans identify more strongly with their favourite team when the team is winning?' It would be relatively easy to make the appropriate measurements (whether the team is winning and how strongly a sport fan identifies with their team) and collect data accordingly. The answer to the research question is likely to be 'yes', in that a sport fan is likely to identify strongly with their team when they are winning (I shall assume for the sake of simplicity that there are no other factors affecting this relationship). That, however, is the only conclusion that can be drawn from such research without a theoretical framework. You would be unable to explain this finding, that is to say *why* it had happened. Neither would you be able to predict the same finding in the future with any confidence. Thus, you would need to place your findings within an appropriate theoretical framework. In this instance it would be appropriate to use a theory such as social identity theory to make sense of the findings. One of the tenets of this theory is that we prefer to identify with groups that positively enhance our self-esteem, that is groups that are seen positively by others. With this theory, we could reasonably hypothesise that people would identify with their team (i.e. be a member of that particular group) if they are seen positively (i.e. by being successful). Using an appropriate theory, therefore, has allowed us to explain the findings. We could also use this theory to try to predict, to a partial extent, future behaviour in this context. Unfortunately, many research projects are examples of what Phillips and Pugh (1994) refer to as 'intelligence gathering'. This refers to the gathering and presentation of data, with no reference to any such theoretical framework. Essentially this is descriptive research, and it simply describes data. For example, it would be relatively easy to collect data to answer the question 'What was the proportion of male to female participants at the 2016 Olympic Games?'. By using appropriate theory, you may be able to propose a plausible explanation of why there were such differences.

You might also encounter the term *model*. In much of the published literature, these terms seem to be used interchangeably, and indeed they are similar in nature. Perhaps the key difference between the two in the social sciences is that a theory, as outlined here, tends to focus on *why* something happens, whereas a model tends to explain *how* something happens. Hence, the Psychological Continuum Model (Funk and James 2006), as an example, explores the stages through which people go before becoming a devoted fan of a team, focusing on *how* they become a fan, whereas Social Identity Theory explains *why* fans may be more willing to support successful teams.

Considering your approach

As I noted earlier in the book, sport can be studied from the viewpoint of a single discipline or from an interdisciplinary or multidisciplinary perspective. This means that there is no single academic subject that we can refer to as 'sport studies', but rather that there are a number of different ways of approaching sport academically, through the various disciplinary approaches. Thus sport can be studied from a sociological perspective, a psychological perspective, a geographical perspective, an economic perspective, as well as from multi- and inter-disciplinary perspectives; the United Kingdom Quality Assurance Agency (QAA), for example, notes 29 different subject areas related to the study of sport.

Within each of these broad disciplines, there are a number of more specific fields, such as 'sport' itself, or 'physical activity', and more specific aspects of each field. Thus, social psychologists may be interested in the aspect of attachment to sport or the relationship between sport and religion, for example. Each aspect will normally consist of a number of theories or models; for example, the attachment to sport will include models such as Funk and James's (2006) Psychological Continuum Model mentioned previously. Thus, in this instance we can see our broad disciplinary framework as follows:

Discipline	➤ Field	➤ Aspect	➤ Theory/model
Social Psychology	➤ Sport	➤ Attachment to sport	➤ Funk and James's (2006) Psychological Continuum Model

If you are undertaking a deductive study, then you need to start thinking about your theoretical orientation and to try to locate your ideas within this type of framework, as it will inform most if not all aspects of the research. As an example, you may be interested in carrying out a study related to Sport for Development and Peace (SDP), evaluating a scheme within a local context. Evaluating SDP practices with no theoretical framework isn't possible in any meaningful way, so you may, for example, identify the "Capabilities Approach" as used by Darnell and Dao (2017) as a framework to explore such initiatives. This approach identifies the importance of not only individual agency, but also their social, political and economic environment. As well as providing an evaluative framework, this also identifies the methodological importance of going beyond exploring either the individual or the environment and expresses the need to examine both. Hence the choice of this theory impacts upon the methodology itself.

CASE STUDY

THE IMPORTANCE OF THEORY FOR QUANTITATIVE RESEARCHERS

BY DR DANIEL LOCK, BOURNEMOUTH UNIVERSITY, UK

Looking at a spreadsheet full of variables, cases and observations can be a confronting experience; especially if the steps that come before data collection are unplanned or rushed. Quantitative research is, typically, premised on a deductive model of theory testing. As such, having a strong coverage of concepts and theories of relevance to a study *before it happens* is an important step in the development of quantitative research for two reasons. First, where a researcher lacks a good foundational knowledge about the concepts and theories of relevance to their study, it is likely that the design of instrumentation will be haphazard and omit (or measure inappropriately) key variables. Second, without knowledge of relevant concepts and theories, a researcher is unlikely to have a good understanding about the 'expected' relationships between variables, which is the cornerstone of sound hypothesis development.

It is for these reasons that 'good' quantitative research starts with a rigorous literature review to identify key concepts and theories, and the 'expected' (based on prior evidence) relationships or differences between them. Framing this process through the statement of testable hypotheses – *developed before the collection of data* – is a sound way of using existing evidence to focus researcher attention on what the data analysis will be about. The creation of a research instrument should seek to interrogate the hypotheses using valid and reliable measurements of the concepts in an operationalised form (e.g. scale measurement of individual personality). If a researcher follows these steps, the opening of a spreadsheet containing a quantitative dataset will, likely, be a less confronting experience because – once the data are cleaned (e.g. missing cases removed) – the analysis is focused and targeted on the study hypotheses (developed from existing theory), rather than random guesswork about where relationships or differences might occur in an unstructured and unplanned analysis. The data collected may not support the hypotheses created; however, if the process followed was rigorous, then the outcomes provide an opportunity to develop theoretical and conceptual knowledge. It is in this final step that the interpretation of the research findings in relation to existing knowledge, the study hypotheses and research aim is crucial to inform knowledge of sport studies.

Choosing an appropriate theory or model

At an early stage, it is likely that you may find it difficult to locate appropriate theories or to decide which theory or model is best for you. If you are undertaking a deductive study, you will need to have a clear idea of your theoretical framework at the outset. Even if you are undertaking an inductive approach, it is useful to have an idea of some of the appropriate theories that may be able to inform your study, without necessarily restricting yourself to any specific theories. There is no easy answer at this stage. It is generally a case of reading around the subject and trying to identify which theories have been used in past studies. Your review of literature should alert you to the theoretical approaches adopted by other researchers in the past. Alternatively, you may want to read around some of the broader, non-sport-related literature and identify theories and models from these sources. As always, don't restrict yourself if possible, and be prepared to search through the wider sociological, geographical, management-based literature and so on. Alternatively, you can always discuss this issue with your research supervisor or tutor, who may be able to put you on the right track. It's important to ensure that you choose your theory because it is appropriate for your research study, rather than it being, for example, one you find interesting, or easy to understand.

Concepts and conceptual frameworks

As I suggested earlier, theories are explanations with which we make sense of our findings. These explanations are built up using concepts. A concept is often easier to identify than it is to define. I would suggest that a concept is a shared representation of an object, a property or a behaviour. Examples of concepts are age, intelligence, anxiety, self-confidence and so on. Having a shared understanding of what concepts actually are is important so that researchers may be able to understand or replicate others' work. Thus, when one researcher discusses a particular concept, such as 'intelligence', others will know exactly what they are referring to. By having a shared understanding of the appropriate concepts and conceptual framework this is possible. As Miles and Huberman (1994, p. 18) describe:

> Categories such as 'sociocultural climate', 'cultural scene', and 'role conflict' are the labels we put on 'intellectual bins' containing many discrete events and behaviours. Any researcher, no matter how inductive in approach, knows which bins are likely to be in play in the study, and what is likely to be in them. Bins come from theory and experience and (often) from the general objectives of the study envisioned. Setting out the bins, naming them and getting clearer about their interrelationships lead you to a conceptual framework.

The conceptual framework describes and explains the concepts to be used in the study – not just those that build up your theory, but also those other concepts that may affect your findings. It outlines the relationships between concepts and how they are to be measured. Thus it is important in helping you plan your overall methodology, what exactly you are going to explore and why. Developing your conceptual framework requires five main steps:

1   Identifying the relevant concepts.
2   Defining these concepts.
3   Operationalising the concepts.
4   Identifying the relationship between variables.
5   Identifying any moderating or intervening variables.

We can illustrate the process with reference to a hypothetical research proposal based upon Chelladurai's (1990) work on leadership styles in sport and the further work by authors such as Ehsani *et al.* (2012) who have subsequently built upon this body of knowledge in varied sports. Say, for example, that you are interested in whether there is any relationship between the leadership style of sport coaches and the consequent satisfaction of the athletes that they coach. Thus, your research proposal was based on the following question:

How does the leadership style of a sport coach affect player satisfaction?

The first step is to identify your concepts, or 'building blocks', within the statement.

In this instance, these are:

- Leadership style.
- Sport coach.
- Player satisfaction.

Second, you must be able to define these concepts. This will help you clarify exactly what you are investigating. These definitions should, if at all possible, come from existing literature and use commonly accepted definitions, so that your research can easily be compared to both existing theory and the findings of others. Here, *leadership style* could refer to whether the coach displays autocratic or democratic leadership behaviour. *Sport coach* could be defined as an individual with responsibility for the strategy, tactics and training of the team. *Player satisfaction* could, from the literature, be defined as the satisfaction with three elements – satisfaction with training, satisfaction with individual performance and satisfaction with their personal treatment.

At this stage, if there is sufficient evidence within the existing literature and you are adopting a positivist methodology, you may want to suggest a hypothesis and a null hypothesis rather than a research question. As I noted in Chapter 2, a hypothesis is a suggested relationship between concepts to be tested empirically. A hypothesis generally requires four things:

1 It must be adequate. A hypothesis must be able to explain findings or relationships that are determined by subsequent data collection.
2 It must be testable. Unless a hypothesis can actually be tested empirically, then it has little value.
3 It should require relatively few assumptions, for example a hypothesis should not only be valid if a considerable number of conditions have to be met.
4 A good hypothesis must be better than other possible or rival hypotheses; that is, it should have better explanatory power than alternative hypotheses that could be considered.

Whether you decide upon a hypothesis or a research question, the next step in developing your conceptual framework is that of operationalising your concepts. Operationalising a concept means deciding how that concept is to be measured. Being able to produce an outstanding piece of theoretical work as the background to your research is of little use if you are unable to subsequently test your theories empirically or if your measurements of the concepts do not actually reflect what you think they do.

The term *measurement* may suggest a purely quantitative approach. Even if you are undertaking a qualitative study, however, it is important to have a clear idea as to how you are going to 'measure' your concepts. If you were going to undertake a qualitative approach on the effects of leadership style, trying to explain why the coaching style had a certain effect on satisfaction, then how would you identify and evaluate the qualitative data provided by the players of that sport team? Here, you would revisit your ontological and epistemological standpoint, as outlined in Chapter 2, to guide you. Often, within a qualitative study, this is a more emergent process, and you will develop your understanding of the appropriate concepts throughout the data collection and analysis process (see Chapter 14 for a more in-depth account of qualitative analysis).

KEY TERM

EMPIRICAL

Often you will see reference to good research as being 'empirical' in nature. This simply means that the conclusions drawn are based upon evidence (or data) rather than conjecture or speculation.

As is the case with defining your concepts, try to use generally accepted measures of a concept (you should be able to identify these when you are reviewing the literature). There are two reasons for this. First, it will allow you to compare your findings with existing literature more effectively, and second, for quantitative data, it will give you confidence that your measures are actually valid and reliable. (I will explain these terms later on in this chapter.) Using the earlier example, leadership styles can be operationalised by using Chelladurai and Saleh's (1980) Leadership Scale for Sport, a 40-item scale that can assess the coach's leadership style. Operationalising the concept of sport coach is not appropriate here, as the clear definitions provided at the first step should be sufficient, and it is simply a case of ensuring that your sample reflects these criteria. Operationalising 'satisfaction' could again be done with reference to existing research; for example, the *Athlete Satisfaction Questionnaire* (Riemer and Chelladurai 1998) could be used.

DIFFICULT TERMS TO OPERATIONALISE

Within sport studies, there are a number of terms that are difficult to operationalise accurately, and you should critically assess your own operationalisation of your concepts. Performance, for example, is difficult to operationalise and often is done incorrectly by measuring wins. This is an obvious way of measuring performance, yet is it a valid measure of performance? There are a number of factors that are of concern here, for example the obvious point that a team may perform well and yet still lose. Conversely, a team may play badly and defeat inferior opposition. Are we interested in the performance of the team as a whole or of individual players? Thus, the concept of performance is likely to be a problematic one in this research project and will need to be reconsidered.

Another common concept used rather vaguely is that of 'effect', such as in 'what has been the effect of commercialisation on the Olympic Games?'. There are so many ways that 'effect' could be operationalised that, until you can clarify exactly what is meant by effect and how it will be measured, the question is almost meaningless. In the same way terms such as *change* or *influence* are also difficult to define unambiguously. Thus, throughout stages 2 and 3 of the conceptual framework development, you should always ensure that you have clear, unambiguous, and valid definitions and operationalisations.

Types of quantitative measurement

Quantitative data collection tends to involve the collection of factual or directly measurable data, yet, as I have just shown, this is not always straightforward. Although the data itself may be clear, how it is operationalised has important implications for the validity of the research (we shall discuss this concept in more depth later in this chapter) and also for how your data is to be analysed. Take the following example. You may be interested in the relationship between income and interest in sport. To determine income, a number of different questions could be asked:

1   What is your gross annual income? _____

2   Is your gross annual income:

- under £30,000?   ❑
- £30,001 – £35,000?   ❑
- £35,001 – £40,000?   ❑
- above £40,000?   ❑

3   Do you earn more than £40,000 per year? Yes ❑ No ❑

These questions are asking roughly the same thing, but in a different way, and each will give you a different response. These responses will all provide correct data, yet they may all result in different types of conclusion to your question. These questions show respectively an example of interval level data, ordinal data and finally nominal data. Each of these types of data can be analysed differently and may give you differing results to your research question. This will be dealt with in more depth in Chapter 13. At this stage, however, it is important for you to consider exactly what you will be measuring and why such measurement is being adopted. Variables can be quantitatively measured in four different ways: Nominal, ordinal, interval and ratio (although some statistical software combines interval and ratio data under one heading).

- *Nominal scales* group subjects into different categories. For instance, grouping football players on the basis of the team they play for is an example of a nominal scale. A nominal scale does not suggest any relationships between the groups; for example, grouping together those playing for team X under the label '1' and those playing for team Y under the label '2' does not suggest that those in team Y are somehow different or 'better' in any way. Nominal data is sometimes referred to as categorical data. If there is any order to the categories, however, then this becomes ordinal data.
- *Ordinal data* have a rank order but do not indicate the difference between scores. Think, for example, of placement on a squash ladder. The person on top has performed better than the person second, and so on. Thus data is ordered, but there is no indication of how much difference there is between players. The player assigned a score of '1' is not necessarily twice as good as the player assigned '2'. They might be slightly better, or considerably better – there is no measure of this. The only information we have is that of the order itself.
- *Interval data* have equal intervals of measurement between values, for example a gymnastics scoring scale. There are equal intervals between each score, i.e. there is the same difference between an 8.00 and a 9.00 as there is between a 9.00 and a 10.00. It is not necessarily the case, however, that a 10.00 is worth twice as much as a 5.00.
- *Ratio data* are also based on order, with equal units of measurement, but they are proportional and have an absolute zero. For example, if a basketball team scores 50 points, then that is worth twice as much as a team that scored 25 points.

Once a concept has been operationalised, it becomes a variable. The two most important types of variables are independent and dependent variables. Independent variables are the presumed cause of the effect being researched. For example, if gender influences attitudes towards violent sports, then it is gender that has the presumed effect upon the attitudes; therefore it is the independent variable. Dependent variables are those that can be explained by the effect of the independent variable, which in this instance is the attitude towards violent sport. In the example I have already discussed, leadership style is predicted to influence satisfaction. Therefore leadership style is the independent variable, and satisfaction is the dependent variable. You need to ensure that you correctly identify your independent and dependent variables; otherwise you run the risk of your conclusions becoming erroneous. This can be illustrated by reference to a hypothetical study that explores the impact of physical activity on well-being. It might well be that people who take part in such activity demonstrate higher well-being as a result of activity, but it could also be the case that they are more likely to participate in physical activity because they have higher well-being in the first instance.

Therefore, superficially at least, it would seem that by measuring leadership style and satisfaction we could identify whether there is a relationship between the two. Unfortunately, research is rarely this straightforward. Leadership style will not be the only influence upon satisfaction. Other variables may also have an effect on the relationship, and we will need to identify them. These are called moderating, or extraneous, variables. Thus, the next stage of developing your conceptual framework is to identify these variables. This is important, as too many unaccounted moderating variables will affect the validity of the research, in that any effect you identify may well be attributable to moderating factors. Moderating variables for our hypothetical example may include:

- Gender.
- Team cohesion.
- Team performance.
- Rewards.
- Past experiences.

With so many moderating variables, it may be difficult to conclude that the satisfaction has been affected as a consequence of leadership style. One option for the researcher is to systematically identify and remove as many moderating variables as possible, for example undertaking the study on males only, to remove gender as a moderating variable, or, where possible, to use a control group, where all variables are the same for both groups, with the exception of the independent, or treatment, variable. Often, however, you won't be able to control for all variables. Therefore a further option is to measure such variables and attempt to account for them in your analysis. However, this can often involve some very complicated statistics, and you need to consider your expertise in being able to undertake and evaluate such analyses. Generally, the more focused your research question, the fewer moderating variables you can anticipate, and this is a good reason for focusing your study as much as possible!

In some cases you will also encounter intervening variables. As the name suggests, these are variables that intervene between the independent and dependent variables. For example, rather than a direct relationship between leadership style (independent variable) and performance (dependent variable), it may be the case that there is another relationship involving a different variable:

> Leadership style (independent variable) ➤ affects self-efficacy (intervening variable) ➤ affects satisfaction (dependent variable)

You need to be able to control such intervening variables if you are to determine the true influence of the independent variable upon the dependent. Alternatively you need to assess the influence of the independent variable upon the intervening variable, and then the influence of the intervening variable upon the dependent variable. By ignoring intervening variables, you may well end up with an apparent relationship that does not actually exist; for example, there may be a strong correlation between leadership style and athlete satisfaction, yet it is not necessarily the case that leadership style does affect satisfaction. Instead, it may be that self-efficacy is actually influenced by leadership style. Self-efficacy may also influence satisfaction, with the consequence that the researcher makes a link between leadership style and performance that doesn't actually exist.

A similar, though slightly different, hypothetical case can also be provided to demonstrate some of the potential dangers in not assessing carefully the relationships between variables. You may be interested in the relationship between education and attitudes to competitive sport, i.e. education (independent variable) affects attitudes to competitive sport (dependent variable). You may well find a relationship between the two and conclude that our attitudes towards competitive sport are shaped by our education. There may be an alternative explanation, however. Our education is often dependent upon the socio-economic class of our parents. What if our attitudes to competitive sport were also shaped by our socio-economic background? This would mean there may be no connection between education and attitudes towards competitive sport, yet your measurements would suggest there is. (You may get a significant correlation between the two.) This is an example of a *spurious relationship*, and you need to ensure that you are measuring relationships that actually exist.

Once you have identified your variables, you can graphically represent the relationships between them, as, for example, Madrigal (1995) did when he explored the idea of sport fan satisfaction (see Figure 6.1). This can be useful in clarifying the objectives of your research, and it also can provide you with a framework for the analysis and interpretation of your data.

A CONCEPTUAL FRAMEWORK FOR SPORT FAN SATISFACTION

Madrigal (1995) was interested in fan satisfaction in attending a particular sporting event. Rather than a single independent variable affecting satisfaction, he identified a number of relevant concepts from the literature that could have an effect, for example:

- Expectancy disconfirmation – or the difference between the expected and actual outcome.
- Team identification – or the extent of the involvement of the fan with their team.
- Quality of the opponent.
- BIRGing – or the tendency to 'bask in reflected glory' of the team. Madrigal suggested that this was influenced by the three factors already cited.
- Enjoyment – this was also influenced by the same three factors.

Madrigal's conceptual framework is graphically represented in Figure 6.1.

Figure 6.1 An example of a conceptual framework

Developing a conceptual framework is important for a number of reasons. As well as providing an overall framework to guide us through the data we need to collect, and our subsequent analysis, it also identifies potential issues before data collection commences. We can see that through developing our conceptual framework with the example presented here that our initial research question raises a number of potential problems, these being the difficulties in defining and operationalising performance, and also the issue of having too many moderating or intervening variables. By undertaking this process you can be made aware of these problems before the research commences and can refocus your research topic.

The role of a conceptual framework does differ between quantitative and qualitative research. Whereas, in quantitative research I would always recommend developing your conceptual framework before data collection, it has more of a guiding role in qualitative research, and often, in such research, your data analysis will lead you to developing and refining your conceptual framework at the conclusion to the study.

Assessing the quality of quantitative data

The process described here will allow you to identify the measurements that you are going to make. It is now a good idea to assess the extent to which your operationalisation of your concepts will actually provide a 'true' answer to your research question, that is the quality of your measures. Two key concepts by which the quality of quantitative research is assessed are those of reliability and validity, and these are often used to assess how 'truthful' a piece of research actually is.

Reliability

Suppose that you are researching brand usage of products of sport sponsors. You ask your sample whether they have used a particular brand, and the affirmative response is 75 per cent. You ask the same sample the following day, and the positive response is 51 per cent. Which is the correct answer? Obviously, to be sure that you had the correct answer, you would have hoped for approximately the same answer on both occasions. Reliability generally refers to the consistency of the results obtained. A number of forms of reliability are important to the researcher, three in particular:

- Inter-observer reliability.
- Test/retest reliability.
- Internal consistency reliability.

Inter-observer reliability assesses the extent to which different observers would give similar scores to the same phenomenon; that is, would two researchers measuring the same behaviour at the same time give such a behaviour equal scores? This is especially important if there are a number of people involved in collecting data for a research project; for example, if you had a team of researchers observing the ratio of hostile and instrumental acts of aggression in a sporting event, then how do you ensure that they would all assign the same interpretation to similar acts of aggression?

Test/retest reliability is the extent to which the research would provide the same measurements if repeated at a different time; thus the test would give the same score over and over again (provided that what was being measured wasn't actually changing!). If a measurement was taken of an athlete's ability at a particular sporting task in week 1, and then the same measurement was taken in week 2 resulting in a different score, then what is the athlete's true score on the task? Such a measure would be considered unreliable. One of your tasks as a researcher is to identify reliable measurements of the phenomenon under investigation. *Internal consistency reliability* refers to the extent to which each question within a measure is actually measuring the same phenomenon. Thus, if you are assessing an individual's commitment to sport using a five-item scale, that is five questions that are analysed together to give an overall measure, then all five questions should be assessing commitment. This is more important when you use scales as a measurement technique. (I will discuss the use of scales in Chapter 8.)

Threats to reliability

Reliability is a prerequisite for any successful research project. A number of potential threats to reliability exist. These include:

- *Subject error.* The subject may respond differently depending upon when they are asked to supply data. If you question sport participants as to their predictions of future participation, you may find that your results are different if you ask participants directly before rather than directly after a match. This can be overcome by choosing a 'neutral' time to question them, for example in between matches.
- *Researcher error.* Two researchers may take slightly differing approaches to collecting the same data, which may result in different responses. If multiple researchers are to be used, then it is vital that each follows the same procedures. A study might involve, for example, multiple observers recording the number of aggressive checks made by ice hockey players. If they have differing views as to what constitutes an 'aggressive check', then reliability will be threatened.
- *Subject bias.* Participants may give the response they think the researcher wants or try and give the 'correct' answers. Anonymity should be stressed by the researcher if possible, as well as reminding the participant that there are no 'right' or 'best' answers.

Validity

A second important research issue is that of 'How do I know that the method I am using is really measuring what I want it to measure, and are my conclusions drawn from these measurements therefore valid conclusions?' This is the concept of validity. Validity has several different components. You should consider all of these components before rather than after you carry out your data collection.

Face validity – Does your method appear appropriate to measure what you want it to measure at first glance? Ask a sample from the population that you are going to research. Do they think it measures adequately the concept you intend to measure? Although establishing face validity on its own is normally not sufficient, you should not overlook this stage, as without face validity it is impossible to achieve the other components of validity. Face validity is also important to prevent participants from becoming frustrated by having to answer questions that they may feel are irrelevant or unrelated to the subject under investigation.

Content validity – This is similar to face validity, except that it refers to the initial assessment from an expert's point of view. The expert should be aware of some of the more subtle issues and nuances of the concept, and be able to critically assess whether you have accounted for these.

Predictive validity – Can your measures predict future behaviour? If someone scores highly on a test of positive attitudes to sport participation, will it predict their future sporting behaviour?

Construct validity – Do your data correlate with other measures? If you have measured people's attitudes towards their own health and fitness, do the scores you obtained correlate with other scores such as attendance at health/fitness facilities, weight, diet, sport participation, etc.? This is the most rigorous form of validity, and you should aim to ensure this as far as possible.

VALIDITY AND RELIABILITY – FEAR OF FAILURE

Fear of failure can be a positive and a destructive force affecting athletes, and it can lead to increased stress, anxiety, poor performance and eventually drop-out from sport. Initially, it was measured as a unidimensional construct, which, although allowing relatively easy measurement, provided data that lacked validity, as it has subsequently been shown to be a multidimensional phenomenon, with most dimensions remaining unmeasured. Only by acknowledging all five dimensions of fear of failure (experiencing shame and embarrassment, devaluing the self, the effect on the future, losing social value and influence, and upsetting important others) (Taylor *et al.* 2021) has a valid and reliable measure, in this case the Performance Failure Appraisal Inventory (PFAI), been developed to gain an accurate measure of the concept of fear of failure.

The relationship between reliability and validity

Although I have looked at reliability and validity as separate concepts, they are related. A number of possible relationships exist between the two:

1   The measure is neither reliable nor valid. The lack of reliability means that sometimes the correct measurement is taken, but that measure lacks validity anyway. You may be interested in an individual's perceived competence

at sport. You may wish to measure this by asking them to rate their competence on a poorly designed scale of competence. If you ask them after a heavy defeat, you are likely to get a different score than if you were to ask them after a good performance. Thus the measure is unreliable. On rare occasions valid measures may occur, although by chance. On most other occasions, however, a different, invalid score will be obtained.

2   The measure is reliable but not valid. The measure may be consistently measuring the concept incorrectly; thus reliability is achieved, but the scores are invalid. Using the prior example, individuals may consistently report the same level of perceived competence in their sport after a number of separate heavy defeats using the same scale. Thus the measure is reliable, as the measure results in a consistent score each time it is used.

3   The measure is valid but not reliable. Although unlikely, it is possible that the spread of unreliable scores averages out to give an overall valid score for the population. The scores for each participant may vary from test to test, but the overall mean is an accurate measure.

4   The measure is valid and reliable. This is what you must strive for in your research. Thus you need to identify a measure that accurately reflects the phenomenon and results in the same score at different times.

Enhancing reliability and validity

As well as some of the considerations highlighted here, there are some other steps you can take to make your data as reliable and valid as possible. The first is to ensure all of the concepts to be measured are clearly defined and operationalised. If possible, use existing definitions and measures from peer-reviewed literature. Additionally, have the data collection instrument assessed by others with expertise in the subject area to obtain feedback. Think about other measures or data that may be available to compare your findings with. Finally, consider the volatility of the context. If volatility is high, and behaviours, attitudes and so on are likely to fluctuate, then carefully consider how to account for this within your research design. Use existing studies to help you here by seeing how other researchers have coped with such issues.

Assessing the quality of qualitative data

There has been considerable discussion regarding the means by which qualitative research is assessed and growing consensus that the traditional concepts of reliability and validity are inappropriate. Lincoln and Guba (1985) are primary among those who have argued for an alternative view of assessing qualitative data using alternative criteria. These criteria include:

> *Reliability* – This term is used in a different way to that normally associated with its quantitative application. Whereas, earlier in the chapter,

reliability was referred to as the extent to which the results would be repeated, in qualitative research reliability refers more to the consistency of methods by which the data were collected. Within the interpretative perspective, interpretation may well differ between different researchers, or even between the same researcher at different times; thus concepts such as test/retest reliability become inappropriate. The key is to ensure that sufficient detail is provided so that the study could be repeated by others, even if the findings would not be exactly replicated. Some authors (e.g. Lincoln and Guba 1985) also use the term *dependability* to refer to this concept.

Rigour – Related to the concept of reliability is rigour. Whereas reliability focuses upon the procedure, rigour examines the appropriateness of the methodological choices made by the researcher. Thus, as well as providing a detailed account of the methodology, choices such as the choice of theory, the selection of respondents, the method of data collection and analysis and so on should be justified by the researcher.

Credibility – This relates to how believable the findings and interpretations of a study are, and how they are related to the idea of internal validity. Do the findings accurately reflect participants' experiences? Would participants recognise the story presented by the researcher as an accurate representation? Would they see the researcher's analysis as credible? Credibility can, where appropriate, be assessed on an ongoing basis by a technique known as 'member checking', where the researcher can discuss their interpretations and conclusions with participants of the study.

Authenticity – A study is authentic when the strategies used are appropriate for the true reporting of the participants' ideas and the study actually helps participants, as well as readers, understand their social world. Authenticity consists of the following (Holloway and Wheeler 2009):

1   Fairness. The researcher must be fair to participants, gain their acceptance throughout the study and continue to obtain valid informed consent.

2   Ontological authenticity. Both readers and participants of the study will have been educated in terms of understanding the social world that has been investigated.

3   Educative authenticity. Through the understanding of ontological authenticity, participants could develop a greater understanding of others within that social world.

4   Catalytic authenticity. Decision-making by participants should be enhanced by the research.

5   Tactical authenticity. The research should empower participants.

Transferability – Although we don't generalise from qualitative data in the same way as with quantitative data, we do use the idea of transferability; this refers to the extent to which our findings could be applied within other contexts.

Enhancing the quality of qualitative research

Jones *et al.* (2013) identify a number of strategies that you can use to enhance the quality of your qualitative research. These include strategies such as:

1   Keeping an audit trail of all parts of the process, including the key decisions made and the underlying thought processes. Your audit trail should start at the very beginning of the process and cover every element, such as your search strategy for literature, your process of analysis and so on. The audit trail is something to be continually referred to and assessed in terms of being able to help you understand your role as part of, rather than outside of, the research and how this involvement has influenced the whole process.

2   Member checking, as briefly outlined earlier. This is not always appropriate; for example, it is difficult to discuss complex theories or ideas with participants, and some groups, such as young children, will not be able to provide feedback.

3   Triangulation within and between methods. Using interviews and observation together, for example to explore a phenomenon.

4   Searching for alternative theories and explanations. This essentially means being open to alternative ideas, theories and explanations rather than remaining focused on your initial assumptions.

Reflexivity, in terms of assessing your own characteristics, implies the relationship between you and the research, and how this relationship might impact upon all elements of the research process. As Brackenridge (1999, p. 399) notes, 'Reflexivity is becoming an increasingly important research skill'. Defined simply, reflexivity is a process whereby the effect of the researcher – and their own characteristics, background, values, attitudes and so on – upon the subject matter is taken account of. As Brackenridge notes, an assessment of the position of the researcher, and the power relations between the researcher and participants, is important in achieving an evaluation of the 'truth' of any findings.

ENSURING THE QUALITY OF QUALITATVE DATA – A NEW APPROACH TO PREVENTING CHILD MALTREATMENT IN SPORT

Owusu-Sekyere *et al.* (2021) set out to apply the concept of 'safety culture' to the safeguarding of children in sport. They undertook a large number of interviews (n=45) and focus groups (n=7). With such a quantity of data, ensuring quality is highly important, and the research team undertook a variety of activities to maximise the quality.

Credibility was enhanced through member checking, where participants were asked whether or not only the words used, but also the impressions generated, were accurate. Reliability was achieved by keeping a detailed record of all research-related activities completed, including interviews, field notes, journals and details of the coding process. To assess transferability, contextual information was provided that 'allows consideration of the applicability of findings to other organisations, situations, countries, and people' (p. 9).

Summary

- Theory plays a crucial role in most research projects. Having an understanding of the importance of theory, and of the particular theories to be used in your research, is an important element of the research process.
- Developing your conceptual framework is also an important stage of the research process. Undertaking this process will allow you to clarify the important concepts within your study, their relationships to each other and their measurement.
- You also need to consider issues of validity (the extent to which what you are measuring actually reflects the phenomenon under investigation) and reliability (the extent to which the findings would be the same if the research were repeated). Validity and reliability are two of the key areas upon which your research will be assessed if you undertake quantitative research. If you are undertaking qualitative research, then how will you ensure your approach is trustworthy authentic, reliable, rigorous and credible?

Activity

Go back to some of the research articles that you have already read. Try to answer the following questions:

1   Can you identify the theoretical framework used by the author(s)?
2   What are the important concepts within the study?
3   How have they been defined?
4   How have the concepts been operationalised? Have the authors used their own measures, or have they used existing measures from the literature?
5   Are there any moderating or intervening variables within the study? How have they been accounted for?
6   How have the authors addressed the quality of their measurements? How have the ideas of reliability and validity been addressed if the study is quantitative? Alternatively, if the study is qualitative, then are other measures of quality addressed?

Now is the time to start identifying and reading past studies that have also used the same theoretical approach. Reading such studies may help you with the next activity.

■ Develop your conceptual framework, paying particular attention to the operationalisation of your concepts. How will you measure (either quantitatively or qualitatively) the necessary concepts?

■ Can you identify any moderating or intervening variables? If so, how do you plan to account for these?

■ What are the threats to reliability and validity in your research project if you are taking a quantitative approach? If you are taking a qualitative approach, how will you ensure the quality of the data that you collect?

■ What steps can be taken to minimise the threats to the quality of your data?

Further reading

There's quite a dearth of sources for the novice researcher in sport looking to understand more about theories and concepts, but if you have access, it's worth reading Volume 16, Issue 1 of *Sport Management Review* for a good selection of articles linked to the use of theory in sport management.

Chapter 7
Research designs and research ethics

Research designs and research ethics

This chapter will:

- Describe the different types of research design that you may adopt within your research project – experimental, cross-sectional, time series, longitudinal, case study, grounded theory, action research, ethnography and autoethnography.
- Introduce the concept of sampling and describe some of the sampling techniques that you may use.
- Describe some of the methods you may use within your research design to collect data from your sample.
- Introduce the concept of triangulation as a means of strengthening the validity of your research.
- Outline some of the ethical considerations to be made when considering your research design.

Introduction

Once you have developed your research question and objectives, clarified the role of theory within your research and developed your conceptual framework, two questions now need to be considered. These are:

- What data do I need to provide with the information to answer my research question?
- What is the best way to collect this data?

DOI: 10.4324/9781003195467-7

It is important to think about the overall methodology (rather than just the methods and sample) that will allow you to collect the data you need, while at the same time maximising the quality of the data you obtain. Your methodology is, essentially, the principles, practices and procedure underpinning the way in which you collect your data, and it is thus strongly related to your epistemology, or philosophy of how knowledge is acquired. Thus, if you have taken a particular epistemological approach, then this should be reflected in your methodology.

 KEY TERMS

METHODOLOGY AND METHODS

There is sometimes confusion over what is meant by methodology and how this differs from methods. Methodology is the overall research strategy that outlines how you go about answering your research question and justifying decisions about things such as what to study, who to study, what type of data to collect, what to do with that data, ethical concerns and so on. Methods, on the other hand, are the techniques used to collect the data. Thus they are an integral part of a methodology, but a methodology consists of a lot more than just the collection of data through various methods. Sometimes there is confusion between the two; for example, as Bryman (2016) acknowledges, we often see reference to a 'case study method' when it is actually a research design.

The first stage in planning your methodology is to consider your research design. The research design is the overall plan that guides you in terms of all activities connected to data collection. In later chapters I will deal with the specifics of data collection itself – questionnaire design, interviewing and so on – but in this chapter I will focus upon the wider context within which such collection occurs. Nine research designs are outlined here, these being:

- Experimental.
- Cross-sectional.
- Time series.
- Longitudinal.
- Case study.
- Grounded theory.
- Action research.
- Ethnography.
- Autoethnography.

Experimental designs

Experimental designs are an under-used design in the social sciences, given their potential to identify causal relationships between variables, specifically whether an independent variable influences a dependent variable (hence, they tend to be approached from a generally positivist epistemology, although they have great potential for the qualitative researcher, where, rather than exploring causality, they can be used to explore more qualitative concepts such as 'impacts' or 'experiences'). The simplest form of experimental design involves measuring a dependent variable from a single group (X1), exposing the group to a particular treatment (independent variable) and measuring the dependent variable again (X2). The effect of the treatment is thus assumed to be the difference between the two measures.

$X1 \blacktriangleright$ treatment $\blacktriangleright X2$
Effect of treatment $= (X2 - X1)$

You may be interested in the effect of mental rehearsal upon shooting performance in basketball. This design may involve you asking your participants to shoot 20 free throws. This would give you a success score of between zero and 20 (X1). You would then ask them to spend some time visualising a successful shot (the experimental treatment) before asking them to repeat the shooting task, again giving you a score out of 20 (X2). The effect would then be calculated by working out the difference between the mean score after the visualisation and the mean score before, for example:

Mean score before visualisation = 11.25
Mean score after visualisation = 13.00
Effect of visualisation $= (13.00-11.25) = 1.75$

Using a single treatment group, however, has considerable limitations that will severely impact the validity of your findings. While it may be possible that any improvement may have been due to visualising the task, it may also be that simply by practice, participants' performance on the task improved, and you have identified an apparent effect of visualisation that does not exist in reality. Alternatively, it may be that participants tired during the second set of shots, and the improvement caused by mentally rehearsing the shots was lost due to fatigue. To account for these moderating variables, you need to introduce a control. This requires two groups, assigned on a random basis. One group is exposed to the treatment (for example being asked to mentally rehearse the shots). The other group (the control group) is not exposed to the treatment (they are not asked to rehearse the shots). The other moderating variables (such as practice, fatigue, etc.) should cancel each other out, as they are equivalent for each group. Measurements of the dependent variable are taken from each group before the treatment (pre-test) and again from each group after the treatment has been administered to the non-control group (post-test). The overall effect of the treatment is thus the overall difference in scores between each group:

Group 1
X1 ➤ treatment ➤ X2
Effect of treatment = (X2 − X1)

Group 2 (control group)
X3 ➤ no treatment ➤ X4
Effect of non-treatment = (X4 − X3)

Net effect of treatment = (X2 − X1) − (X4 − X3)

Thus, repeating the earlier experimental design, we could more accurately assess the effect of visualisation:

Mean score before visualisation (treatment group) = 11.25
Mean score after visualisation (treatment group) = 13.00
Mean score before visualisation (control group) = 11.00
Mean score after visualisation (control group) = 11.90
Effect of visualisation = (13.0–11.25) − (11.9–11.0) = 0.85

Experimental designs may be carried out in either a controlled (laboratory) setting or in the natural environment. In a more contrived setting, Dijksterhuis and van Knippenberg (1998) carried out an experiment where some participants spent a few minutes describing the behaviours, lifestyle and appearance attributes of a professor, whereas others described those of a soccer hooligan. Participants then performed a multiple-choice general knowledge test. Those describing the stereotypes of the professor scored more highly on the test than those describing the hooligan. The main disadvantage with such 'laboratory'-based designs is the possibility that participants will behave differently if they are aware that they are part of a research project. This may be overcome by undertaking the data collection in a more natural environment. Luna *et al.* (2020) did this when exploring the effectiveness of the Sport Education Model (an approach that focuses on authenticity in sport education) on subjective well-being and anxiety. They randomly assigned 146 students to either a control or a treatment group before applying the intervention in lessons over the school year. They showed that the experimental group had significant improvements in subjective well-being and reduced anxiety compared to the control group. They were fortunate in being able to assign a control group, which isn't always possible in such natural settings (either for practical or ethical reasons).

Demonstrating causality using experimental designs

Experimental designs are generally used to demonstrate causality, that is whether the independent variable (such as reading about a football hooligan or experiencing the Sport Education Model) actually causes the effect upon the dependent variable (such as performing worse on a subsequent general knowledge test or impacting upon well-being and anxiety). To achieve this, four conditions need to be met:

- Covariation. This simply means that as the independent variable changes, then so does the dependent variable. Thus, if we ask individuals to mentally rehearse a basketball shot, then their performance should change as a consequence if causality is to be demonstrated.
- Time order. It is important to ensure that the independent variable (i.e. the cause) actually happens before the effect upon the dependent variable, for example that performance does not start to improve before the mental rehearsal.
- Non-spuriousness. As I explained in Chapter 6, some relationships may be due to the existence of another variable. Thus, all variables need to be accounted for. In the case of shooting basketballs, it may be that practising the task has led to the improved performance.
- Theoretical support. Ideally there should be a strong theoretical underpinning to explain why there should be an effect.

Cross-sectional/survey designs

As the name suggests, this design takes a cross-sectional sample from the overall population of interest, for example taking a sample from a list of registered players in a sport league. Data are collected once from each participant, most commonly through interviews or questionnaires. Findings can – provided the sampling has been done randomly – then be generalised back to the population. One example of a cross-sectional study was that of Cronin et al. (2013), who were interested in the availability and use of defibrillators in amateur sport clubs in Ireland following a number of high-profile cases of sudden cardiac arrest (SCA) in sport. Rather than sampling the population of every hurling, football and rugby club within Ireland, they took a cross-section of clubs, 171 in total. This allowed them to generalise their findings about the number of clubs that had a defibrillator, the various barriers encountered by those that did not and the extent to which clubs had used the equipment in an emergency situation. They were thus able to confirm the widespread availability of defibrillators in sport clubs in Ireland. More recent cross-sectional research was undertaken by Yamada et al. (2020), who undertook a cross-sectional study to explore the effect of COVID-19 on the physical activity levels of older adults in Japan. To collect data from all such individuals was clearly not possible, hence a cross section of 1,600 older adults was selected, allowing the researchers to suggest that, across the entire elderly population, physical activity dropped by over a quarter due to the pandemic.

The strengths of such a research design are that it is convenient to the researcher with limited resources. Obtaining a cross-sectional sample is often easier than obtaining an experimental sample, attrition rates are less of an issue and random samples may be taken from the population to allow the findings to be generalised to the wider population.

Time series designs

A time series design involves measuring the dependent variable over an extended period both before and after the effect of the independent variable, or the measurement of a single variable a number of times across a specified period, to assess trends in data. This can be over a relatively long period of time, for example the study of Jakobsen *et al.* (2013), who were interested in the impact of hosting the Olympics or a major football tournament on foreign direct investment (FDI). To do this, they explored levels of FDI over a 40-year period involving measurements of FDI a number of times before and after hosting an event, allowing them to determine that hosting a football tournament seems to have a small positive impact upon FDI in the years preceding a football tournament, whereas the Olympics has no effect at all. Alternatively, a time series design can involve a much shorter period of time, such as the study of Lloyd *et al.* (2013), who explored the impact of sporting events on alcohol intoxication cases in Australia, demonstrating that increased cases of intoxication could be identified the day preceding sporting events such as the Melbourne Cup and the Australian Football League Grand Final, perhaps reflecting the drinking culture associated with these events.

Longitudinal designs

A longitudinal study is one that uses the same sample group and measures particular variables over an extended period of time. For example, you may wish to examine the behaviour of employees of a sport organisation after a change in managerial policy to assess the effects of such a change, or you may wish to track the sport-related skills of a cohort of students throughout their education. You would take a measure of behaviour at X1 (beginning of the study), X2 (after six months), X3 (after 12 months) and so on. The period of time involved could range from just a few weeks to several years. Chen *et al.* (2014), for example, were interested in how destination image (DI) changed among sport tourists in the months following their participation in a marathon event at that destination. Through undertaking a longitudinal study collecting data two weeks, 10 months and 20 months after the event, they were able to identify that cognitive DI, that is the beliefs and knowledge about a destination, remained unchanged over a 20-month period, affective DI (related to the emotions generated about the destination) significantly declined in the first 10 months, but then rebounded in the following 10 months, while conative DI (behavioural aspects, such as an intention to revisit) showed a continuous decline over the 20 months.

Longitudinal research needs to be approached with caution. It can take more time and resources than cross-sectional research, and there is always the issue of attrition, or dropout from participants. One alternative, although not totally desirable, is to approximate a longitudinal study using a cross-sectional research design. This is done by asking the sample to recall past attitudes and behaviours, describe their present attitudes and behaviours, and predict their future attitudes and behaviours. This is obviously a less desirable research design, but it may prove useful where issues of time constraints and attrition are important or during times when the context makes it difficult to undertake, such as during the COVID-19 pandemic. Another alternative to the traditional longitudinal approach is to choose groups at different stages in their development. For example, you may be interested in how attitudes towards competitive sport are developed during adolescence. Rather than take measurements with a single cohort over an extended period of time, a sample could be selected from different age ranges at the same time, and these could be compared, which would essentially be a cross-sectional research design.

Case study research

Case study research involves the intensive study of a specific case; a case refers to a specific instance. For example, you could undertake case study research on:

- An organisation.
- A team.
- A school.
- An individual.
- A policy.

The use of case study research is based upon the argument that developing a rich understanding of an issue requires analysis of both its development over time and the context within which it occurs. Such issues are often researched using a variety of methods over an extended period of time. Gall *et al.* (1996) note four characteristics of case study research:

- Phenomena are studied through focusing on specific cases.
- Each case is studied in depth.
- Phenomena are studied in their natural context.
- Case study research takes the perspective of those within the case, rather than the researcher's perspective.

You may consider the use of a case study design in three instances, according to Yin (2008):

1   Your theory suggests particular outcomes in a particular context. Thus, you would need to choose a case that provided such an appropriate context.
2   You want to be able to describe and explain a unique or rare situation.
3   You want to describe and explain a case that has yet to be studied in any detail.

A CASE STUDY OF AN INDIVIDUAL ATHLETE

The positivist dominance of early sport research focused very much on identifying larger sample sizes, the findings from which could be generalised back to the broader population under investigation. The case study approach seeks to identify patterns of behaviour, and phenomena within a particular context, and thus seeks depth, rather than breadth, meaning that small sample sizes, even to the extent of a sample size of one, are appropriate. McGannon and Pomerleau-Fontaine (2020) explored identity meanings of extreme athletes in the context of their health and well-being. To do this, they focused on a single case – that of the skyrunner Kilian Jornet – and through analysing autobiographical material they were able to discover two narratives, those of discovery and relational, and were able to develop an understanding of extreme athletes that went beyond over-simplistic explanations based on them as pathological risk-takers or as motivated by certain personality traits.

The case study of a single athlete was able to provide such findings, as it allowed the researchers a much more nuanced view of an athlete, a depth of study often only available with the case study method. Had a larger sample been taken, then it would have been entirely possible that some of the depth, and thus understanding, would have been lost to the researcher.

There has been a growing acceptance of the use of smaller sample sizes over recent years, with a number of high-quality studies utilising small numbers of participants. Anyone thinking that a sample size of one is too small for any meaningful research should read Barker *et. al.*'s (2011) text on single-case research in sport psychology or many of the increasing number of excellent case studies being published in a varied range of disciplines.

Grounded theory designs

Grounded theory is strongly associated with the inductive approach to research (see Chapter 2) but has its own specific procedures of sampling and analysis. Rather than enter the research field or setting with any pre-determined theories or ideas, the researcher will usually have no more than a generalised idea of the intended outcomes of the research. Theory is still an important part of the research, but it is developed from the initial data collection, rather than testing pre-determined hypotheses. These theories can then be tested, and the theory modified. More data can then be collected, and the theory continually modified through a combination of inductive and deductive approaches. This ensures that the theory is 'grounded' within the data. While this approach has its undoubted strengths, it can be time consuming, and the continual process of data collection and analysis can mean it is often beyond the scope of many research projects. It can also be a risky strategy for student research. Grounded theory is also often misunderstood or conflated with inductive research, especially in terms of how difficult it is to carry out, especially with its use of specific techniques, such as constant comparison and theoretical sampling (Jones *et al.* 2013).

Action research

Action research is a form of applied research (see Chapter 1) that involves the researcher actively participating within a specific group or organisation to solve a particular problem or improve a process through a continual cycle of research and reflection to create value for practitioners rather than developing more general knowledge, hence applied, rather than pure research. In some ways, this can be seen as analogous to the researcher carrying a series of experiments. The aim is to bring about change and for that change to be based on empirical evidence, for example the research of Rovio *et al.* (2012), who explored team-building processes in ice hockey, choosing action research because of its abilities to 'enable opportunities for continuous planning, acting, and reflecting on the data-collection processes, feedback generated discussion, and problem solving' (p. 587), making it an ideal design with which to approach the longitudinal nature of team building. Action research can address more than one aspect at a time; for example, Voldby and Klein-Døssing (2020) used action research to not only develop coaches' own practices but also to develop broader coach educational practice.

Ethnography

I will deal with ethnography in some depth in Chapter 11 but will briefly outline the main concepts here. Essentially, ethnography involves the in-depth study of a group or community through immersion into the culture of that group, often, but not always, for an extended period, using multiple methods of data collection. The aim is to understand the behaviour or culture by seeing it through the perspective of members of the group themselves. This involves the researcher becoming immersed within the day-to-day activities of the group.

Data collection is much more flexible, and data are collected as and when appropriate from available sources to create a "rich" description of the group and its members. There are some similarities between ethnographic and case study research, with the key differences being those of immersion within the group and focus on observational methods within ethnographic approaches.

Autoethnography

Autoethnography is an approach where the researcher focuses upon their own experiences and connects those experiences with the wider context within which those experiences are enacted. Essentially you become the primary participant and source of data. Autoethnography may lie on a continuum from descriptive autobiography to more analytical (and preferable) accounts that attempts to make sense of the experiences of the researcher in light of their connection to the wider social context with a strong link to theory. Anderson (2006) identifies six features of an autoethnography, these being:

1   The researcher is a 'complete member' of the social world being investigated, either through opportunistic means, such as having innate knowledge of the group through day-to-day involvement, or being thrown into a group through chance circumstances or covert means, such as developing a research interest first and subsequently joining the group as a means of data collection.
2   There is a need for analytic reflexivity, or the ability of the researcher to be able to locate themselves within the research situation, their effects upon it and the subsequent impacts upon the analysis.
3   The researcher should be visible and active within the reporting of the research and be part of, rather than hidden from, the analysis.
4   Recognising that although the self is the primary source of data, dialogue with others in the group is important to develop knowledge.
5   The need to follow an 'analytical agenda', that is the research should not simply report experiences but attempt to analyse them through reference to, refinement of or development of theory.
6   An understanding that writing the autoethnography differs from other forms of academic writing, with a strong autobiographical element. As such, autoethnography requires the researcher to present themselves to an audience, and you need to be comfortable with this if this is an approach you are considering.

Chen's (2021) analysis of his experiences as a non-white international sport student in Canada, as well as his place within a context of "settler colonialism", demonstrates many of these characteristics. Through both documenting his own experiences as they happened and undertaking "reflexive journaling" (a more retrospective account of past experiences and observations), he was able to identify a number of broader tensions in the relationship between colonialism and international sport education. Autoethnographic data can also be augmented by other data; for example, dialogue with others was demonstrated in Butterworth and Turner's (2014) account of the first author's progression from being an undergraduate sport studies student to working within an elite performance analysis environment, and it showed how stepping out of his 'comfort zone' allowed accelerated personal development augmented by further data from the second author, explaining how the student's own progression related to his own educational philosophies and background as a lecturer on the programme.

Despite the emergence of a number of high-quality autoethnographies, there remains some resistance to their use, with accusations of being opportunist, self-indulgent and lacking interest to the wider academic community (which, unfortunately, is certainly true in cases). As with any research design, done badly, an autoethnography can demonstrate a number of weaknesses. On the other hand, however, it can also provide a different, innovative and insightful way of examining sport. It is not, as may wrongly be perceived, an easy option, and can be a difficult task. As Edwards and Skinner (2009, p. 190) suggest, *researchers must be adept at identifying pertinent details, introspection, descriptive and compelling writing, and confronting things about themselves that may be less than flattering*. As such, it is not for everyone.

AUTOETHNOGRAPHY: EXPERIENCES OF ANOREXIA, EXCESSIVE EXERCISING AND PSYCHOSIS

Brendan Stone (2009), in a frank and honest paper, presented his experiences of anorexia, excessive exercising and psychosis as a teenager. His autoethnography involved an interaction between his 'current' self, that is the researcher whose role is to remember, describe and interpret, and his 'historical self', that is the subject of the research, which, in effect, has shaped the current self. Stone's autoethnographic approach was justified by the subject matter, something that is difficult to research at any time, noting (p. 68) that:

> To experience trauma or madness is to traverse a realm which reason and narrative cannot adequately describe. I have long thought that the conventions governing traditional academic discourse could have been designed to exclude the unsettling truths of those who have known that strange country.

The interpretation of the historical self by the current self allowed Stone to identify insightful findings about his past, findings of which he was previously unaware, to link his anorexia and excessive exercise to the repression of traumatic memory, which are described within the paper.

Choosing a research design

There is no hierarchy of research design, in that certain research designs cannot be said to be 'better' than others. The research design is, effectively, the link between the research question and the data collected to answer that question. Thus, your overall choice of design should be coherent with both your onto-logical and epistemological standpoint, and the aim of the research. Hence, you will normally have only a single research design. Although this will nor-mally be chosen once the question has been identified, you can also use a pre-ferred research design to help guide you towards a question. Thus, you might be interested in experimental design, intrigued by the nature of an autoethnog-raphy, or be a member of a sport team and thus be in a position to carry out ethnographic research. You can then use your preferred research design to aid in developing your question. As long as the final link between your research question and research design is coherent, then the order in which you make your decision isn't that important; the overall coherence is what counts.

Choosing your sample

Once you have decided what information you need, and the design with which to collect data to yield this information, you need to identify from where the data is to be collected. In most cases, the population under investigation will be too large to collect data from each member. Thus a sample must be taken. A sample refers to a subset of a specific population. The population refers to everyone who shares those characteristics defined by the researcher as rel-evant to the investigation; thus, for a study on anxiety among professional male tennis players, your population would be all professional male tennis players. For quantitative research the purpose of sampling is, in most cases, to gain information about that overall population by selecting a smaller but representative number of individual cases. The responses of the sample, if it has external validity, can then be applied to the overall population. An example of this would be if you were identifying the most common reasons why NBA fans attended their first basketball game. It would be impossible to question every NBA fan. Thus, a smaller number of fans who are representative of the popu-lation are chosen. If, from this sample, it was determined that 50 per cent were taken to the game by their fathers, then it can be suggested that this is likely (within certain limits) to be the case for the entire population of NBA fans.

For qualitative research, sampling is less about identifying a representa-tive group from which to collect data and more about identifying a group that is of relevance, for example selecting a sample that demonstrates a certain theory or model particularly well, or simply investigating a single group that is of particular interest to the researcher. In such cases, the results cannot (and should not) be generalised to the overall population, and indeed generalisation isn't important for many qualitative studies. You can general-ise to theory, that is your findings could be used to develop, refine or simply confirm an existing theory, which could then be applied to different samples. Alternatively, qualitative researchers talk about the idea of transferability, or the extent to which findings could apply to other similar samples within similar settings. Thus, qualitative research involves non-probability sampling, as certain members of the population are much more likely to be chosen than others based on certain factors or characteristics.

Selecting a quantitative sample

A number of sampling techniques can be used. The most common associated with quantitative research are:

- Random sampling.
- Stratified random sampling.
- Cluster sampling.
- Systematic sampling.

Random sampling

A random sample is where every member of the population has an equal probability of being selected. This is considered the best technique to obtain a representative sample and produce findings that will be – to an extent – generalisable to the overall population. The first stage is to define your population. The next stage is to ensure that each member of this population has an equal chance of being selected. The easiest way to do this, if you know your entire population, is simply to place the names of all the population in a container and pick names until the desired sample size has been achieved. Alternatively, each name can be assigned a number, and appropriate software can be used to select the sample. In many cases, provided you have a suitably focused question, a random sample is possible. If you have a broad question however, it is unlikely that you will be able to undertake a simple random sample, and an alternative sampling strategy will be required.

Stratified random sampling

If there are certain subgroups within the population, for example based on age, sex and so on, then it may be necessary to ensure that they are adequately represented in the final sample. In this case, the population is divided into subgroups. Random samples are then taken from within these groups. Thus, you may divide your population into 'male' and 'female' and randomly select 50 per cent of your sample from the list of your male participants, and the remaining 50 per cent from the list of your female participants. This will ensure your initial sample reflects the appropriate subgroups that are present within the population.

Cluster sampling

Cluster sampling is where groups are randomly selected, rather than individuals. Thus, if the researcher was interested in the attitudes towards intimidatory behaviour in little league baseball, rather than select a random sample from the population of little league baseball players, a number of teams could be selected at random, and all players within those teams questioned. It is important to select a number of clusters to ensure generalisability with this method. Chen *et al.* (2015) used this method when exploring physical activity in older people living alone within China. They randomly selected two towns, and subsequently nine communities from within those towns. They were then able to approach all individuals meeting their criteria from those communities.

Systematic sampling

Sampling using this method involves selecting every Kth case, for example taking every fourth name from a list or every seventh person to enter a sport facility, as in Dixon *et al.*'s (2013) approach to measuring the economic impact of sport tourists attending university baseball, where they approached, after a random start, every fifth person entering the stadium. Systematic sampling is best recommended when the list from which the names are taken is randomly ordered, otherwise some bias is likely to occur.

There will always be some form of sampling error, in that you are unlikely ever to get a truly representative sample. You can take steps to reduce this error though, and Kim and Lee (2019) identify strategies that you need to consider when thinking about your quantitative sampling strategy, two of which are particularly relevant for undergraduate research.

1   Have an adequate sample size – the larger your sample, the lower the chance of error. Hence a sample of 50 respondents is likely to have significant level of error, whereas increasing to over 200 respondents will give much more confidence in the findings. You can determine your sample size though either looking at similar peer reviewed studies and targeting similar samples or by using a sample size calculator, such as that provided by Qualtrics at www.qualtrics.com/blog/calculating-sample-size/.

2   Use a stratified sample wherever possible – if you know the various strata, or groups within the overall population, then by randomly sampling each strata, rather than the overall population, your sampling error will be reduced.

Selecting participants for a qualitative study

Although you will still see some qualitative studies refer to the use of random samples, the qualitative researcher generally has no interest in such a sample and will focus instead on the range of non-probability sampling. The term *sampling* is perhaps less appropriate here, and *selection* more reflective of the process, as generalisability is not the prime concern of the qualitative researcher, with the focus more upon participants who can describe, explain and illuminate the phenomena being explored. The means by which the qualitative researcher can select their sample include the following:

Purposive sampling

You choose your participants because they possess certain characteristics or traits, for example the strategy of Khasnis *et al.* (2021), who chose their participants based on their 'elite' positions in Indian sport, with a level of influence over sport-related issues within the country, or, Muslim *et al.* (2021), who in their study of talent identification in Malaysian golf chose interviewees because they were identified as 'information rich'(p. 121).

Theoretical sampling

You identify cases that demonstrate a particular theory particularly well, or allow you to develop a theory. You may be interested in explaining the influence of the influx of foreign expertise upon the managerial culture of sport organisations, for example. You would therefore sample those from organisations that had experienced such expertise. As you develop your ideas, you then continue to select cases that help you further inform, refine and develop your emerging theory. Theoretical sampling is often associated with, but not exclusive to, grounded theory research.

Maximum variation sampling

You choose the full range of experiences, demographics and so on to capture the full range of the subject being explored. Examples of this include Jowett and Frost's (2007) study of the impact of race and ethnicity on the coach/athlete relationship in football, which sampled male black football players from different levels of professional football, playing in different positions, from a variety of racial/ethnic backgrounds, and being both first generation and second generation British, and South *et al.*'s (2020) study of Commonwealth Games volunteers, where the maximum variation sample was designed to reflect the varied characteristics of volunteers.

Snowball sampling

You locate your initial participants, and these initial participants identify further potential participants themselves. Smith-Tran (2021), for example, in her study of *Black Girls Run!* found a number of participants through personal networks and referrals. Alternatively, you may find access to a 'gatekeeper', or influential member of your population. They can then introduce you to other participants. One potential advantage of being introduced by a known member of the population is that you may be able to engender greater trust between researcher and subject, with subsequent improvement in the quality of your data.

Typical case sampling

Your sample is chosen on the basis that they are 'typical' of a particular context; for example, you may wish to assess the impact of changing legislation affecting those using sport stadia with reference to a particular stadium that you consider 'typical'. The findings can then be generalised to those using other 'typical' stadia. What is 'typical' can be determined by any available secondary data, your own informed judgement, or – as Fuller *et al.* (2013) did in their study of an afterschool sport programme – use knowledgeable stakeholders (such as staff on the programme) to help determine what is 'typical'.

Extreme case sampling

You choose cases that are unique, or special in some way, for example an investigation into the personality characteristics of elite athletes may involve you sampling Olympic medal winners as extreme cases (remember that this is a hypothetical example. In reality your chances of getting access to such a sample is minimal at best!). Another example is that of Gross (2021), who explored experimentation in recreational running in Estonia and chose runners who had demonstrated the greatest levels of experimentation in their own practices.

Opportunistic sampling

You select samples as they arise, taking advantage of unexpected opportunities. For example, you may be introduced to a particular key informant at an unexpected time. Alternatively this might also be where certain samples suggest their willingness to take part in the research, such as Howells *et al.*'s (2019) study of the *Daily Mile* initiative, where three schools expressed their willingness to participate.

Key informant sampling

Individuals are chosen on the basis of specific knowledge that they possess, for example, they may have a particular role or responsibility within an organisation, such as Swart and Maralack's (2020) study of the cancellation of the 2020 Two Oceans Marathon due to COVID-19, which involved interviewing the race director and board members.

USING KEY INFORMANTS TO OVERCOME OVERTOURISM IN HOST CITIES OF MEGA SPORT EVENTS

BY DR RAMI MHANNA, WINCHESTER UNIVERSITY

Host cities of mega sport events may experience 'overtourism', where the number of tourists may result in negative impacts, such as crowding, pollution, congestion and impacts upon local residents. My study (Mhanna *et al.* 2019) set out to identify and recommend initiatives to overcome overtourism in host destinations of mega sport events, based on the perspectives of practitioners.

To achieve this, key informants were identified using the stakeholder salience model of Mitchell *et al.* (1997), using the criteria that they held organisational or managerial roles within organisations which were actively involved in the staging of the event, in this case the 2012 London Olympics. This allowed 20 semi-structured interviews to be carried out from organisations such as VisitBritain, VisitEngland, UK Trade and Investment, the Tourism Alliance, London and Partners, various London 2012 sponsors, local government representatives and members of Olympic research centres. Data from these key informants identified the need to spread tourists beyond the host city, with three initiatives emerging: (1) spreading domestic tourism outside the host city, (2) showcasing destinations beyond the host city and (3) promoting regional collaboration.

Convenience sampling. The sample is chosen as it is convenient in terms of location, accessibility and so on. Try to avoid convenience samples as far as you can – it is always tempting to hand out questionnaires to those you are in day-to-day contact with or to interview people you know, but try to consider this as a last resort and always acknowledge the limitations if you have to choose this route.

PURPOSIVE SAMPLING – EXPERIENCES OF INJURY AND RETURN TO SPORT

Podlog *et al.* (2013) were interested in the extent to which basic psychological needs theory could explain adolescent athletes' experiences of injury and return to sport. To do this, they interviewed 11 athletes using a purposive sample, with the criteria for selection being:

Sport involvement as determined by membership on a regional sport academy squad or a state/national team.

A current musculoskeletal injury requiring a minimum one-month absence from sport participation.

They were undergoing physiotherapy treatment for the injury at the time.

The intent to return to a similar level of pre-injury participation or higher.

This allowed four themes to emerge, these being:

- Injury stress (the range of stressors and strain responses reported across the recovery phases).
- Coping (the specific strategies used to maintain motivation and reduce uncertainty).
- Experiences with social support.
- Recovery outcomes (perceptions of a successful/unsuccessful recovery).

Mistakes made in selecting a sample

Your choice of sampling technique can be an important one for the success of your research project, so it is worth spending time considering your approach. Some of the common errors made in sampling – especially at undergraduate level – include:

- Selecting individuals who are convenient, or readily available, for example individuals who are already known to the researcher.
- Selecting individuals who volunteer to take part as well as those who are more randomly selected without reference to the potential differences between these.
- Introducing bias through selecting a non-random sample, for example through posting a link on social media.
- Using a random sample when other sampling methods would be more appropriate, for example in a qualitative study.
- Not having an appropriate sample size for the purposes of the project. For quantitative studies, small samples have a number of inherent risks, such as not being representative of the wider population, or increased false positives. On the other hand, having too large a sample can sometimes be an issue for qualitative research, which generally benefits from greater depth from fewer participants.

Determining the sample size

A frequently asked question is 'How big should my sample be?'. Unfortunately there is no simple answer to this question, other than to say, 'Make sure it is big enough'! For the type of quantitative analysis typically collected as part of a quantitative study, you will need to balance the need for as large a sample size as possible with constraints based upon the issues of cost and time required for analysis (although online surveys do partially mitigate against these to some extent). The sample size calculator mentioned earlier will help you determine this, but it has to be balanced against the constraints, especially at undergraduate level, of actually achieving this, especially for experimental studies. For experimental designs, then there is always the trade-off between sample size and the simple pragmatics of undertaking your experiment. You will find that time and resource issues have implications for how much data you can collect. This will vary among projects, but you must ensure that you maintain the integrity of the experimental design, rather than look for shortcuts in the design to allow you to increase the sample size. A well-designed experiment that has fewer subjects is always preferable to a poorly designed study with more subjects. Cross sectional studies may seem easier to achieve larger samples, but there is sometimes a balance between achieving a large sample and maintaining its truly random nature; for example, it can be relatively easy to achieve many hundreds of responses through online surveys, but the online nature of the survey has implications for its representativeness, not being random for most populations. It is crucial to acknowledge the limitations of the sample size in your analysis.

Sample sizes for qualitative research are much lower and will depend on many different factors. The key with qualitative data is not the size of the sample but the depth and quality of the data. Thus, sample sizes will range from one upwards. A study with too little data will be a weak one, but (counterintuitively perhaps) too much data can also be detrimental to a qualitative study where time and resources are limited. Too much data may result in weaker analysis, and you should bear this in mind. Six rich, detailed, informative interviews that are really well analysed are always preferable to 12 shorter, less detailed interviews that have had limited analysis. You need to consider first the question of the nature of the sample, in that a homogeneous group will require a smaller sample than a group containing a high degree of variation. Second, you will be guided by the issue of 'saturation', that is when you are collecting data but, in essence, not learning anything new (which is actually quite difficult to achieve in many cases). Finally, you need to consider the nature of the study, with narrative and phenomenological studies (see Chapter 9) requiring smaller sample sizes than generic qualitative approaches. The question you need to ask is not 'Have I collected data from enough people?' but 'Have I collected enough data?'.

Case study sampling

There are a number of issues of sampling that are specific to case study or ethnographic research. Your choice of case should rarely be random; rather it is more likely to be purposive, that is chosen to illustrate a particular situation. Often it may be a choice of convenience or access; for example, you may have access to a particular organisation or sport-related body. When you are undertaking such research, the questions that you need to consider are:

- How many cases are required? Am I looking to provide a detailed analysis of the factors affecting one particular case, or would I like to be able to compare two or more cases to be able to assess the relative importance of such variables?
- Am I looking for a typical case, with which the results I obtain can be generalised to other cases? If so, how will I identify what is 'typical'?
- Am I looking for an extreme or important case that will demonstrate a particular theory or model well?
- Am I likely to get access to my sample?

Non-response bias

It is extremely unlikely that you will get responses from your entire sample, especially if you are using methods such as an online questionnaire. Respondents may not have sufficient time, motivation or expertise to respond, they may fill in the questionnaire incorrectly or they may simply not be reachable. As a result, the data you eventually collect may not always be representative of your population. This is less important for qualitative studies, but for a quantitative study it is good practice to assess whether this is the case before you can generalise your findings, and this can be done in a number of ways:

- Initially you should examine the characteristics of the achieved sample to try to identify any features that may suggest non-response bias, such as looking at the age and gender profiles, as well as any other variables that you may feel are important. Using a computer package such as JASP (see Chapter 13) you could always display the response for certain variables graphically to examine response patterns.
- If the information is available, compare the characteristics of your respondents with those of the population under investigation. Thus, for example, at the very simplest level you should be able to compare the gender distribution of your achieved sample with that of the population. If the gender balance of your population is equal, yet either males or females are under-represented in your achieved sample, then your sample is likely to be biased in this respect.
- Send a follow-up to those who have not responded. If any further responses are obtained, then you can compare the characteristics of those who didn't initially respond with the original respondents to see if they differ in any way from your original respondents.

Choosing methods

So far in this chapter, I have covered the issue of research design, whereby you consider the overall framework of your data collection. I have also covered the issue of sampling, that is from whom this data is collected. The next issue within this chapter is that of how such data is to be collected. Thus the choice of appropriate methods becomes the final consideration of this part of the research process. Methods are, simply, the techniques by which you collect your data. The key methods that you may encounter include:

- Questionnaires.
- Interviews.
- Observation.
- Participant observation.
- Content analysis.

The choice of method is obviously important to the success of your project. Chapters 8–11 of this text examine each of the methods in turn, so I will only provide a brief outline here.

By this stage of the research process, you should be able to identify your own epistemological stance. You should also have an idea of the type of data you need to collect, this being qualitative, quantitative or a combination of the two. Finally, you should also have an idea of your likely sample in terms of who you would like to collect data from and the desired sample size for a quantitative study. You can now begin to approach the issue of choosing your methods. There is no one set way to do this; however, the following questions can guide your approach:

- Am I looking to collect quantitative data? If so, then if those data can be directly observed, consider the use of observation as your data collection method (Chapter 10). If not, then consider the use of a questionnaire (Chapter 8). Alternatively, if you are intending to analyse texts, such as newspapers, blogs, television programmes, letters, speeches, etc. then use content analysis (Chapter 10) or undertake online research (Chapter 12).
- Am I looking to collect qualitative data? If you are looking to explore the thoughts, feelings, emotions and perceptions of others, then consider the use of in-depth interviews (Chapter 9). If you are looking to explore your own subjective experiences, then use participant observation (Chapter 10).
- Am I looking to carry out an in-depth investigation of a particular group or culture? Consider the use of an ethnographic approach (Chapter 11) or a netnographic design (Chapter 12).
- Am I looking to strengthen the validity of the findings through triangulation? If so, consider using more than one method. I outline the concept of triangulation in the next section.

You should also consider your own personal skills and preferences in making your choice. If you are not happy talking to others, then interviewing may not be the method for you! Or, if you lack confidence in dealing with numbers, then consider alternatives to a strongly quantitative questionnaire, requiring detailed statistical analysis. The most important thing to ensure, however, is that your choice of method is appropriate to meet your research objectives.

Triangulation

While you are considering your research design, you may wish to consider the appropriateness of triangulation. Triangulation in its most common form refers to the use of multiple means of data collection to explore a single phenomenon. Consider the following example. You may be interested in how pupils on a physical education course react to a change in the nature of their course of study. You may collect data using a questionnaire, which suggests that pupils are not overly concerned provided they can comprehend the rationale behind the change. If you have designed and piloted your questionnaire carefully, you may have some degree of confidence in these findings. Now imagine that you have followed up this initial data collection by using an additional method, for example by interviewing a sample of pupils. These pupils also suggest they are not overly concerned, again provided the rationale behind the change is clear to them. Now, your confidence in the findings should be increased, as you have data from different methods, which allows you to draw the same conclusions. This is the basis of triangulation, which refers simply to the use of more than a single source of data (although poorly thought out triangulation can also have the effect of increasing error rather than reducing it!). You could consider:

1   Data triangulation. This may refer to the use of different data sources, for example, interviews and questionnaires. Alternatively it may involve using different informants, such as interviews with pupils and teachers, or informants with the same sample but at different times.
2   Investigator triangulation. Different researchers may collect and draw their own conclusions from the same data (obviously less feasible, for example, for an individual undergraduate project).
3   Theoretical triangulation. The same situation may be examined using different theoretical viewpoints. Generally, this form of triangulation will be beyond the scope of most student research projects, but it might be worth considering in some instances.

As I have said, it is possible for triangulation to increase the error in your conclusions. In our example, pupils may have felt that the data from the questionnaires may have been made available to their tutors and, not wishing to be seen to be causing trouble, may have responded positively towards changes in their course. They may have been even more concerned about this during their interview and again responded positively towards the changes. The researcher, meanwhile, writes up the report under the impression that the data triangulation has strengthened the validity of their findings. Thus, you need to be cautious in triangulating your data and identify any potential problems that may arise.

Combining quantitative and qualitative approaches

So far in this chapter I have suggested that your design will lead to the collection of either quantitative or qualitative data. In nearly all cases this is advisable, for example in terms of the expertise required in both approaches, the extended time required to actually carry out the study and the need to keep the research focused. As I noted in Chapter 2, however, it can sometimes be appropriate to collect both types of data, and sometimes this can enhance a piece of research in a number of ways. As already mentioned, triangulation from using different data collection techniques can strengthen the validity of the research. The two types of data may complement each other; for example, quantitative data may describe a phenomenon well, and qualitative data may be appropriate to gain an understanding of the phenomenon. Quantitative data may throw up questions that are more suited to qualitative analysis, and vice versa. Using qualitative and quantitative data does not, however, always make a study better, and very often will make it worse, with a lack of depth or rigour on either or both elements, the mixing of different ontological and epistemological standpoints, and finally the very real danger that studies that attempt to combine qualitative and quantitative data will end up as two separate, albeit related studies, and this needs to be avoided. In most cases, a single approach done well will always be superior to a combined approach that isn't done as well, and there has to be a strong justification for you mixing approaches in your research project.

Ethical considerations in research design

Whatever research design, sampling techniques and choice of methods you choose to adopt, you will also need to consider the ethical issues associated with the research, that is the question of whether your research design is socially and morally acceptable or has the potential to cause physical, social or environmental harm. Carrying out research into social phenomena such as sport is difficult to do without coming across some ethical issues, and all research designs raise important ethical questions. Addressing these questions is non-negotiable before commencing any data collection, even if it would seem to have no ethical issues, and your research project must have some form of formal ethical approval before any data is collected. Make sure you read the codes of conduct laid down by your specific discipline. For example, if you are interested in the psychology of sport, then you should familiarise yourself with the guidelines of the American Psychological Association (APA) or the British Psychological Society (BPS). Such codes generally include the following key requirements:

- Risks to participants are outweighed by the benefits of the research programme.
- Participation should be voluntary.
- Risks to participants are eliminated or minimised as far as possible, including psychological and social, as well as physical, risks.
- All information should be treated as strictly confidential.
- The participants have the right to be informed of the purpose of the study.
- Participants may withdraw at any time.
- Participants should be debriefed after the research programme.

Some of the key ethical issues are outlined in the next section.

Voluntary participation, involuntary participation and informed consent

In almost every case, all participants in the research need to have provided informed consent. Once they have been identified as a potential participant, they should be informed as to the nature of the study, why they have been selected and the use of the data that they will provide. This information is normally provided through the use of a participant information sheet. The important point about informed consent is that it must provide participants with a clear understanding of what is involved rather than being, as McNamee *et al.* (2007) note, a mere 'box-ticking' exercise, where in many cases, the level of information actually provided to participants fails to meet the necessary standards, in terms of failing to provide detail of the exact requirements of the study, omitting key details that may mislead the participant or writing in jargon or specialist terminology that participants may not fully understand. Thus it is essential that informed consent is not simply seen as a paper exercise, but that the participant is given, and genuinely understands, all the necessary detail to allow them to make a fully informed decision to participate or not. Berg and Latin (2008) refer to this as 'valid consent', which summarises the principle well. In terms of the decision not to participate, it is also important that no undue pressure is put upon participants that may make them feel obliged to take part. Direct coercion should not be used under any circumstance to ensure participation in any way, and even more subtle forms such as intense persuasion are to be avoided. Subjects must also be given the right to withdraw from the study at any time, and they must be made aware of this. If it is highly likely that informing the participants as to the exact nature of the study would bias or invalidate the results in some manner, then the participants should be given as much detail as possible but be informed of the true purpose of the study after data collection.

THE PARTICIPANT INFORMATION SHEET

You should always provide a participant information sheet so that participants are able to make a fully informed decision about their participation in the research. The information sheet should give a summary of the research project, clearly outlining the entire process in a clear and accessible manner.

The following list is not exhaustive but gives an idea of the main topics to be covered:

- Outline the nature and aims of the research.
- Explain that participation is always voluntary and that participants can withdraw at any time.
- Explain exactly what participation means in practice (how long participation takes, where it takes place and what it involves).
- Outline clearly the inclusion criteria, that is, why participants have been chosen.
- Outline any risks, inconveniences or discomforts that could reasonably be expected to result from the study.
- Describe the benefits for participants and for the wider society.
- Explain how privacy and confidentiality will be maintained, including how data will be stored.
- Describe what will happen at the end of the study; for example will it be published, or written up as a dissertation?
- Provide full contact details of the researcher, their institutional affiliation and the name of the relevant person to contact in case of concerns about the research process.

Language and Layout

- Use clear, non-technical language.
- Use appropriate language for the target audience. For example, consider the different ways needed to communicate to primary school children as opposed to their teachers, or people with expertise in the area of study as opposed to people with no such expertise.
- Divide the text into paragraphs for ease of reading.
- Consider using sub-headings for clarity.
- Make sure the font is legible.
- Have someone else read through your information sheet before it is circulated.

These should all be checked through the relevant ethics process or your institution, which may well request changes to the research itself or to the participant information sheet. Hence, the process of approval may take some time.

Deception

The issue of deception is a complex one. The primary argument for deception is that if the subject is aware of the nature of the investigation, then this may affect the results. The argument against is that deception is basically unethical in society. Some deception may be acceptable if there are no questionable outcomes to the subjects or if the subjects are not harmed or affected in any way. Other deception is more questionable. For example, in a well-known study in a non-sport context, Rosenthal and Jacobsen (1968) informed teachers which children were likely to show better academic performances and which were not. Despite the fact that the two groups were actually chosen at random, those expected to do better actually did so, compared to those who were expected to fare worse. Such an experiment, it could be argued, may have had an extremely harmful effect on the subjects, both in the short and long term. In this instance, I can suggest no justification for the research and would take the overall view that such deception is very rarely justified. I would again stress that, at the very least, if you feel that deception is warranted, you should ensure that you strongly justify your argument and an ethics committee at your university or organisation assesses your research proposal.

Confidentiality

All participants should be informed as to who will have access to research data. In many countries this is governed by broader legislation, such as GDPR legislation in Europe, which restricts access to those who actually need access to such data (in many cases this may be only the researcher), and you must ensure that once data is collected, then no one will have access unless authorised to do so, with good reason. A further step is to ensure that individuals cannot be identified; this can be done by using pseudonyms or assigning numbers to individuals in the data set (but if you keep a key that allows real names to be linked to numbers, for example, then this must be stored in an entirely separate location). Again, precise detail needs to be considered, and McNamee *et al.* (2007) identify some key questions, including:

- Precisely how are the data being recorded?
- How and where are the data stored?
- Who has access to the data?
- How long are the data held for?

Using ethics to improve your research

It's important to remember that ethical considerations are an aspect of the research process that you must get right without exception, as they ensure the safety and well-being of others. You should ensure that you gain ethical approval from the relevant committee at your institution before any research programme commences. You mustn't see getting such ethical approval, however, as a tick-box exercise or a barrier to be overcome. Ethics and methodology are closely related, and careful consideration of ethical issues can only ever improve the overall research design, and that's how you should approach research ethics. Although it is not the job of an ethics panel to comment on your research design as such, their advice can only ever strengthen your project and, equally important, ensure the well-being of those participants involved.

Summary

- You should have a carefully considered approach to the collection of your data, in terms of who you will collect data from, when such data will be collected and how such data will be collected. This is your research design.
- I have identified nine research designs: experimental, cross-sectional, time series, longitudinal, case study, grounded theory, action research, ethnography and autoethnography.
- Whatever research design you adopt, it is unlikely that you will be able to collect data from the entire population. Thus you will have to collect data from a smaller group within that population – your sample.
- You will also have to choose the methods by which you are going to collect data from that sample. Those methods should be appropriate to the type of data required and characteristics of your participants.
- It may be possible to increase the validity of your research by under-taking some form of triangulation. Triangulation means collecting data from more than one perspective; for example, it may involve collecting qualitative as well as quantitative data.
- You will also need to consider the ethical issues involved in your research, and you should gain approval from the committee responsible for ethical issues at your institution before you begin data collection.

Activity

Look again at some of the pieces of research that you have already read. Can you answer the following questions about each article?

- What research design has been adopted for the research? Do you feel this is appropriate for the research in question? Can you identify any alternative research designs that may have been considered?
- What methods have been adopted in the study? Why?
- Can you identify any ethical issues that may have arisen? If so, have the authors addressed these issues?

ABOUT YOUR RESEARCH PROJECT

- Can you clearly identify and justify the research design you are using?
- Have you considered any alternative designs?
- What type of sample are you going to choose? Why?
- Have you considered using triangulation as a technique to enhance the validity of your research?
- What are the ethical issues involved with your research project?
- How will you ensure that your research project will not breach any guidelines?
- Have you ensured that your research has been assessed by the appropriate ethics committee?

Further reading

Although it covers a wide range of material beyond this chapter, it is certainly worth reading Creswell, J., and Creswell, D. (2017) *Research Design: Qualitative, Quantitative, and Mixed Methods Approaches*, London: Sage. This book provides a wealth of information to the sport researcher on all aspects of the research process. It's also worth searching peer reviewed journals for methodologically focused papers, such as Hoeber and Shaw's (2017) discussion of qualitative research methods in sport management. Finally, there are a number of special issues of journal focusing on specific designs, for example volume 27, issue 4 of *Sport Marketing Quarterly*, which devoted an issue to undertaking experimental research in sport consumer behaviour.

The ethics of any study are of paramount importance, so I would strongly recommend reading:

McNamee, M., Olivier, S. and Wainwright, P. (2007) *Research Ethics in Exercise, Health and Sports Sciences*, London: Routledge. For a more global view of ethics, it's also worth exploring Nakray, K., Alston, M. and Whittenbury, K. (eds) (2015). *Social Science Research Ethics for a Globalizing World – Interdisciplinary and Cross-Cultural Perspectives*, New York: Routledge.

Chapter 8
Collecting data I:
The questionnaire
survey

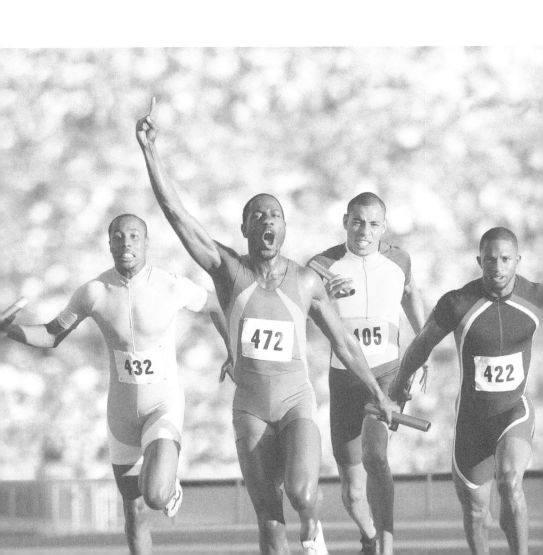

Collecting data I: The questionnaire survey

This chapter will:

- Discuss the use of questionnaires as a method of data collection, including a brief introduction to internet-based questionnaires.
- Introduce some of the advantages and disadvantages of using questionnaires in your research project.
- Outline some of the issues of questionnaire design and administration.

Introduction

So far, I have largely dealt with the background to your research project in terms of reading and assessing the literature, clarifying the role of theory, developing your conceptual framework, deciding upon a research design and gaining ethical approval for the proposed research. The next stage in most cases is to plan your collection of primary data. The next few chapters deal with issues of data collection, beginning in this chapter with an examination of the use of questionnaires.

Defined simply, a questionnaire is a standardised set of questions to gain information from a subject. They are often (though not always) associated with quantitative research designs, when relatively simple measurements are required from a large sample group (although you can use questionnaires

DOI: 10.4324/9781003195467-8

for a qualitative study, as outlined later in the chapter). Questionnaires generally fall into one of four categories:

1   Online questionnaires. These are now the most common form of questionnaire, delivered through software such as Qualtrics, Google Docs or Survey Monkey.
2   Postal questionnaires. Now much more rarely used, postal questionnaires are given or posted to the participant, who completes it in their own time. The participant then posts the completed questionnaire back to the researcher.
3   Telephone questionnaires. The researcher questions the participant over the telephone or platforms such as Skype, Zoom or Microsoft Teams, and the researcher fills in the responses.
4   Face-to-face questionnaires. The researcher and participant are in the same location, and the researcher asks the questions 'face-to-face' and fills in responses as they receive them, generally using a laptop or smartphone.

Questionnaires can thus be designed for completion either by the researcher (interviewer completion) or by the subject (respondent or self-completion). Interviewer completion questionnaires are effectively the same as structured interviews, and the issues associated with this particular technique will be dealt with in the next chapter. This chapter will provide an overview of respondent completion surveys, the type of questionnaire that you are most likely to use.

When is the use of a questionnaire appropriate?

The first consideration that you must make is whether a questionnaire is an appropriate method to collect the data you need. Once you have developed and focused your research question, considered the relevant concepts and developed your conceptual framework (see Chapter 6), and determined your choice of research design (Chapter 7), you should be able to list your information needs, that is the information you require to answer your research question (including information needed to account for any moderating variables). Three questions can now be asked:

1   Can I get the information I need using data from a questionnaire?
2   Is a questionnaire the best or most appropriate method, or are other methods more appropriate to collect the data?
3   Are other methods excluded, for example interviews, because of time and cost restrictions?

Questionnaires are appropriate in a variety of contexts, where relatively simple, generally quantitative information is required from a large sample group. This data can then be summarised through the use of tables or charts or analysed statistically to answer a research question. Moyo *et al.* (2020), for example, used questionnaires to investigate whether fans who had attended the 2010 FIFA World Cup in South Africa had revisited the country since. They used a questionnaire to 'collect numerical data and factual information', which was analysed 'using mathematically based methods to explain a social and cultural phenomenon' (p. 61). Their population was international football tourists who had visited South Africa in 2010 from the UK, Germany and France. To gain information about fan behaviour, they developed and administered a questionnaire consisting of closed questions, using a systematic sampling method, to 391 fans. This allowed them to identify patterns and motivations of travel to South Africa, allowing them to identify the importance of hosting sport mega-events on awareness of, and willingness to, travel to a destination.

Advantages of using questionnaires

As you will learn over the next few chapters, each of the methods you may adopt as part of a research project has its own advantages and disadvantages. In most cases you will have to assess these when considering your choice of method. What you will ultimately need to do, however, is to be able to justify your eventual choice, utilise their advantages and minimise the potential disadvantages. The advantages of using a questionnaire include the following:

- *Accessibility.* Questionnaires, especially those administered online, allow you to collect data from a geographically dispersed sample group at a much lower cost than interviewing a similar sample. In addition, questionnaires allow a much larger sample to be investigated.
- *Potential reduction in bias.* With a well-designed questionnaire there is little opportunity to introduce bias into the results as may be the case with interviews, for example through the way you respond to an answer or your body language (see Chapter 9), or simply your presence in observational studies. You should be aware, however, that badly designed questionnaires can lead to bias in your data.
- *Anonymity.* The presence of the researcher interested in certain sensitive issues (for example, player violence, the use of drugs or cheating in sport) may inhibit the respondent. A questionnaire allows anonymity and may therefore improve the validity of your responses in certain cases.
- *Structured data.* Questionnaires tend to provide highly structured quantitative data that is easily comparable, either between subject groups or between the same group studied over an extended time period. Such data is generally straightforward to convert into tables and charts, and to analyse statistically.

- *Increased time for respondents.* Respondent-completed questionnaires allow the respondent to fill in the questionnaire at a convenient time if necessary or to be able to go back to the questionnaire at a later time if they recall anything further.

Disadvantages of using questionnaires

- *Potential problems over complex questions.* The questions have to be clear enough for all participants to understand, as there will often be no opportunity for the respondent to seek clarification. If complex questions are required, then you may need to be present to explain them. Thus, to a large extent, you are restricted to relatively simple questions.
- *No control over who completes the questionnaire.* Unless you specify exactly who is to fill out the questionnaire, an inappropriate party may complete it. Even if you do specify that it has to be completed by a particular individual, it may be that the respondent delegates the task to somebody else without your knowledge.
- *No opportunity to probe.* Once the respondent has answered the question there is no opportunity to get them to expand upon or explain any of the points that may have been made.
- *Potentially low response rates.* Response rates from questionnaires are notoriously poor and can range from as little as 5 per cent or so upwards. Low response rates may have a serious effect on the reliability and validity of the study. Potential means of improving your response rates are highlighted later in the chapter.

Using internet-based questionnaires

The internet, through tools such as Qualtrics, Survey Monkey and Google Docs, is now the primary means by which questionnaires can be administered, and it offers the sport researcher a number of advantages. Wright (2005) has summarised these as follows:

- Greater access to certain populations. Online surveys may allow you to identify and access certain groups more easily; for example, you may be able to access fans of a particular sport team through the team's online forum or through social media sites. They also allow you to reach samples at a global rather than national level.
- Larger sample sizes. In the past couple of years, I have supervised a number of final-year dissertations that have achieved sample sizes of well over 500 respondents.

- 'Cleaner' data. Lonsdale *et al.*'s (2006) study of New Zealand athletes determined that the group who was sent online questionnaires provided fewer missing values when compared with a control group who was assigned paper-based questionnaires.
- Time efficiency. As well as being quicker to send out, data is also quicker to analyse in that responses can be downloaded to a database or statistical package rather than having to be manually input.
- Cost. The costs of postage and printing are removed through use of online surveys, although this needs to be weighed up against the costs involved when using certain online survey tools. Many sites allow a certain amount of free usage but will involve a cost for things such as being able to access more than 100 respondents or downloading directly into software packages such as SPSS for Windows. This will generally be cheaper than the costs associated with postage, however.

In addition, as Hoon Lee *et al.* (2018) note, internet-based questionnaires also have environmental benefits, having fewer environmental impacts than paper-based or researcher administered questionnaires.

The technical skills required to design and use internet-based questionnaires are, in most cases, relatively simple, and it is something that you will be able to pick up fairly quickly if you have basic IT skills. It is worth trying a number of different options, as there are advantages and disadvantages to whichever you will choose, so my advice is to test a couple of options before you go into 'live' data collection.

USING ONLINE QUESTIONNAIRES – WHO ARE THE SPORT GAMERS?

Stein *et al.* (2013) have noted how little is known about those who play sport video games such as *FIFA14* or *Madden NFL 11*. To fill this void in the literature, they decided to utilise an online survey to explore gamers' playing habits, their experiences of games and the links between their 'real' and virtual sporting experiences. Once the questionnaire had been designed and launched on a server, the researchers recruited participants through posting information and a link to the survey on social media sites such as Twitter and Facebook, as well as related game blogs and web sites. Over a period of approximately 1 month, they were able to achieve a total of 1,718 respondents. This allowed them to determine a range of information, such as gamers tending to be overwhelmingly young and male, and to identify strong links between their real life sporting activity and their virtual sporting activity.

There are, however, potential disadvantages, and you shouldn't necessarily see the use of online surveys as a simple solution to overcoming issues of paper-based surveys. You need to consider:

- Sampling bias. Online surveys will generally not involve random samples from the population under investigation, and the sample may be skewed to younger, more committed respondents, and to countries that have greater internet access.
- Potentially low response rates. Increasing numbers of 'spam' emails may make it difficult to get respondents to open, let alone read, the covering email. Lonsdale *et al.* (2006) have, however, indicated that online questionnaires may actually result in a higher response rate, so the evidence is equivocal.
- Incentives. The offer of incentives to overcome low response rates may encourage individuals to fill in multiple responses to increase their chances of winning.
- Access issues. Members of an online community may resent researchers getting in contact and respond by ignoring the message, moderators of the group may delete the message or the researcher may encounter abusive responses, especially if they are seen as an outsider to that group.

Designing the questionnaire

Once you have decided that it is an appropriate data collection technique, the second stage of questionnaire-based research is that of the initial design of the questionnaire. A good questionnaire is difficult to design and takes considerably more time than is often anticipated. While a questionnaire that may seem to have some relevance towards the research objectives is relatively easy to put together, designing questions that actually fulfil all of the researcher's needs and is both reliable and valid is more time consuming. As Oppenheim (1992, p. 7) notes:

> Too often, surveys are carried out on the basis of insufficient design and planning or on the basis of no design at all. 'Fact-gathering' can be an exciting and tempting activity to which a questionnaire opens a quick and seemingly easy avenue; the weaknesses in the design are frequently not recognised until the results have to be interpreted – if then!

Three questions need to be asked at the beginning of the design stage. These are:

1   What information do I need to answer my research question?
2   What questions can I ask that will provide me with data that will, when analysed, give me such information?

3   How am I going to analyse the data that I get from such questions to give me the answer to my research question?

Thus, before designing the questionnaire, it is important that your information needs have been clearly identified. Here, the conceptual framework that you have identified (see Chapter 5) can be extremely helpful. As a rule of thumb, you should try to keep the questionnaire as short as possible, yet ensure that it will provide all of the necessary data. Do not be tempted to include questions that are not required, even if you consider them to be interesting! You should be able to justify the inclusion of each question and identify how that question will help answer your research question. You also need to think ahead in terms of how you intend to analyse your data, which will influence you in the type of data that you decide to collect. (For example will you need your responses to provide you with ordinal or ratio data?) In terms of the data that you need, you should be guided by the aim and objectives of the research, the literature review and your conceptual framework, which should be related. If the research objectives are detailed and specific enough, then these should provide a clear starting point. There are a number of different question formats that you can adopt when designing your questionnaire. The most common formats are described here.

Closed/pre-coded questions
The respondent is asked to choose one or more responses from a series of choices pre-determined by the researcher, for example:

Q.1 How many competitive matches have you played so far this season? (Please tick one box.)

0–5 ❑   6–10 ❑   11–15 ❑   16–20 ❑

This format can be used if the question requires relatively simple information and you know all of the available responses beforehand. Such questions are also easier for respondents and take less time than other question formats to complete.

Open questions
Sometimes it is not possible to anticipate all the answers you are going to receive, or you may anticipate a wide variety of different answers. Here you will need the respondent to write their answer with no prompting. For example:

Q.2 What, in your opinion, are the attributes of a good sport coach?
. . . .
. . . .

You can use open questions within a questionnaire to obtain qualitative data (as discussed later in the chapter), although you need to be careful, as participants are unlikely to be willing to write down lengthy answers to your questions. Open questions can be harder to analyse, as the respondent can give a wider range of answers, or the answers might be difficult to interpret. For example, the answers to any open questions will need to be coded for qualitative analysis or converted into numbers if you are going to quantitatively analyse your data (see Chapters 13 and 14 for an overview of data analysis).

Often, you will have the choice between using open and closed questions. Rather than make an arbitrary choice, you should think about the purpose of your questionnaire. The following guidelines may be of use. Use closed questions if:

- You require quantitative data.
- You have a clear idea of all of the likely responses.
- Responses are likely to be simple.
- It is important for respondents to answer using a pre-determined set of responses.

Use open questions if:

- You require qualitative data.
- You are unsure of the likely responses.
- Responses are likely to be complex.
- The respondent's own words are important.

An alternative approach is to combine open and closed questions, so that a number of responses are provided but the respondent has the opportunity to respond in an alternative manner if none of the responses are appropriate or to elaborate on a particular response. For example:

Q.3 Who was the most important influence on your decision to take up your chosen sport? (Please tick one box.)

Father ❑
Mother ❑
Brother ❑
Sister ❑
Teacher ❑
Other ❑ (Please state.) . . . .

Using scales

Occasionally you may need to measure a concept using a scale. A scale is a series of questions designed to gain a single measure of a concept, such as an attitude towards or opinion on something. Thus, several questions will contribute to an overall score. A number of different scaling techniques exist.

Likert scales

These are generally used to assess attitudes. A Likert scale allows the respondent to indicate the extent to which they agree with a certain statement. At its simplest level, such a scale may provide a statement and the respondent may be asked whether they agree or disagree. Often, however, a respondent will be unhappy about being forced into such an either/or choice. Likert scales can be used to measure the extent to which participants agree or disagree with a particular statement, and they are useful for questions where there may be no clear responses such as 'yes' or 'no'. Responses can be scored; for example, if there is a five-point scale (respondents have the option of ticking one of five possible responses), then a response that ticks the first box scores one; a response that ticks the next box scores two; and so on, thus providing ordinal data.

Q.4 Do you agree that sponsorship of major sporting events is an effective marketing strategy for major corporations?
Yes, very much so. ❑ ❑ ❑ ❑ ❑ No, not at all.

USING SCALES TO EXPLORE THE USE OF HOMOPHOBIC LANGUAGE IN MALE TEAM SPORT

Denison *et al.* (2021) used different scales in their exploration of homophobic language use in male team sport. Questionnaires were administered to rugby union and ice hockey players to identify both their attitudes to and use of such language.

To explore the use of such language, the *Homophobic Content Agent Target* (HCAT) was used, which listed various words such as *fag* and then provided a scale for respondents to report how many times they had used such words, with response options being (0) never, (1) 1–2 times, (2) 3–4 times, (3) 5–6 times and (4) 7+ times.

To explore homophobic attitudes, two scales were used. Firstly, a semantic differential scale was used. The question *'When you think of gay men, as a group, what words describe your feelings?'* was followed by five sematic differential scales – respect/disapprove, negative/positive (reverse-coded), friendly/hostile, trusting/suspicious, dislike/admire (again, reverse coded) – which were each measured using a six-point Likert scale. Secondly, the Attitudes Toward Gay Men (ATG) scale was used, consisting of three statements about homosexuality, such as *'I think male homosexuals are disgusting'*. This was again scored on a six-point Likert scale and combined with the scores from the semantic differential scale to develop an overall measure of attitudes.

Semantic differential

This format measures the respondent's reaction to a specified concept using a scale with contrasting adjectives at each end. For example:

Q.5 Just before I start a football game I feel:

Relaxed	❑ ❑ ❑ ❑ ❑	Anxious
Optimistic	❑ ❑ ❑ ❑ ❑	Pessimistic

The responses are scored in the same way as for a Likert scale. Semantic differential scales are also useful to assess respondents' attitudes towards a particular phenomenon without forcing them into an extreme choice. You should ensure that the two adjectives are related, however. For example, you couldn't use *anxious* and *confident*, as respondents may score highly on both.

Using existing scales

Inexperienced researchers often feel that to add to the originality of their research, they should always develop their own questions or scales, and that the use of somebody else's questionnaire lays them open to the charge of plagiarism. In reality, you are, in almost every case, better off using existing questions and scales, especially if they have been designed to measure the same concepts that you are interested in (provided, of course, that you fully acknowledge the source of the original questionnaire!). These will already have been assessed in terms of their reliability and validity, and using existing questions allows you to compare your findings with those of others much more easily. Valid and reliable scales are difficult and time-consuming to develop, and even apparently straightforward concepts may be difficult to measure using a scale. Sport is a complex social phenomenon, and the concepts within it are rarely one-dimensional, that is they cannot be measured using a single question. Scales therefore have to measure the multidimensionality of concepts, and developing such scales can often be a task that is time-consuming even to experienced researchers. Thus, when searching the literature, you should be prepared to look for information not only about the relevant concepts and ideas, but also about how such concepts and ideas have been measured in the past.

Ranking questions

Ranking questions ask the respondent to place responses in order of importance. These are appropriate when you want respondents to consider the relative merits of particular items.

Q.6 Please rank the following sports in order of preference from 1 to 3, with 1 signifying the sport you like most, and 3 signifying the sport you like least:

Field hockey	❏
Basketball	❏
Tennis	❏

Ensure that you don't have too many choices to rank with this type of question. Asking respondents to rank ten items in order is an extremely difficult task.

List questions

These questions allow the respondent to indicate several responses to one question. For example:

Q.7 Which of the following companies have sponsored sports events to your knowledge in the last 12 months? (Please tick as appropriate.)

Rolex ❏   Ford ❏   Gillette ❏   Coca-Cola ❏

One of the issues that you need to be aware of with questions such as this is that when you come to enter this data, you will have to treat each response as a separate question, so instead of analysing Q.7 as a single question, you will have to analyse each sponsor separately, and whether the response was 'yes' or 'no'.

Filter questions

It is important that you don't alienate potential respondents by asking them to read through and respond to large numbers of irrelevant questions. Filter questions can be used where appropriate to prevent this. Often some of your questions will be inapplicable to certain respondents. Rather than forcing respondents to read each question and decide whether or not it is relevant, questions that are not applicable can be filtered out using the following format:

Q.8 Have you bought any PlayStation sports games in the past 12 months?

No ❏   Please go to question 9.
Yes ❏
If YES: What game(s) did you buy? . . . .

Using filter questions can minimise the time taken to complete the questionnaire and reduce the potential frustration that respondents may feel when reading through a number of questions that don't apply to them. This can be a useful way of helping to increase your response rates.

Ordering the questionnaire

Once you have designed the specific questions, it is then important to consider their sequence within the questionnaire. There is no set order, but you should consider the following points:

- Try to begin the questionnaire with a few straightforward, closed questions requiring factual answers if at all possible. It is important to get the respondent to actually start completing the questionnaire. Once the first few questions have been completed, it is much more likely that the respondent will persevere.
- You should therefore avoid putting complex questions, questions requiring detailed thought or questions requiring lengthy responses at the beginning of the questionnaire.
- Group questions on a similar theme together and avoid jumping from topic to topic.
- The location of personal, or what might be perceived as potentially threatening, questions needs to be carefully considered. Some authors suggest that they are placed at the end of the questionnaire; however others argue that this may give the impression of them being 'hidden away' and that it is better to be open and include them at the beginning. You need to firstly think about whether such questions are actually needed and make a judgement using your own competence as a researcher.

Designing online surveys

There are two broad means by which you can collect survey data online. The first (and preferable) is to undertake an internet survey, which involves the questionnaire being hosted online, using specialist survey software such as Qualtrics or Survey Monkey, or a tool such as Google Docs. An alternative is to undertake an email survey, which involves including the survey in the body of the email or as an attachment. Including the survey within the body of the email does restrict the design and layout of the questionnaire, and the use of an attachment does involve greater effort on behalf of the respondent, with a subsequent risk in terms of response rates. You also lose many of the benefits of a hosted questionnaire, such as the option to download data directly to your analysis software.

The process of undertaking an internet survey differs slightly from that of paper-based survey. The stages are as follows:

1 Initial design of the questionnaire.
2 Piloting of the questionnaire. This can be done, at this stage, using a paper-based copy of the questionnaire. This stage is key to ensuring that the nature and wording of the questions are appropriate, clear and so on.

3   Create the questionnaire electronically, using a package such as Qualtrics, Google Docs or Survey Monkey.
4   Pilot the online survey. As well as testing the wording, this stage is to test the experience of completing the survey, the clarity of instructions, ease of navigation and so on.
5   Invite potential respondents to complete the survey, for example through emailing the relevant URL to your population.
6   Monitor the progress of data collection, sending reminders if appropriate.
7   Close the survey, and download data for analysis.

Poynter (2010) provides useful guidance in terms of designing an online survey:

- Ensure a welcoming first page that includes the necessary information and a last page that thanks the respondent for taking part, provides any relevant informant about how the data will be used or any incentives that may be offered and allows the respondent to make any comments by answering an open question. Use a multi-page design, where no scrolling is necessary, rather than including all questions on a single page where the respondent has to scroll down.
- Put related questions together on the same page. Otherwise, one question per page is acceptable.
- If a single question is too long to be displayed on the screen without scrolling (e.g. there are a large number of potential responses), then tell the respondent that scrolling is necessary to read the entire question.
- Consider having a brief section at the top of each page or section where the questions are set in context and any useful information can be given, for example a line such as 'The following questions are designed to examine your attitudes towards the cost of televised sport. For each question, please read the statement carefully and indicate your level of agreement with that statement'.
- Provide an indicator of progress. Some packages will allow a graphical indication of how much progress has been made; if this isn't available, then a simple text-based indication, such as 'page 3 of 4' is helpful.

In addition, you should also ensure the following:

- Respondents should be able to move back and forwards between sections.
- Don't overuse graphics, and ensure that colours and fonts should be appropriate and allow the content to be easily read.
- Make error messages both as precise and friendly as possibly.
- Avoid too many forced questions if possible. A forced question is one that has to be answered before progressing to the next one. Too many

may encourage the respondent to fill in an arbitrary response simply to move on, or to abort the survey.

- Put personal questions at the beginning, rather than the end of the survey. Andrews *et al.* (2003) note that attrition rates are higher when such questions are placed at the end of the survey.

Enhancing the online survey experience

Whatever the data collection method, one of your responsibilities as researcher is to ensure that the experience is a positive one for the respondent, and this is certainly true for an internet survey. Poynter (2010) outlines a range of issues to improve the survey experience for an online participant. Two important aspects are:

1 Being 'better with people', making it clear to respondents why they have been asked and why their help is important. It is also important to be honest about how long the survey will take to complete and to ensure that all instructions are politely worded.
2 Improving the survey itself. You should thus ensure that the survey is as short as possible while collecting all of the required data. Questions should make sense and have no mistakes (this should, of course, be picked up during the piloting).

Problems in questionnaire design

Unlike many other forms of data collection, questionnaire surveys, whether paper, telephone or online, generally only allow the researcher a 'one-off' chance at research. If the questionnaire is badly designed, then it is unlikely that you will get another chance to collect the data, due either to time restrictions or the difficulties in finding further participants. Therefore, you should be aware of some of the potential errors in designing a questionnaire.

Ambiguous/complex wording

Keep the questions as simple as possible. Questions that may seem clear to the researcher may not be clear to the respondent, especially if the sample group is likely to be diverse. You should also avoid using technical or 'academic' language. The questions should be understandable to the lowest level of education or understanding that the sample may encompass. For example, if you are collecting data from a broad cross-section of the population, then your questionnaire must be understandable to children. Otherwise, you are likely to under-represent this group in your achieved sample, leading to non-response bias.

Incorrectly pre-coding closed questions

An easy mistake to make is to incorrectly identify the pre-determined responses that you provide for your respondents. An example of this would be the following question:

Q.9 How many times a week do you train?

Never	❏
1–2 times	❏
2–3 times	❏
More than 3 times	❏

Those respondents who train twice a week could fill in more than one box, leading to problems of reliability and validity. Alternatively you may omit possible responses, so that none of the available responses are appropriate to the respondent.

Leading questions

Questions such as 'Do you agree that potentially dangerous performance enhancing drugs should be banned?' should be avoided, as respondents may feel pressured to agree with such statements. Try not to influence respondents in any way by your question wording.

Double-barrelled questions

Avoid asking for respondents' views on two separate issues in the same question. Questions such as 'Do you agree that boxing is an inherently dangerous sport and should therefore be banned?' asks two different questions, yet only allows for a single answer. Ensure that each question measures a single concept.

Vague questions

Questions such as 'Do you regularly take part in physical activity?' may be interpreted in different ways by respondents. Some may interpret 'regularly' as meaning once a week; for others it may mean once a year. Both interpretations are valid in their own way. In the same way that you have to be able to clearly define each concept in your conceptual framework, as outlined in Chapter 6, you should be able to clearly define the concepts in each question and ensure that your understanding of those concepts is the same as the person completing the question. If necessary, define any terms.

Threatening questions

It is often difficult to obtain valid information if the respondent is likely to feel threatened at all. When undertaking research into violence in sport or the use of performance-enhancing drugs, for example, the respondent may well under-report or even deny such activity. The researcher must first identify any threatening questions and, second, carefully word these questions to reduce bias. Try to word such questions in a neutral manner. If you are asking such questions, then you should clearly highlight the confidential nature of the data to potential respondents.

Incorrectly operationalising concepts

If the concept has not been suitably operationalised, then it will be impossible to collect valid data. An example may be that you have operationalised commitment to playing for a particular amateur sport team in terms of how many times a respondent plays a season. It may be that an individual is extremely committed yet can only play irregularly, perhaps due to work or family commitments. In such an instance, the data obtained would lack validity.

Questions being subject to a positivity bias

Matlin and Gawron (1979) described something called the Pollyanna effect, or the tendency for people to tend to agree with positive statements about themselves. Thus, asking people to agree or disagree with statements such as 'I am generally an honest person' are less likely to receive responses that disagree. This is also related to the Forer effect, which is an effect whereby individuals are also likely to rate vague and generalised statements as highly accurate for them individually. Thus, statements such as 'You are someone who enjoys taking part in sport and physical activity on a regular basis' are likely to produce high ratings in terms of agreement.

Not including a 'Don't know' or 'Not applicable' option

There may be questions where respondents simply do not know, can't give or don't want to give an answer. Ensure that they have the option not to respond.

Piloting the questionnaire

No matter how well-designed you think your questionnaire is, it is vital that it is piloted beforehand. A pilot survey refers to a small-scale administration of the survey prior to the main administration. The pilot survey performs a number of important functions, including:

- To check that the wording of the questionnaire is clear, unambiguous and understandable to the intended sample.

- To check that the sequence of the questionnaire is clear and logical to respondents.
- To assess the likely completion time of the questionnaire.
- To check the administration of the questionnaire, from its initial distribution to receiving the completed questionnaire.
- To allow you a 'dry run' at analysing the data collected from the questionnaire.

The last point is one that is often overlooked. It is worth inputting your preliminary data from the pilot questionnaires into whatever package you are going to use for analysis, for example JASP or SPSS (see Chapter 13), and using this data to try to answer your question. This ensures that the data you collect is suitable for your purposes.

Your pilot survey should be carried out in conditions as close as possible to the main survey, and with as similar a sample group as possible. Thus, if your questionnaire is going to be administered to a sample that includes children, then the pilot sample should also include children. The results of the pilot should be closely monitored. Once changes have been made, then the survey must be re-piloted and the need for any further changes assessed. You should then continue to pilot your questionnaire until you are completely happy with its design, even if it takes a number of attempts.

MEASURING THE ECONOMIC IMPACT OF VISITORS TO SPORT TOURNAMENTS AND SPECIAL EVENTS

UK Sport (1999) provided a set of guidelines for those conducting research into the economic impact of major sporting events. These studies are generally done through visitor surveys, and the additional expenditure generated within a city as a consequence of hosting an event can partially be evaluated through self-completion questionnaires. Through examining the design of their questionnaire, we can develop an idea of how questionnaires should be designed to achieve their research objectives. It is important that a questionnaire of this type is kept as short as possible to maximise response rates. Thus, as with any good questionnaire, each question has a particular purpose related to the objectives of the research.

The objectives of the research were as follows:

- Objective 1. To quantify the proportions of respondents who live in the host city and those who are from outside the host city.
- Objective 2. To determine the catchment area of the event by local, regional, national and international responses.

Economic impacts refer only to expenditure made by out-of-town visitors. Thus a question is required to differentiate between local and non-local respondents. This question also allows researchers to identify the proportion of out-of-town visitors to the event, as well as enabling the catchment area of an event to be identified.

Q.1 Where do you live? (Please specify town or city.) . . . .

Note that an open question is used, as it is not possible to list all potential responses. It is important to specify the level of detail by ensuring respondents specify the town or city, otherwise unhelpful answers such as 'England' may be returned. At this point, those who live within the host city can be identified, and the data collection terminated.

▨   Objective 3. To group respondent types by their role in the event, for example, media, spectators, competitors, officials, etc.

Different groups will show different characteristics; therefore it is important to know which group the respondent belongs to.

Q.2 Which of the following are you?

Athlete   ❏
Official   ❏
Spectator   ❏
Coach   ❏
Media   ❏
Other   ❏

In this instance, all the appropriate responses are known; thus a closed question is appropriate. This allows easy analysis of responses, as well as being easier and quicker for the respondent.

▨   Objective 4. To identify the basic characteristics of respondents.

Certain characteristics – such as gender – are easily observed. Other characteristics, such as the size of the group of which the respondent was a part, are included on the questionnaire. Note the use of a filter question to minimise the need to answer irrelevant questions:

Q.3 Are you attending the athletics alone? Yes ❏ No ❏
If YES, please go to question 4a.
If NO, how many other adults (over 16) are there in your party today?
If NO, how many other children (under 16) are there in your party today?

▨   Objective 5. To quantify the number of people from outside the host city staying overnight in the host city and from this subsample to quantify how many are staying in commercially provided accommodation. Accommodation is by far the largest expenditure item, and those staying overnight are likely to spend more elsewhere. Thus, it is important to quantify such individuals. By using two questions, the location where respondents are staying, the type of accommodation utilised and the proportion of day to overnight visitors could be ascertained:

Q.4a In which town/city are you staying tonight? . . . .
Q.4b Is this:

At home ❑   With friends/relatives ❑   A guest house ❑
A hotel ❑   A camp site ❑   Other ❑
If OTHER, please specify. . . . .

Note the importance of allowing respondents an alternative option if none of the given options are appropriate.

■ Objective 6. To quantify how many nights those staying in commercial accommodation will spend in the city and how much per night such accommodation is costing. The revenue from visitors staying in commercial accommodation is, as we noted, the largest source of economic revenue. To calculate this revenue, two questions are again needed:

Q.5a How many nights are you staying in town/city X? . . . .

If you are not staying overnight in town/city X, go to question 6.

Q.5b If you are staying overnight in town/city X, how much are you spending on accommodation per night? . . . .

Simple analysis thus allows the number of commercial beds/nights (number of visitors X number of nights stayed) and revenue (commercial beds/nights X average cost per bed/night) to be calculated.

■ Objective 7. To quantify the amount spent per day on six standard categories of expenditure.

For such a study, it is also important to quantify the amount spent on other products and services by all respondents (not just overnight visitors).

It is important that only expenditure made in the host town or city is included, and thus the question is designed to reflect this:

Q.6 How much will you spend in town/city X TODAY on the following?

Food and drink . . . . Programmes/merchandise . . . .
Entertainment . . . . Shopping/souvenirs . . . . Travel . . . .
Other (parking, petrol, etc.) . . . .

■ Objective 8. To quantify how much people have budgeted in total to spend in a host city and on how many other people this expenditure will be made. People may combine an event with another activity, such as a mini-break or business, for example.

To identify additional expenditure that would not otherwise be picked up, a question is included to quantify the total amount individuals have budgeted to spend in the host city. The final part of this question asks how many other people this expenditure is being made for. Response to this question enables any amount of expenditure already identified to be put on a per capita basis.

Q.7 How much have you budgeted to spend in TOTAL during your stay in town/city X?

Total expenditure. . . . .
Does this include expenditure on others? Yes ❏ No ❏

If YES, for how many others is this expenditure? . . . .

■ Objective 9. To establish the proportion of people whose main reason for being in the host city is the event under investigation. It may be that, in certain instances, those attending the event are not in the host town or city specifically for that event. Thus, any economic impacts from such visitors cannot be attributed to the sporting event itself. A question is needed to identify such individuals:

Q.8 Is event Y the main reason for your being in town/city X today?

Yes ❏ No ❏

■ Objective 10. To determine whether any respondents are combining their visit to the host city with a holiday. For some, an event may lead to a decision to take a break or a holiday. For example, the World Cup may lead to supporters spending an extended period of time in the host nation. For such individuals, the economic impact is clearly greater than on the day or days of the event. Thus, it is important to have some data about these people:

Q.9 Are you combining your visit to event 'Y' with a holiday? Yes ❏ No ❏
If YES, where are you going? . . . .
For how long? . . . .
Can you provide us with a rough estimate of your total budget for this part of your trip? £ . . .

The results of this question allow the wider economic impacts of an event to be assessed. For some events (such as the World Cup, Olympic and Commonwealth Games, etc.) such extended impacts are significant and an important consequence of hosting them.

Increasing your response rate

As well as the design of the questionnaire itself, you need to be thinking about its administration (that is, how it will be given to potential respondents), how it will be returned and how you will ensure that as many are returned as possible. It is important to maximise the response rate for both academic and pragmatic reasons. A low response rate leads to the questions of whether there are any particular groups that have not responded and why, what are the effects of the non-response on the findings and whether there is bias in the data as a consequence. If children, for example, have not completed the questionnaire because it was too complex, then how can an accurate overview of the entire population be made?

Ethically, it is important to remember that you cannot coerce participants to complete a questionnaire – it has to be done voluntarily. You can take steps to persuade them gently, however, but without putting undue pressure on them. Frankfort-Nachimas and Nachimas (1996) have identified a number of techniques that may be adopted to increase response rates. You should not focus on only one or two of these techniques, however – all of them should be considered.

- Follow-up – a gentle reminder at an appropriate time, for example after two weeks, will encourage non-respondents. Make sure the tone of the follow-up is appropriate and not coercive.
- Inducement – an incentive may encourage responses, provided that it is valued, appropriate to the potential sample and seen as a 'fair' amount.
- Sponsorship – support from an organisation or individual of which respondents are aware may be helpful.
- Method of return – the easier the method of return, the higher the response rate. Online surveys are advantageous here.
- Format – the layout must be totally professional and user friendly.
- Appropriate target audience – a population that is interested in or familiar with the subject will result in a higher response rate, as is one that feels that the survey may be of some use.

The covering letter

You should always include with any questionnaire a covering letter or accompanying email that includes the information required in your participation information sheet (Chapter 7). As well as fulfilling your ethical requirements to provide your participants with information about the study, it is extremely important as one method of maximising the response rate. It should be separate to the main survey (i.e. as a separate letter, never as a few lines at the top of a questionnaire, or as an introductory email followed up with a separate email linking to the questionnaire). If you are carrying out an online or face-to-face survey, you should also cover the same points as would be included in your covering letter. This can be done using a 'script' that has been prepared in place of the covering letter. Covering letters should also be piloted to ensure that you have not been ambiguous or said anything that lacks clarity or relevance to your sample.

Administering the questionnaire at sporting events

Although having an appropriately designed questionnaire is important, it is not simply a case of distributing questionnaires wherever and whenever possible. If you have access to details about your population, then it is generally straightforward to provide them with the questionnaire. In some cases, however, you will need to distribute your questionnaire during a sporting event (provided you have appropriate permission). The following process is suggested by the Sport Industry Research Centre (SIRC).

Preplanning

Each potential respondent group must be considered, so that a strategy can be implemented for optimum data capture. Thus, the following issues need to be assessed:

- How many of each respondent group will there be?
- When will they be arriving?
- Where will they be staying?
- How will it be possible to get convenient access to them?
- Are there any unique circumstances relevant to any group that may have an effect on the research?

You will also need to consider how the questionnaires will be given to potential respondents and how many assistants you will need to undertake this task.

Collection

You then need to consider whether questionnaires will be left with the sample, to be returned at a later date through the post, or whether they will be completed face-to-face. Postal questionnaires (distributed either at the event or through lists of attendees where available) are considered cost-effective, and they allow participants to complete the questions in their own time. However, response rates may be low, and two or more follow-up letters may be required to achieve a desired response rate. An alternative is to hand participants the questionnaire and wait with them while they complete it. This can be problematic, as during the event spectators are unlikely to have the time or inclination to complete a questionnaire, and this method is also much more resource-intensive. Unless you have a team of helpers, it is unlikely you will be able to collect sufficient data unless you are prepared to spend a considerable time within the field. One possible answer to this is to use the approach of Pol and Pak (1994), obtaining names and addresses during the event that can then be used after the event has finished.

Following up non-respondents

After the final date for questionnaire returns has passed, you will need to contact those who have not returned their questionnaires. This is usually done by sending a follow-up letter or email and a copy of the original questionnaire or reminder of the link to the questionnaire, as well as a pre-paid envelope in which to return the questionnaire if appropriate. Do not send the original covering letter, as this was obviously unsuccessful in eliciting a response first time round! Instead, one approach is to suggest that the failure to return a completed questionnaire was an oversight on the participant's part, rather than a straight refusal. Stress the importance of the study and the value of the contribution that would be made by completing the questionnaire. You must ensure as before, however, that you do not coerce the respondent into completing the questionnaire in any way. Remember to include a further cut-off date as appropriate.

CASE STUDY

QUESTIONNAIRE ADMINISTRATION AT SPORT EVENTS IN SOUTH AFRICA

BY DR JANICE HEMMONSBEY, CAPE PENINSULA UNIVERSITY OF TECHNOLOGY, CAPE TOWN

Our research study was titled 'Leveraging home-grown sport tourism events for strategic destination branding outcomes'. A quantitative research approach was adopted to elicit responses from sport event attendees on the brand messages of South Africa as a host to major events. The study's results hold practical and policy implications to the stakeholders of events, destination and tourism organisations.

Interviewer-administered questionnaires were used to collect quantitative data that would lead to achieving the research objectives. This questionnaire method was favoured for its ability to increase participation, allow for clarity, as well as ensure fewer unanswered questions. Well-trained fieldworkers were positioned at strategic locations in and around the precinct of selected sporting venues. These were supervised by experienced researchers who presided over the quality of the data. Sport event attendees were purposefully selected and approached to participate in the study. The study brief, including research ethics, was explained prior to participation.

Advice to consider when administering questionnaires

■ Your justification of the adopted methods is imperative to the credibility of the study – use the literature and previous related studies here.

■ Use screening questions to maintain your focus on the targeted respondents.

■ Ensure you pilot the questionnaires for reliability and validity. This will help to identify and address any gaps that might emerge.

Using questionnaires to collect qualitative data

Often questionnaires are seen as too inflexible to collect rich qualitative data, lacking the opportunity to probe for further information and including the perceived difficulties in persuading participants to provide detailed written (or typed) accounts. Yet, as Braun *et al.* (2020) highlight, questionnaires can provide a number of benefits to the qualitative researcher, and their use should not be automatically ruled out. These include:

● The application of a "wide-angle" lens on the topic allows the researcher to capture a wider range of experiences and voices, especially if the population is large or diverse, which may allow otherwise overlooked or marginalized voices to be heard, creating a true maximum variation sample (see Chapter 6).

● As with quantitative questionnaires, they allow greater access to participants, some of whom whose voices may otherwise be unheard.

● They may encourage participants to discuss sensitive topics, where a face-to-face interview may be more difficult for the participant to disclose information.

● Participants have a degree of control over the process, being able to complete the questionnaire in their own time without having to travel to meet, or to host, a researcher.

● They allow follow-up data collection, for example by inviting respondents to provide a contact email if they would like to participate in further data collection.

● They may be cheaper for the researcher, a key consideration for undergraduate projects.

The disadvantages do need to be acknowledged, however, and these are also outlined by Braun *et al.*

● They require participants to have a level of literacy, and hence they may exclude those less literate or lacking language ability.

● Access to the internet is still unequal, and thus this method may exclude the least privileged and most vulnerable.

- Data may lack detail and richness – although as Braun *et al.* point out, this critique doesn't always stand up, and qualitative questionnaires have been shown to create rich, often more focused, data. The key point is to explore the data as a whole, rather than focus on individual responses. As they note, "While an individual response may lack the meandering detail of an interview transcript, if surveys are a good 'fit' for the research question, topic and population, then the dataset as a whole will likely be rich and complex" (p. 4).

In terms of designing a qualitative survey, many of the key principles of quantitative surveys apply, for example the need to carefully pilot the questionnaire to ensure questions are clear and unambiguous, to keep questions as short and simple as possible, to avoid specialist terminology and to make the overall questionnaire as short as possible.

Summary

- Questionnaires are generally an appropriate method to collect large amounts of relatively simple data.
- The advantages of using questionnaires include the accessibility of your sample, reduced bias, anonymity, structured data and allowing time for respondents.
- The disadvantages include the need for relatively simple questions, no control over the completion of the questionnaire, no opportunity to probe responses and relatively low response rates.
- The design of the questionnaire is crucial. Careful design and piloting are required.
- There are a number of means whereby you can improve your response rate. Of these means, following up with non-respondents, inducements, sponsorship by an outside body and an appropriate covering letter seem to be the most effective.

Activity

1 Use your research question developed in the suggested activity at the end of Chapter 4. Design a preliminary questionnaire suitable to obtain data to answer this research question, using a range of question formats.
2 Pilot this questionnaire to a sample of approximately five others. Get your sample to critically comment on the design of the questionnaire.
3 Redesign your questionnaire in light of the pilot study.
4 Produce a covering letter for the questionnaire. Again, pilot this to a small group, asking them to critically comment upon it, and redesign as necessary.

5   Explore one of the online survey tools, such as Qualtrics, Survey Monkey or Google Docs. Create a short questionnaire to get the feel of designing an online survey. Email the link to the questionnaire to 4–5 people and, as before, get them to critically comment upon its design and layout.

ABOUT YOUR RESEARCH PROJECT

If you are thinking of using a questionnaire, consider the following questions:

- Can I justify using a questionnaire as the most appropriate method by which to collect my data? How?
- What type of questionnaire is most appropriate; for example, would an online survey be preferable?
- What steps can I take to ensure the validity and reliability of the data that I collect using this method?
- What will be the effect of a low response rate on the reliability and validity of the data that I collect? How can I maximise my response rate?

Further reading

Although a little old, Oppenheim's work is still incredibly useful (Oppenheim, A. (1992) *Questionnaire Design, Interviewing and Attitude Measurement*, London: Pinter.). For a more up-to-date resource on online surveys, it's worth a look at Cleland, J., Dixon, K. and Kilvington, D. (2020) *Online Research Methods in Sport Studies,* London: Routledge.

Chapter 9
Collecting data II: Interviews

Collecting data II: Interviews

> **This chapter will:**
> - Discuss when interviews are an appropriate data collection tool.
> - Introduce the different types of interview that you can undertake.
> - Discuss some of the issues of interview design and administration.
> - Introduce the concept of the focus group, or group interview.

Introduction

The interview can be contrasted with the structured nature of the questionnaire (Chapter 8) in both the type of data that is collected and how it is collected. Whereas the questionnaire collects highly structured, generally quantitative data and is often completed without the presence of the researcher, the researcher is a key element of the interview process, and their skills, attributes and interviewing technique are all an integral part of the success of this method in obtaining 'rich', qualitative data. The interview is undoubtedly the most common method by which qualitative data is collected in sport research.

When is interviewing appropriate?

Interviewing is often associated with the collection of qualitative data – that is, the 'why' and 'how' of a phenomenon from the respondent's perspective – and hence is associated with non-positivist epistemological standpoints. Interviews can collect data concerned with concepts that are

DOI: 10.4324/9781003195467-9

difficult or inappropriate to measure, usually allow respondents much more freedom in terms of their answers and tend to explore questions of 'why' and 'how' rather than 'how many' and 'when'. Interviews tend to provide much richer data than, for example, a questionnaire survey, where respondents are generally limited to short and relatively simple responses by the format of the questionnaire or lack the motivation to provide long, written answers. Whereas questionnaires are appropriate for collecting limited data from a large sample group, interviews are better at gaining richer data from smaller sample groups. As well as their effectiveness in collecting qualitative data, Veal (2006) notes three further situations where interviews tend to be used:

1   Where there is only a low population, making the quantitative approach of the questionnaire inappropriate.
2   Where the information is expected to vary considerably among respondents, and such information is likely to be complex and thus difficult to measure using other methods.
3   Where the research is exploratory, and interviews may be used to identify information that could be used to refine and develop further investigation.

As always, the key questions are those of 'What is my ontological and epistemological standpoint?', 'Based on my standpoint, what data is needed?' and 'Will this method provide such data?'. If rich, qualitative data are required, or you are looking for explanation, rather than description, then interviews are likely to be an appropriate method. If relatively simple descriptive data are required, then it is likely that questionnaire surveys will be a much more efficient method.

The different types of interview

Interviews can generally be classified under five categories: the structured interview, the semi-structured interview, the unstructured interview, the narrative interview and the focus group (or group interview).

- *The structured interview.* This is essentially a questionnaire where the questions are read out by the researcher, who also notes the responses. This has the advantage over a respondent completion questionnaire in that the respondent can seek clarification over questions that may be unclear or ambiguous.
- *The semi-structured interview.* This approach uses a standard set of questions or schedule. However, the researcher adopts a flexible approach to data collection and can alter the sequence of questions or probe for more information with subsidiary questions.

- *The unstructured interview.* Here the researcher has a general idea of the topics to be covered, but the respondent tends to lead the direction of the interview. Further questions are developed by the researcher as the interview progresses. This allows the respondent to provide information from their own perspective and to develop areas that are important to them, rather than being led by the interview schedule. Phenomenological interviews, for example (see later in the chapter) tend to be unstructured. They are difficult to undertake for the inexperienced researcher but can be hugely rewarding when they go well.
- *The narrative interview.* This is an approach whereby the interviewee allows the participant time to describe and develop a story, and relive their experiences, and life histories, and how they see or make sense of things that have happened to them with very little involvement from the interviewee. The story emerges almost entirely from the participant. Although there are guidelines and areas to cover within a narrative interview (see later text), the researcher takes less of a role guiding the narrative interview than would be the case with an unstructured interview.
- *The phenomenological interview.* Again, this is covered in later text, but essentially phenomenological interviews focus on individuals' accounts of their experiences and feelings to generate in-depth descriptions of a phenomenon.
- *The focus group.* Essentially this is an interview involving a group, often consisting of between four and eight participants, rather than one-on-one interaction, and interaction between members of the group is an important element in obtaining data. Focus groups tend towards being semi-structured in nature.

Advantages of interviews

Interviews have a number of advantages that make them appropriate in certain situations. As with any other methods, the important thing is to take advantage of the strengths of the methods while minimising any potential limitations.

- Interviews enable participants to talk about their experiences in their own words and allow them to elaborate on any areas of particular interest or importance.
- The interview can be more insightful than other methods. As Yin (1994, p. 80) notes, the interview 'provides perceived causal inferences' from the actor's, rather than the researcher's, point of view. This allows the respondent to become more of an 'informant', providing data from their own perspective, which is often desirable, especially within inductive research.

- Interviews allow unexpected data to emerge. Unstructured or semi-structured interviews allow the emergence of important themes that may not emerge from a more structured format. This enables the subjects to reveal insights into their attitudes and behaviour that may not readily be apparent to the researcher from their prior awareness of the phenomenon. Questionnaires are restricted to a series of questions developed by the researcher, and respondents are limited to these questions, with the occasional final directive along the lines of 'If you have any further comments, please write these below', which can be less than ideal in persuading participants to introduce new areas of information.
- A face-to-face interview allows you to assess the participant's body language, facial expressions, tone of voice, etc., which may be useful in some cases.
- By using interviews, the researcher can introduce themselves to the subject and establish trust and rapport, especially if any information is considered confidential or sensitive.
- Interviews allow you to investigate target groups that may be less able to complete surveys (such as the less well-educated, or older or younger respondents).
- Interviews may allow the researcher to develop a sense of time and history, rather than providing a series of 'static' responses, which may be the outcome of a survey. They allow the responses to be put into context, rather than providing a 'snapshot' picture.

Disadvantages of interviews

As well as the undoubted strengths of interviewing as a data collection method, it does have several potential weaknesses that need to be considered before you carry out any interviews:

- Interviews require more resources than questionnaires. They may be expensive both in terms of time and travelling, and they may preclude you from interviewing certain individuals.
- It is possible that you may add bias as a result of your – often unconscious – verbal and non-verbal reactions, for example through nodding at certain responses, which may encourage the informant to answer in the manner that they think you want. It may be the case that the participant thinks that they have to provide the 'right' answers, rather than their own views, which may be exacerbated by you nodding or shaking your head after each response.
- The interviewee may become dominant and lead the interview in unwanted directions. The researcher must be prepared to guide the interviewee back to the interview schedule.

- Analysis of the data may be difficult. The analysis of quantitative questionnaire data is often relatively straightforward and requires little or no interpretation on the part of the researcher. Analysis of qualitative interview data may be more difficult, especially where there may be ambiguity. As Fontana and Frey (1998, p. 47) suggest: 'Asking questions and getting answers is a much harder task than it may seem at first. The spoken word always has a residue of ambiguity, no matter how carefully we word the questions and report or code the answers'.
- As with all self-report measures, the quality of the data is dependent upon the responses of the interviewee. Interviewees are subject to problems of recall, misperception and incorrect knowledge.

Thus, as with all methods, the strengths of the interview need to be consolidated, and the weaknesses eradicated as far as possible. The use of appropriate probes, neutral body language and validation of your interpretation of the data by others (more on these points later) can be used to minimise such bias.

Designing the interview schedule

Designing the interview largely follows the same process as designing a questionnaire; that is, you need to identify what information is required and how you will get that information using an interview. The two key differences are that first, your interview schedule is likely to be much less prescriptive than a questionnaire and may simply include a list of bullet points regarding topics that you are looking to cover (or even less, if undertaking an unstructured or narrative interview); and second, once you have determined the structure of your questionnaire, you are generally unable to alter it, whereas you will be able to continually develop and refine your interview guide to some extent between or even during interviews. A few points to note when constructing your initial interview guide are as follows:

- Introduce the purpose and structure of the interview beforehand. In much the same way that a covering letter for a questionnaire provides the respondent with important information, your introduction should also 'set the scene', and you may find it useful to apply the guidelines about participant information sheets in Chapter 7 to your introduction to the interviewee.
- Group questions about the same concept together, and try to avoid jumping back and forwards between topics. Keep the interviewee on your side; one way to ensure you don't do this is to have an illogical structure to your interview.

- Begin with one or more 'easy' questions that will put the respondent at ease, and encourage them to begin talking comfortably. This question need not be directly relevant to the research – it is more important at this stage to gain the cooperation and trust of the interviewee. Don't spend too long on background questions, though, as the interviewee may be busy and have limited time, and you do not want them to have to end the interview before you have elicited all of the required information.

- Ensure that the questions are clearly worded, unambiguous and understandable to the interviewee. Make sure too that the relevance of each question is clear. If the relevance is not apparent, or if the interviewee seems unclear, then take time to explain the purpose of the question.

- Ask personal, or potentially threatening, questions (if necessary to the research) towards the end of the interview, once you have had a chance to develop trust between interviewer and interviewee. Again, make it clear as to why such questions are being asked.

Once a preliminary interview schedule has been developed, then it is important to pilot it, in much the same way as you would a questionnaire. As well as testing the questions, piloting an interview provides a further important function. It will provide a useful run-through for the interviewer and may increase confidence when it comes to the actual interviews, especially for the inexperienced researcher. You will find your first interview difficult, so a pilot will be helpful to you.

USING INTERVIEWS TO EXAMINE SPORT AND BELONGING AMONG NORWEGIAN MUSLIM WOMEN

Walseth (2007) wanted to explore the commonly held belief that sport creates and enhances a sense of belonging to a community by collecting data from a number of young immigrant Norwegian Muslim women. To do this, she decided upon a life history approach, an approach that aims to get the respondent to provide a rich, detailed narrative of their life in their own words, in chronological order. The requirement for rich, detailed data from a life history normally (although not always) makes asking respondents to write this detail impractical, thus making one-on-one interviews the logical choice. Second, the need for respondents to be able to focus on areas they, rather than the researcher, considered important is more suited to such a method. The interviews consisted of three parts. The first covered descriptive data, such as family background. The second involved respondents being asked to describe their lives as a book, where their life story was divided into different chapters. The final part allowed the researcher to ask about areas of interest that did not emerge in part two, focusing on sport and physical activity.

The findings from the interviews demonstrated that for some Norwegian Muslim women, sport acted as a source of social support and allowed reciprocal friendships to develop, leading participants to feel part of a wider, 'imagined' community. Second, sport was a place of 'refuge' for some, whereby it provided an avenue to escape from the trials of everyday life. Third, sport provided a means for positive identity confirmation and image building. For some, however, sport contributed to feelings of exclusion, especially where barriers were perceived between respondents and others within the sport.

Carrying out the interview

It is important for you to project professionalism, enthusiasm and confidence to the interviewee. Both appearance and demeanour are important in projecting these. As well as being appropriately dressed (even if you are undertaking a Zoom interview), you should ensure that you appear knowledgeable about the subject under discussion and can discuss this confidently. Thus, it is not a good idea to rush into interviews before you have become proficient in your field of study. The location of the interview is important. It needs to take place where the interviewee is comfortable answering questions, especially in light of the COVID-19 pandemic, such as their own home or office. The location should be relatively private so that there will be no bias from the presence of others (ensure that the interview cannot be overheard, as this can be extremely off-putting to the participant). Finally, the interview should take place in a location free from high levels of background noise, especially if it is being recorded.

The skills required by an interviewer are more than those of simply being able to talk to others. Always remember that the overall objective of the interview is to gather rich, detailed data to answer your research question. To achieve this, Hannabus (1996) suggests the following techniques:

- Establish rapport. This should start from when you first contact your interviewee.
- Keep the discussion going. Short periods of silence may actually be beneficial, in that the interviewee may be persuaded to provide further data, but try to avoid periods of lengthy silence. Know when not to interrupt and let silences work for you, but be prepared to step in with a comment or further questions if appropriate.
- Avoid asking questions that can be answered with simply a 'yes' or a 'no'.
- Avoid jargon and abstractions with which the interviewee is unlikely to be familiar.
- Avoid double negatives and loaded expressions.

- Be non-judgmental in your reactions to the interviewee's responses, and avoid reacting in any way that may influence further data collection.
- Remember to keep focusing on your research objectives, and try not to stray from them.

USING PROBES

One key advantage of the interview as a research method is that of your opportunity to probe. For many interviews, the most important questions that you can use are not the initial questions from your interview guide, but the questions you use to follow up the initial responses, such as:

- 'Why do you think that is?'
- 'Can you tell me more about that?'
- 'Can you give me an example of that?'
- 'How did this make you feel?'
- 'What happened next?'

These are examples of probes. A probe is where the researcher can gain additional information from the respondent through using particular techniques. Two types of probe can be used:

- Clarification probes. These allow you to clarify any point that was not clear or was open to misunderstanding by the interviewee, or to clarify your understanding of a point made by the interviewee.
- Elaboration probes. These are used to elicit a more in-depth response about a particular point related to the interview. For example using phrases such as 'Why is that?', 'Could you expand on that?' or 'Could you tell me more about that?' will often enhance the richness and quality of your data. You may be interested in the reasons why people purchase sport equipment. Their initial response may be something along the lines of 'I like the appearance'. You would then ask something along the lines of 'What is it about the appearance you like?', and then follow up with a further probe, such as 'Why is that important to you?'. This method allows you to collect a lot of rich detail from relatively few questions.

Interview skills do need to be practised. Although they may be relatively easy to achieve in an informal or social setting, the artificial nature of an interview makes them harder to attain, and it is likely that you will feel after your first few interviews that perhaps things didn't go quite as well as they could. Don't worry – your technique will improve as you persevere. If you have videoed your initial interviews, then it can often be a good idea to observe your own interviewing technique. Otherwise, you may be able to gain feedback from interviewees and develop your technique accordingly.

Phenomenological interviews

Phenomenology is both a philosophical and methodological concept that focuses upon people's experiences and perceptions of the subjective world within which they exist, or their 'life-world', collecting data normally through one-to-one interviews. The aim of phenomenology is to describe a phenomenon as it manifests itself to the person experiencing it using first-person accounts to arrive at an understanding of both the meaning and essence of experience (Jones *et al.* 2013). Phenomenology may be descriptive or interpretive. Whichever approach is adopted, the aims of the phenomenological interview remain similar, firstly to allow participants to express their own world as fully as possible, and also to allow the essence of that life world to be captured, such as achieved by Brymer and Schweitzer's (2013) exploration of the 'search for freedom' in extreme sport, which utilised 15 phenomenological interviews to identify six elements of freedom. To develop this type of understanding, the phenomenological interview starts with a request for the interviewee to describe an experience as fully as they can. Rather than any other pre-determined questions, the researcher will then need to rely on relevant probes and prompts to elicit further information, which should be as open as possible. Thus, the phenomenological interview can be a difficult one for the novice researcher.

Narrative interviews

Narrative interviews are designed to elicit stories. These rich, detailed stories then allow us to understand how people make sense of and interpret what has happened to them. A narrative has a number of elements, such as an overall plot or storyline, patterns of events, actors within the story and a temporal element. The role of the narrative interview is to elicit these with the minimum interruption or participation of the researcher, and it's important to only ask questions as and when needed to develop the narrative. Thus, although you may have a list of potential questions, these should only be used sparingly, and the participant should be allowed the freedom to control the interview. Narrative interviews are particularly useful in identifying how individuals' relationships shape their lives and in reflecting their own personal experiences, as well as issues of identity, as demonstrated, for example, through Papathomas and Lavallee's (2013) narrative analysis of disordered eating in sport or Knowles *et al.*'s (2014) narrative analysis of physical activity in adolescent girls.

Motivating the interviewee

The overall objective of the interview is to ensure that the respondent feels willing to provide the desired information; otherwise it is likely that the data will lack richness and depth, especially if the interviewee feels pressurised into taking part or just wants to get the interview finished as quickly as possible. Frankfort-Nachimas and Nachimas (1996) identify four factors that will help motivate the interviewee to co-operate with the researcher:

1   The respondent must feel that the interview will be enjoyable and satisfying. Three factors are important here. First the personal demeanour of the researcher must be such as to create a good impression. Second, the informant must be briefed as to the nature of the interview and how it is to be carried out, and given an indication of the likely length. Third, the location and timing of the interview are important, and it is advisable to let the respondent choose these as far as is practical.
2   The respondent needs to see the study as worthwhile. The respondent should feel that they are making a contribution to a worthwhile study. This can be done when individuals are initially approached to take part in the interview, as well as in the briefing beforehand.
3   Perceived barriers in the respondent's mind need to be overcome; for example, they might not feel best placed to offer an opinion or might not have sufficient experience.
4   Trust needs to be developed. This can be done by explaining who you are and why you are doing the study, as well as how the respondent came to be chosen, and by ensuring the confidential nature of the research.

A further factor is also important here, this being the perceived credibility of the interviewer. You also need to project your competence and credibility to be undertaking such research, and demonstrate an awareness of the key issues related to your interview. You will need to demonstrate a level of knowledge about the subject area yourself, but also demonstrate a willingness to learn from the interviewee.

Asking sensitive questions

You may, at some stage in the interview, need to ask questions that the interviewee may perceive as sensitive or even potentially threatening in some way. It is often tempting simply to play safe and not ask these questions; however, it may be that such sensitive information is important to your research. If you do have to ask sensitive questions, you should ensure that you follow a number of guidelines:

●   Ensure that the respondent is aware of the confidentiality of the data.
●   Be careful in your use of language when you first approach the interviewee for help. Avoid phrases such as 'I want to investigate. . . ', which may imply that you are looking to uncover something underhand, and instead use neutral language, such as 'I am hoping to explore. . . '.

- Don't ask sensitive questions at the beginning of the interview. Wait until you have established trust and rapport with the interviewee.
- Try not to ask such questions in any way that could be construed as 'loaded'. This is one area where piloting of the interview can be extremely useful.
- Ensure that it is clear to the respondent, if at all possible, why you are asking the question. If the respondent can see the face validity of the question, then they are more likely to give you a response.
- If you are seriously worried about asking a particular question or series of questions, then acknowledge this to the interviewee.
- Do not coerce the respondent into giving an answer. They are entitled not to answer any questions, and they cannot be forced to do so.

Using visual methods within interviews

When designing your interview, you don't need to focus purely on verbal questions. There are other techniques to elicit information, and these are often referred to as 'visual methods'. (You can also embed these within questionnaires, but information using these methods is generally elicited through interviews.) One example of this is *photo-elicitation*. This is a method whereby images are introduced into the interview and used to stimulate discussion. These images may be produced by the researcher or created by the interviewee themselves, but they are used to develop deeper analysis and reflection; for example, the research of Mills and Hoeber (2013) used photo-elicitation to examine the perceptions of skaters towards various artefacts in a figure skating club through asking their interviewees to take 20–25 photos that were later discussed in the interview. The term *photo voice* refers to the method whereby participants are given the means to record data themselves to reflect their own lives (generally through photographs or video) and to present their own contexts or circumstances, rather than that of the researcher.

CASE STUDY

VISUAL PARTICIPATORY METHODS IN RESEARCHING URBAN PHYSICAL CULTURES AND INEQUALITIES

NICOLA DE MARTINI UGOLOTTI, BOURNEMOUTH UNIVERSITY

As an increasingly established methodological tool in studies of sport, leisure and physical culture, visual methods use the generation of images, drawings and videos to facilitate "culturally sensitive, relevant and contextualized"

(Azzarito 2012, p. 296) data, and they are also often used to start processes of participatory research with participants (Azzarito 2012; Azzarito and Kirk 2013). Guillemin and Drew (2010, p. 178) have suggested that the use of visual methods by respondents may be a part of a participatory and emancipatory research agenda that takes participants seriously as knowers, or "experts of their own lives" (Azzarito 2012, p. 297), thus reducing researcher/researched power relations. Within my research addressing how racialised and (post) migrant young men negotiated identity, place and belonging through capoeira and parkour, the use of visual methods enabled me to capture the visual but also emplaced dimensions of the observed practices.

The use of images, generated both by the researcher and the research participants such as that shown in Figure 9.1, thus allowed a multiplication of the perspective accounted in the research process. Visual participatory methodology placed participants' views, rather than researcher's assumptions, in the foreground and helped to contextualize the field of research, therefore reducing a reliance on words both in gathering data and representing respondents' perspectives and insights.

The use of participatory visual methodologies also enabled me to work with a group of participants (see Figure 9.2) in the co-production of a short documentary in which they could describe and discuss their involvement in capoeira and parkour as well as address other significant issues in their lives (identity, racism, belonging, etc.). As a methodological tool, the video project represented a valuable opportunity to access and gain the trust of some of the

Figure 9.1 Photo courtesy of Nicola de Martini Ugolotti

Figure 9.2 Photo courtesy of Nicola de Martini Ugolotti

respondents, as well as to literally hear participants' voices and engage with them in moments of group discussion. As a research *product*, the participatory video provided a meaningful means of public engagement on the themes and issues addressed in this research, and it represented a valuable means of disseminating this study beyond the academic audience of specialized peer reviewed journals and conferences (Finley 2005, p. 682). The documentary video was presented across 2015 and 2016 in Italy, the Netherlands and the United Kingdom.

Employed in aiming to co-create research and public narratives with the research participants, visual participatory methods thus can constitute acts of *border crossing* between researcher and researched, through which a rigorous process of inquiry can also be significant for the groups of people amongst whom the research is conducted or has originated (Finley 2005, p. 682). In crossing some of the multiple borders that define mine/our, academic, and social, roles in everyday life I situate this methodological instrument within an "emerging tradition of participatory critical action research in social science" (Finley 2005, p. 682) that reflected a recognition of the "power of form to inform" (Eisner 1981, cited in Finley 2005, p. 684).

These are, again, discussed within the interview. Such techniques are useful additions to the sport researcher, yet perhaps under-utilised, and certainly worth considering.

USING PHOTO-ELICITATION – INDUSTRY AND ANIMAL ADVOCACY PERCEPTIONS OF HORSE RACING PRACTICES

Sports involving animals are always subject to scrutiny in terms of animal welfare, and horse racing is no different. Bergmann (2020) wanted to explore how both those involved within the horse-racing industry and those involved in animal advocacy viewed common practices within the sport, and to do this, she used photos with interviewees as a way of 'foregrounding their experiences' (p. 5), showing them photos of 'common' scenes of a race day focusing upon the horses themselves. Four images were used to 'elicit spontaneous responses drawing on the informants' personalised and emotive levels, experiences and memories' (p. 9). Three questions followed the images:

1   Describe briefly what it is that you see, what comes to your mind first, your immediate reaction, please.
2   Is this a common thing that you see on the racetrack?
3   Is there anything else you would like to say in relation to this image?

This technique allowed her to identify how each group had different ideas about what was deemed acceptable practice within the sport.

Recording the interview

Interviews should be recorded in some form – it is simply not possible to rely on recall alone. The choice is generally between that of written notes or audio/video recording. Sometimes the respondent will determine the choice of method, in that certain individuals may be uncomfortable with it (you must ask for their consent before recording). Taking written notes has two main advantages: First, it precludes potential problems created by using recording equipment, such as inaudible responses, excessive background noise, battery failure and so on. Second, if the researcher records only data that are relevant to the research question, then time may be saved in identifying and discarding irrelevant data (although this can be a dangerous tactic, as data that may seem initially irrelevant, may actually turn out to be very important). Writing notes can, however, result in a loss of rapport between interviewer and interviewee, and the interviewer's focus may be divided between the respondent and writing down notes. Recording the interview will allow more rapport to develop, which may result in more information being divulged from the respondent. This will, however, result in much more data to be analysed, and a great deal of irrelevant material to be identified and discarded. As you are likely to have only one chance to undertake each interview, I would suggest that the best option is to record it (with the interviewee's permission), as well as making limited written notes.

HOW TO BECOME A GOOD INTERVIEWER

Some years ago, Baker (1994) noted five basic rules that you should follow for every interview. These are still as valid now, and they are as follows:

1   Understand the interview. You need to know the purpose of the interview and clearly understand the concepts under investigation.
2   Be committed to completing the interview. There may be the temptation to complete the interview in the shortest possible time, or to end the interview early. You should be committed at every interview to spend sufficient time to gather enough data (although the participant must be able to withdraw at any time).
3   Practise the interview. In the same way that a questionnaire survey is piloted, or pre-tested, an interview must be rehearsed beforehand.
4   Minimise the effects of your personal characteristics. Factors such as your age, dress, demeanour and so on may all affect the responses given. Depending on the nature of the interview, you should minimise these through appropriate dress, language and so on.
5   Use common sense. Be prepared to use common sense if things seem to be going wrong or problems arise. Take each situation as it comes, and be prepared to exit the interview if things do go wrong.

Maximising the quality of the interview

As I have already noted, the concepts of validity and reliability relate less to qualitative methods such as interviews and focus groups. If you are using these as criteria to assess your approach, however, then reliability can be enhanced through a standardised interview schedule, maintaining a consistent interviewing environment and recording with the interviewees' permission, which should then be transcribed within as short a time as possible by the researcher. Validity is harder to ensure, given that transcriptions are a tool for interpreting the interview, rather than an analysis in themselves. The key is to achieve those criteria by which qualitative research is more appropriately assessed, such as plausibility, truthfulness and credibility. A number of problems need to be considered at the outset. These are:

- Will the informant interpret the question correctly? This will be more of an issue with younger or less-educated participants.
- Are informants able to verbalise their thoughts, to say what they actually feel? That is, are they able to accurately convey their feelings and experiences through their own command of language? Responses need to be critically questioned by the researcher. The researcher's own experience through participant observation will be important in this respect in being able to tacitly assess responses.

- Is the informant giving a response that is applicable only to that moment in time, or are their views more long-term? Although their behaviours may be relatively stable, responses may be affected by events or occurrences at the time of the interview.
- Will the informant's own values affect the response? That is, will people provide information based upon what they think is the correct response, rather than their own attitudes?

Dean and Whyte (1978) have noted that the interviewer needs to take into account four major factors prior to the interview. These are:

- Does the informant have any motives that may influence their responses? This may be the case if the informant stands to benefit in any way from a particular response. Thus the researcher should stress the confidential, or 'blind', nature of the interview.
- Are there any 'bars to spontaneity'? That is, are there any instances where the informant hesitates to mention things that will show them in a negative light?
- Will the informant attempt to please the interviewer?
- Are there any idiosyncratic features that may affect a response? An example of this potential effect may be a particular news story related to a sporting event on a particular day that will have a short-term effect on the respondents' attitudes.

All of these considerations need to be accounted for before each interview. Two suggestions are made by Dean and Whyte (1978) to maximise the quality of the data obtained. First, it is important to ensure that the subject is aware of the confidentiality of the interview. Second, it is generally a good idea to structure the interview so that a range of questions may be asked on any areas that may cause concern in terms of the data provided, thus using a form of 'within-interview triangulation'. The interviewer cannot always assume a relationship between responses and actual behaviour. This framework will allow a more reasoned evaluation as to what is reality and what is distortion.

Gender and race can be important issues when collecting interview data. Watson and Scraton (2001) discuss both of these issues, demonstrating that the researcher must be aware that their own personal characteristics may have implications in terms of the data obtained. Will a white female collect the same data as a black male in a certain context, for example? They stress the need for reflexivity throughout the research process, and it is an issue that you should consider. As well as the personal characteristics, the ability of the researcher should also be critically questioned. Before undertaking interviews, the question of whether the interviewer has the appropriate

188   CHAPTER 9

skills and experience to undertake the interview needs to be evaluated. This is rarely done, and, as Biddle *et al.* (2001) note, it is rare for this issue to be addressed, even in research published within international journals.

Telephone and online interviews

Not all interviewing is carried out face-to-face, and telephone or online interviewing can be an appropriate method in some cases. Telephone interviews maintain many of the characteristics of face-to-face interviews, with the obvious exception of not being able to see each other and assess body language. Online interviews will vary, depending upon whether they are synchronous (taking place in real time), such as via Skype, Zoom or Microsoft Teams; asynchronous, such as through qualitative questionnaires (as discussed in Chapter 8); or asynchronous interviewing, where the researcher will post a question and may wait some time for a response before asking further questions. Whichever form is chosen, there are both advantages and disadvantages. Let's begin with the advantages: First, cost is greatly reduced, especially if the participants are geographically dispersed, and in certain cases one of these methods may be the only feasible option. Second, some individuals may prefer to be contacted by such methods, rather than by the interviewer in person. Third, these methods may be appropriate if face-to-face interviewing would involve access to restricted or potentially dangerous locations. There are disadvantages with these methods, however. First, it may be more difficult to develop a rapport and trust from the participant. Second, it is not possible to observe non-verbal reactions to questions as well as with a face-to-face interview (even if you are able to see the participant). Third, for telephone interviews it can be difficult to record interviews without specialist equipment (although using Zoom, for example, makes it much easier to record).

USING SKYPE INTERVIEWS TO EXPLORE MARGINALSED GROUPS IN SPORT

Hussain and Cunningham (2020) explored how traditional, more localised sports such as Kabbadi and Kho-Kho offered opportunities for marginalized Pakistani women to take part in sport. To do this, they undertook 16 semi-structured Skype interviews. Although the lack of proximity to participants was cited as a potential weakness, this was certainly outweighed by allowing participants to be in a 'comfort zone' (i.e. at their home), as well as lowering the potential anxiety caused by the gender difference between interviewer and interviewee.

How many interviews do I need?

The issue of sample (or 'selection') size in the collection of qualitative data is a common area of confusion. As I noted in Chapter 7, unlike quantitative analysis, where there is often a requirement for the largest possible sample size that represents the overall population, qualitative research has different requirements. Quantitative methods such as questionnaire surveys tend to obtain relatively shallow information from a large sample. The purpose of qualitative research is to generate 'rich' data from a small sample group, with many published studies interviewing fewer than six participants (the minimum sample size for a qualitative study is one). It has been argued that a large sample group in qualitative research may be detrimental. Kvale (1996, p. 103) suggests, with reference to qualitative research, that

> many research projects would have profited from having fewer inter-views in the study, and from taking more time to prepare the interviews and analyse them. Perhaps, as a defensive overreaction, some qualitative interview studies appear to be designed on a quantitative presupposi-tion of 'the more interviews, the more scientific'.

As a qualitative researcher, the issue of sample size is not one that you should determine at the beginning of a study. Instead, you should aim to achieve what is referred to as 'saturation'. This refers to the stage in the fieldwork where any further data collection will not provide any different information from that you already have; that is, you are not learning anything new. This point can be difficult to determine, however. If you undertake, for example, three or four interviews consecutively where no additional data are obtained, then this would be a good indication that saturation has occurred. Occasionally you may find that saturation does not occur, and in certain instances other considerations such as time or cost may be more important factors. If you do not reach saturation in your data collection, then the advice is to complete as much data collection as possible within your constraints.

QUALITY RATHER THAN QUANTITY IN INTERVIEW SAMPLING

Sparkes (2000) was interested to find out the 'complex ways in which a strong athletic identity can act as an Achilles heel in terms of both shaping an indi-vidual's reactions to a disruptive life event, and the consequences of these re-actions for personal long-term development' (p. 15), that is how an elite sport person would react to the ending of their athletic career. The objective was not to generalise the findings to a wider population, but rather to gain an un-derstanding of the processes by which the athlete coped with the termination of their athletic identity. In this instance a purposive, rather than a random sample was chosen, consisting of a single subject – Rachel. Through examining Rachel's reactions to the end of her sporting career, Sparkes was able to explain some of the issues, which could then be generalised to other athletes. By having a small ($n = 1$), non-random sample, Sparkes was able to discover a great deal of information and demonstrate that, in qualitative research, it is the amount of data that is important, rather than the amount of subjects.

The key informant interview

You may be able to identify one or more key informants who will be able to supply you with specialist knowledge, based upon their position or relevant experience. Often, the key informant interview can complement data collected from other sources. For example, you may be researching the impact of a change in policy upon sport participation, and you may be able to collect data from the individual responsible for such a change. This, while not answering the question itself, will be able to provide you with useful background information, as well as develop your own knowledge of the subject matter. Be careful to assess each informant's perspective on the issue, so that any particular views can be taken into account. An employee of a sport organisation, for example, is unlikely to provide an opinion that may go against the organisation's policies or show that organisation in a bad light.

CASE STUDY

INTERVIEWING KEY STAKEHOLDERS AT THE 2010 FIFA WORLD CUP

BY DR BRENDON KNOTT, CAPE PENINSULA UNIVERSITY OF TECHNOLOGY, SOUTH AFRICA

For my doctorate thesis (Knott 2014), I wanted to find out more about the nation-branding legacy for South Africa from the 2010 FIFA World Cup. I designed a study that aimed to develop theory based on the practice and experience of definitive stakeholders involved with the event or nation-brand.

Stakeholders were selected based on their first-hand experience and expert knowledge of the mega-event, representing event owners, regional and local government, destination promotion agencies, national government agencies, sponsors and academic researchers. For each, the researcher identified the most suitable candidate to be interviewed as the most senior member of the entity, organisation or department directly involved in the event.

Semi-structured interviews ($n = 27$) were conducted with these stakeholders two to three years after the event. Face-to-face interviews were conducted with all, except for three interviews conducted online. Interview times varied, with most between 35 and 75 minutes. Interviews were guided by a set of questions related to topics identified through an extensive literature review. This guide was tested with senior academics and structured in a way that would allow conversation to flow naturally. In some cases, respondents asked to see the guide in advance of the interview. This was useful as it allowed them to prepare themselves and to be more relaxed in knowing the scope of the questions, even though the actual interview could be more free-flowing in nature.

A good idea is to start the process with a respondent that you are familiar with or have some rapport with already. I found that this allowed me to be more relaxed and also to use the first interviews as learning opportunities.

As the interviewer, you need to consciously think about creating an environment that will make the respondent feel comfortable and free to communicate and focus on the interview. In this case, the interviews all took place in locations and a time of the respondent's choosing. In almost all cases, this was in their office or at a neutral venue free from surrounding distractions.

I prepared for each interview by finding out as much background information about the stakeholder in advance as possible, to ensure that I could get the most out of the time. I also reflected on which questions would be most relevant or areas that I should focus on for that stakeholder. So, although I had a general guide, it was flexible to account for the diversity of stakeholders. I included an introductory section with ice-breaker type questions designed to get the respondent speaking confidently on subjects they were familiar with. For example, 'What were your main responsibilities during the event period?' I found it useful to think about conversation-starting questions in advance to avoid awkward moments.

I made a point of assuring respondents of the confidentiality of their responses. They had the freedom to terminate the interview at any time if they felt uncomfortable. In this study, they were free to express their opinion or perspective without necessarily needing to reflect their organisation's perspective alone. Communicating these aspects further served to relax the respondents and to build trust. Once trust and rapport has been established, the interviewer can then probe or clarify issues raised and explore particular areas of experience or expertise of the respondent.

A particular skill for semi-structured interviews is the ability to lead the conversation. At times you need to redirect the stakeholder to the topic at hand to keep the interview focused. They may be excited to tell you about projects or examples that are not related to your study. At other times, you will need to encourage stakeholders to elaborate on their answers or to pause their conversation to probe deeper into an issue or example that was raised. Even though you may ask a question directly as it was written on your interview guide, you may need to phrase it differently for a particular stakeholder to ensure they understand your focus and intention with that question.

From my experience, the stakeholders were very responsive and supportive of being involved in the research process. Many of them actually indicated that it was useful to reflect on their experiences and pass on observations and lessons learned, noting that there had not been many such opportunities to do so. Most of them asked to see my final results or publications from the study as they were interested in the outcome.

Focus groups

Focus groups are similar in many ways to interviews, with the key difference being that a small group of people, rather than a single respondent, is used. Members of the group are able to interact with each other, with the interaction leading to a greater depth of discussion, in that ideas can be generated and discussed between group members, allowing for 'richer' information to be gathered than if participants were asked individually. The interviewer will take on the role of facilitator and will stimulate discussion while keeping it relevant to the topic being investigated. Focus groups are often used when the information collected would be richer than that from an interview. An example of this would be research into youth groups, where young people may be unwilling to talk to a researcher on their own but would be happy to discuss things as part of a group of other young people.

A focus group can consist of between 3 and 12 people (although you should really aim between 4 and 8, so that everyone has a chance to make some sort of significant contribution) who ideally have not met beforehand. It is important to ensure that everyone within the group contributes and that the discussion is not dominated by one or two individuals. Your role is to channel the discussion in much the same way that you would a semi-structured interview, to ensure that the discussion is relevant and all participants have the opportunity to contribute. This can be a difficult task, and as a consequence it is unlikely that you will be able to make any notes during the discussion. Thus you should ensure that you record the focus group and also use a colleague to make notes of the most salient points. It is preferable to video focus groups rather than record sound only, as this will allow you to identify which data came from which participant much more easily.

Although focus groups are a valuable means of collecting information, they can require much more in the way of organisation and resources than other methods. Successfully running a focus group is difficult to do, and you will often need to carry out a number of them before you feel totally confident, especially if the group needs a lot of guidance. Therefore you should think carefully about the use of focus groups as a method. If you do decide to use focus groups, then much of the earlier guidance given on interviewing applies.

IDENTIFYING THE OUTCOMES OF OUTDOOR AND ADVENTUROUS ACTIVITIES THROUGH FOCUS GROUPS

The benefits of outdoor and adventurous activities (OAA) have been discussed by a number of authors, two of whom (Dismore and Bailey 2005) wanted to explore their impact upon children and how this affected subsequent learning in school. An interpretative qualitative methodology was adopted, given the view that it was important to place the child at the centre of the analysis and allow them to create and report their own accounts of their experiences from their own perspective.

Interviews would have been a possible data collection method, but focus groups were chosen as they were seen to elicit contributions from those who otherwise may not want to be interviewed on their own (the children were aged between nine and ten years old). In addition, those who felt that they had nothing to say would be encouraged to contribute within a group discussion, especially if ideas could be generated by others within the group. This allowed the authors to make tentative suggestions about the benefits of OAA in terms of positive intellectual, affective and social development. The focus group method in this context allowed much richer data from a wider sample than had interviews been used.

Focus groups and difficult-to-research populations

Focus groups can be particularly useful to collect data from groups that may otherwise be unwilling to provide it. Children, for example, may be uncomfortable discussing issues with an adult interviewer. However, they may well be more willing to discuss those issues with other children as part of a focus group guided by the researcher. You should be careful as to the quality of the data you collect in some circumstances, as participants may be tempted to provide false data to make an impression upon others in the group, so do be aware of this.

Summary

- Interviews can be an appropriate method to collect qualitative data.
- They are especially useful when the information to be collected is varied or complex, or when the study is exploratory.
- Three general types of interview can be used – the structured, semi-structured and the unstructured.
- Data collected from interviews can be rich and varied, especially if the interviewer is skilled at using 'probes' to elicit such information.
- Undertaking an interview is a skilled task, and one that should not be approached lightly. The quality of the data can often be dependent upon the skill of the interviewer.

Activity

You should gain interviewing experience by undertaking an interview with a colleague on a sport-related topic of your choice. Try to ensure that you use a range of questions, and practise your use of probes to maximise the information obtained. You should also carry out a focus group, again on a topic that you choose. You should try to ensure that data is obtained from all members of the group and that the group is not dominated by certain individuals.

In both cases, obtain feedback from those involved. Try to assess your strengths and weaknesses as an interviewer and focus group facilitator, and identify how your performance could be improved.

ABOUT YOUR RESEARCH PROJECT

If you are using interviews as a data collection tool, then consider the following points:

■ Think about the design of your interview schedule. How are you going to ensure the quality of the data that you collect?
■ Are there any personal characteristics that may affect the quality of data that you collect? If so, how will you deal with this issue?
■ Can you justify your choice of the sampling method that you used to obtain your interviewees?

Further reading

There are a wide range of resources available for the interviewer; some of the best are as follows:

Brinkmann, S. and Kvale, S. (2014) *Interviews: Learning the Craft of Qualitative Research Interviewing*, London: Sage.

Cyr, J. (2019) *Focus Groups for the Social Researcher*. Cambridge, England: Cambridge University Press.

King, N. and Horrocks, C. (2010) *Interviews in Qualitative Research*, London: Sage.

Kvale, S. (2007) *Doing Interviews*, London: Sage.

Weiss, R. (1995) *Learning from Strangers: The Art and Method of Qualitative Interview Studies*, New York: Simon and Schuster.

Chapter 10
Collecting data III: Unobtrusive methods – observation and content analysis

Collecting data III: Unobtrusive methods – observation and content analysis

This chapter will:

- Introduce two forms of unobtrusive method – observation and content analysis.
- Introduce some of the advantages and disadvantages of using unobtrusive methods in your research project.
- Outline the procedure by which each of the methods described can be carried out.
- Briefly outline the various sources of data that may be used for a content analysis.

Introduction

The questionnaire and interview methods I discussed in Chapters 8 and 9 still dominate the research literature in sport, in terms of both peer-reviewed studies, and undergraduate and postgraduate dissertations. Kellehear's (1993) views of almost 30 years ago are still valid when he suggests that this is due to the fact that these are the obvious methods by which to elicit information from others. As he says (p. 1):

> There is today, in social science circles, a simple and persistent belief that knowledge about people is available simply by asking. We ask people about themselves, and they tell us.

DOI: 10.4324/9781003195467-10

Although there has been steady growth in the use of alternative ways of collecting data, the dominance of such methods is slightly disappointing, although perhaps understandable, especially in terms of student dissertations, where it is perhaps more tempting to stick with a 'safe' approach. Over recent years, however, there has been increasing use of other methods, especially those that can be referred to as 'unobtrusive methods' (sometimes referred to as 'non-reactive measures'). Unobtrusive methods are those that do not have any effect upon the social environment under investigation and require no interaction between subject and researcher that may otherwise influence the data collected. This chapter introduces two forms of unobtrusive method, observation and content analysis, and outlines their potential use in sport-related research.

Advantages of unobtrusive methods

As I noted earlier, there may be a tendency to focus on interviews and questionnaires as a 'safe' approach; however, unobtrusive methods have a number of advantages that can, in certain cases, be beneficial to the research.

- Unobtrusive measures may be stronger in measuring actual behaviour, which is not always the same as reported behaviour. Interviews, focus groups and questionnaire surveys are always prone to the possibility that respondents will provide false or incorrect data. Thus, it could be argued that the validity and reliability of such approaches may be potentially greater in some instances.
- Unobtrusive measures do not involve the researcher disturbing the social environment to the same extent as other methods. Because the methods are unobtrusive, participants are less likely to react to them and alter their behaviours. As a consequence, they are often repeatable, and the researcher can revisit the research site to collect additional data.
- Access to certain data may often be easier. For some unobtrusive measures, such as certain observational data collection, permission will not always be required, and for methods such as content analysis, access to data will be significantly easier; as a result ethical clearance may be more straightforward.

Disadvantages of unobtrusive methods

As with any approach, there will always be limitations with using unobtrusive methods, and these need also to be acknowledged by the researcher.

- As the researcher is not interacting with the participants in the same way, it may be difficult to understand or explain the phenomenon under investigation. While it may be relatively straightforward to describe what is happening, it may be more difficult to gain a clear understanding of why it is happening.

● In the same way that interview responses can be distorted to present a particular image or viewpoint, data collected by unobtrusive measures can also be subject to distortion, especially if the subjects are aware of the research.

● For unobtrusive methods such as observation, data collection may be difficult without the use of specialist photographic or video recording equipment (often a smartphone may not be enough).

Observation and participant observation

Observation remains, arguably, the most neglected research technique in sport, yet it has a number of advantages and can be an excellent choice, whether as a single method or as part of a multi-method study; in addition, it is an essential method in ethnographic research (Chapter 11). Questionnaires and interviews rely on self-reporting by participants in research, which may lead to bias from respondents who may wish to present particular information about themselves, which may not always be accurate, or from those who cannot accurately recall or verbalise events. An alternative is to observe behaviour. Observation is often classified as being on a continuum between non-participant and participant observation. Non-participant observation is the simplest form, where the researcher will observe the phenomenon 'from outside' with no engagement with either the activity or the subjects. An example of this would be observing the behaviour of sport fans during a tournament. This could be done using various techniques, for example video, photography, or simply watching and recording the data on a laptop or smartphone. The other end of the continuum is that of participant observation, where the researcher actually takes a full part in the phenomenon being studied. An example could be where the researcher is investigating issues of customer care at a stadium and becomes a fan, taking a full part in the activities, such as buying a ticket, accessing refreshments, watching the game and so on. They would collect data about their own experience as a fan to try to gain an 'insider's' understanding. Data in this instance would be recorded by the researcher in the form of field notes, whereby their experiences would be recorded. This is not, technically, an unobtrusive method, as the researcher may have some effect upon the social environment, although it could be argued that this impact should be minimal and that the researcher should not, as long as they are careful about their own conduct, alter the behaviour of others in any way.

When is observation appropriate?

Non-participant observation is, simply, an appropriate method when the phenomenon under investigation can be directly and accurately observed.

Harley *et al.* (2020), for example, undertook a simple study to explore the efficacy of the presence of both signs and patrollers on skiers' speed. This could have been undertaken with a questionnaire survey, however respondents are highly likely to respond in a more socially desirable way, in this case by stating that they slow down. By simply observing the presence of either no sign, a slow sign, or a slow sign and presence of patroller and measuring speeds using a radar gun, researchers were able to identify that beginner skiers and snowboarders tended not to adjust their speeds compared to other skiers, findings that contradicted other self-reported data. Non-participant observation, as a result, is generally, although not always, more suitable for descriptive rather than for explanatory research. A second justification for the use of observation would be when other methods are inappropriate. A good example of this would be investigating patterns of play in children's sport. Children themselves would almost certainly be unable to accurately describe how they play sport, therefore interviewing or using a questionnaire would be unreliable and lack validity. Observation would allow you to describe the children's play more accurately, especially – as an unobtrusive researcher – you would be less likely to influence their behaviour in any way. Observation can also be a useful method when researching contentious issues, such as violence or cheating in sport. Respondents may be unlikely to accurately report their own violent or aggressive behaviour, or they may even over-report such behaviour in some cases. Unobtrusive observation would allow you to assess the validity of such claims made by participants. It is often used in combination with other methods, and such triangulation (see Chapter 7) will help strengthen the validity of your research. Observation can also be used in a non-triangulation manner with other methods. Take, for example, the case of sport clothing described earlier. Observation would allow you to identify that individuals do wear their team's clothes more often after they have won. Another method, such as in-depth interviews, may allow you to explain why they do so. Thus, such methods can be complementary.

THE USE OF OBSERVATIONAL METHODS TO EXPLORE COACH-ATHLETE INTERACTIONS

Turnnidge *et al.* (2014) were interested in the relationship between coach behaviour and the experiences of athletes with disabilities taking part in sport programmes alongside their siblings. One element of this research was to actually identify the behaviours demonstrated by coaches. The use of methods such as a self-completion questionnaire was clearly problematic, given the difficulty in coaches being able to accurately recall this information. Thus, they used systematic observation, using an approach called the Para-Coach

Athlete Interaction Coding System (Para-CAICS). This system allows observers to identify the occurrence of a range of coach behaviours such as humour, positive reinforcement/encouragement, technical instruction with modelling and keeping control, plus a range of athlete behaviours, such as helping others, positive responses and general communication with the coach. These observations helped the research team to determine that a successful sport environment within this particular context was characterised by patterned and positive coach-athlete interactions that were focused on the athlete, rather than the disability.

Participant observation is appropriate when you are interested in uncovering some of the more subtle features of group behaviour and trying to uncover meanings that are not directly observable. The researcher experiences, rather than observes, what is going on, and it is this experience that provides the data for the researcher.

PARTICIPATION OBSERVATION TO INVESTIGATE TEACHERS' PERCEPTIONS OF PHYSICAL EDUCATION

Kim and Taggart (2004) explored teachers' perceptions of physical education in an urban Korean primary school, a context where the authors describe the 'loss of the class', where teachers allowed pupils complete freedom, with little or no instruction provided, with difficulties in achieving pupil engagement with physical activity. One of the researchers had previously worked within a school teaching physical education, and this allowed them to undertake participant observation as a method to collect data, as well as take advantage of the close relationships that were formed with teachers, which, arguably, provided better data than that if the researcher had maintained a role as 'outsider'. This was reinforced by the researcher being able to help and support some of the other teachers in their roles, to form trust and thus to allow triangulation between her experiences and those of the other teachers.

Advantages of observational methods

Participant and non-participant observation both have a number of advantages that make them well-suited for data collection in certain circumstances. The advantages can be listed as follows:

- Directness. It is possible to record a phenomenon as and when it happens, rather than having to rely on an individual's recall of a particular event at another time.
- It takes place in a 'natural setting'. The researcher is able to observe the phenomenon in its natural setting ('in situ') rather than in the 'artificial'

surroundings of an interview or while completing a questionnaire. This allows the researcher to observe the context in which such behaviour takes place, and – in the case of participant observation – to experience that context for themselves.

- It allows for the identification of behaviours not apparent to the subject. The individual may simply be unaware of how they behave in a particular situation or believe that they act in an entirely different way. Observation will allow the researcher to identify the 'true' behaviour.
- It allows for the identification of behaviours that the subject may be unwilling to disclose. This is an issue when researching potentially sensitive subjects. Respondents may be unwilling to incriminate themselves in an interview or questionnaire. It may be possible to observe such behaviours, however.

Disadvantages of observational methods

Although observational techniques do have their advantages, there are also a number of potential disadvantages of which you need to be aware:

- Misunderstanding of the phenomenon. A drawback to observational methods is the likelihood that the researcher may simply misunderstand what they are seeing, especially if they are researching a subject in which they have little or no experience. This may be overcome to some extent through using observation in conjunction with other methods, such as interviewing, to ensure that the phenomenon has been correctly understood. As Gilhespy (2006) points out, it is not simply a case of looking and recording. Instead, what we look for and perceive as significant are influenced by our own values, and this must be recognised by the researcher.
- Difficulties in data recording. What to actually look for, and how to ensure that nothing of importance is missed are key issues in observational research. The use of technology, such as video recording, may prevent this to some extent, but this is often an unrealistic option for many researchers. An alternative is to have a number of researchers each recording the phenomenon, in which case inter-observer reliability becomes an issue (see Chapter 6) unless suitable training is given.
- The effect of the observer on the subjects. It is always possible that the researcher will affect the subjects' behaviour to such an extent that it may invalidate the entire research. The option of covert observation exists, where the subjects are unaware that they are being watched. However, this raises two issues: First the ethical question, that is whether it is ethical to undertake research on a group without them being aware of the research or without the option of not taking part in the research; and second, the issue of how the researcher records their data without making the subjects aware that they are doing so.

Carrying out an observational study

As with any other means of data collection, it is important that you don't rush into the data-gathering stage of the research without careful consideration of what data is required. It is often tempting to observe a sporting phenomenon and collect reams of data, only to find that such data are inadequate for the purposes of your research. Thus, you should carefully plan and pilot your data collection (especially if you are observing a one-off event). A number of planning stages can be identified:

1   Defining the variable(s) under investigation. The first stage is to identify the variable(s) to be observed. Are you interested in a particular behaviour, for example? Ensure you are clear about what exactly you are recording. If you are observing usage at a particular sport facility, then are you interested in quantitative measures such as the number of users, the breakdown between male and female users, etc.; or are you more interested in qualitative measures such as how they use the facility, their patterns of behaviour, their interactions with others and so on? You should relate these issues back to your research objectives; that is, determine what information is required to achieve these objectives, and what data is needed to provide such information, and identify the variables as appropriate.
2   Decide on your sample or participants. Your sample should, ideally, be carefully chosen rather than just observing the most convenient. Once you have decided upon your variables, you need to decide from which individual, group or location you will collect your data. As well as sampling particular individuals, behaviours and so on, you may also need to choose a sample of times. Sometimes you will be able to sample an entire event, such as a single match. Otherwise you will need to choose when you will make your observations.
3   Decide how the variables are to be recorded. Will you use video recording equipment, a smartphone or rely upon making notes with a pen and paper? Can you produce a pre-determined data sheet that simply needs to be filled in, or will you collect all data longhand?
4   Pilot your study. In exactly the same way that you would pre-test a questionnaire or interview schedule using a pilot study, then you should pre-test your observation and identify any potential factors that may affect your data collection. This should be done in conditions that are as close to those of the actual data collection context as possible.

Recording data

Provided you have clearly identified the variables under investigation, the recording of quantitative data should be relatively straightforward. Generally it will involve the recording of information using a simple checklist, for example the checklist shown in Figure 10.1, which is taken from a study into basketball tactics and strategies.

For each play made by the sampled individual, tick the relevant action. Player no. 'X'								
Dribbled then shot	✓	✓	✓					
Dribbled then passed	✓	✓	✓	✓	✓			
Immediate shot	✓	✓	✓					
Immediate pass	✓	✓	✓	✓				
Lost possession	✓	✓						

Figure 10.1 Recording data using an observation checklist

It is difficult to record more than one variable at a time, so you should avoid recording large numbers of variables, unless you are using techniques such as video recording or observing existing videos, such as from YouTube. If you do need to record more variables without the use of such technology, then you should either alternate between variables – that is record one variable for a specified period, and then another – or use multiple observers. If you use multiple observers, then you have to ensure reliability through careful training and briefing of all observers to ensure that they are measuring what you intend them to measure.

Data can be recorded directly on a pre-produced recording sheet, dictated into a recording device or recorded onto a laptop or smartphone. The danger with the second option is that, in many sport contexts, the level of background noise may make the recording inaudible. If you choose the third option, then consider pragmatic issues such as battery life.

Qualitative observation data is recorded using field notes. Field notes are a detailed summary of the observations made, and they follow a less structured format. Field notes should be:

- Descriptive. They should include a description of the setting, the participants and the relevant actions and behaviours, as well as any other features that may have relevance for the research.
- Detailed. The description should be as detailed as possible. It is not possible to be able to rely on memory to recall all of the important occurrences.
- Reflective. The field notes should also contain the researcher's account of the situation and any information that may later help interpretation.
- Analytical. You should be prepared to write down initial thoughts about the data, its meaning and interpretation.

OBSERVING SPORT AUDIENCES' PERCEPTIONS OF ENGLISH IDENTITY

BY EDWARD LOVEMAN, BOURNEMOUTH UNIVERSITY

My PhD research involves the observation of sport audiences in their own dwellings whilst watching International Sport Mega Events (ISMEs), a context where the harmful tropes of nationhood are performed, legitimised and internalised. I took full advantage of the potentiality for creativity of participant observation, primarily by videoing participant families/households in 'Gogglebox style'* recording sessions during ISME fixtures. Utilising technology as an observational tool enables researchers to gain deep familiarisation with the data – on account of the ability to re-watch recordings – and uncover behaviours that, arguably, would remain 'unseen' if the researcher simply just 'observes' participants. So, in the context of my PhD, allow the focus to be on immersing myself in the group dynamic and, thus, be intimately involved with the processes of identity creation. This was reinforced by being able to interact with participants as they discussed artefacts that they felt 'represented' their national identity, which allowed for triangulation within the study.

*Gogglebox is a British television programme broadcast on Channel 4. Families and/or households are recorded from their own dwellings watching and reacting to television shows. It is, in many ways, an audience study in itself.

One issue with field notes that you might encounter is that it might seem difficult or inappropriate at times to be taking detailed notes; for example, writing field notes while observing a sport crowd might attract attention. Hence you need to consider a strategy whereby you can take some time to write your field notes preferably during the event by moving to another location, for example, or ensuring that your field notes are written up as soon as possible afterwards. As a reminder, you can always record key points into your phone whilst pretending to take a call if necessary.

USING OBSERVATION WITH OTHER METHODS

Van der Veken *et al.* (2020) wanted to explore the conditions under which community sport programmes could improve the health of socially excluded and vulnerable groups. To do this, they undertook over 100 hours of observation and participant observation of training sessions, team building and tournament-related activity with teams of socially vulnerable people. Observations were recorded in field notes immediately after each activity. This was augmented with interviews with both relevant stakeholders (such as co-ordinators of community sport programmes) and players in the teams. This allowed them to identify that the impact of such programmes was not due to becoming better at the sport, or fitter through participation, but more that broader outcomes, such as increased reflexivity, responsibility and experiential learning from peers, were able to lead to the personal conditions (such as increased self-esteem) for participants to pursue health-related goals.

Mistakes made in observational studies

There are a number of mistakes that are regularly seen within observational studies. You should ensure that these are not an issue within your research!

- Attempting to observe and record too many variables, hence missing key data.
- Not evaluating the effect of the researcher on the subjects.
- Not taking a sample of times and/or locations, leading to a bias in the findings.
- Making inadequate field notes and over-relying on recall.

Content analysis

Content analysis refers to the analysis of the content of communications. It involves the use of systematic procedures to describe the content of a text. This text can be written, audio or visual, for example a television programme, a newspaper, an internet site, various forms of social media, a sport autobiography or a radio broadcast. Sport is now communicated through a huge variety of media, and to a varied range of consumers. As a result, content analysis is an excellent approach to developing an understanding of certain aspects of sport. Content analysis generally involves the researcher determining the presence, meanings and relationships of certain words or concepts within the text. Almost any type of text, image or video can be analysed, either quantitatively (for example, in terms of the number of times a particular word or phrase is used, or the percentage assigned to negative stories within tabloid newspapers), qualitatively (for example, a qualitative analysis of the imagery associated with advertising a sport product) or both. Content analysis can prove to be a rewarding method, especially for those interested in how sport is communicated and for looking more deeply into what can seem to be, at times, fairly ordinary messages about sport.

Stages in doing a content analysis

Once you have identified a research question and chosen to undertake a content analysis, the following steps are useful as a guide.

1 Identify the text to be used. The choice of text will, of course, be largely dependent upon your research objectives, and it may actually emerge before the research question. Thus, you may be interested, for example, in how sport is presented through social media. You may then decide to undertake a qualitative content analysis of athlete Twitter accounts, and then develop a question.

2 Identify the data set to be used. If you have chosen a newspaper as your source text, for example, then you will decide which newspaper(s) is to be used, which editions, how many and so on. Be realistic in terms of your sample and what you can realistically analyse without losing quality, especially within a qualitative analysis.

3 Collect the data as appropriate, given your research objectives.

4 For a qualitative analysis, identify your categories, or codes into which the data will be placed. Codes can be taken from existing theory, or you may develop your own. Ensure that your codes are appropriate to fulfil your research objectives. Place each relevant statement/article/ other data unit into the appropriate code. Analyse the resultant data (see Chapter 14 for an outline of qualitative analysis).

5 For a quantitative analysis, record the data as required using an appropriate framework, for example making a note of the number of times that certain words appear, the number of photographs showing a particular athlete and so on.

6 This data can then be analysed using SPSS for Windows, for example (see Chapter 13).

Fishwick and Leach (1998) carried out a content analysis of BBC television commentaries of the 1994 Wimbledon Tennis Championships. They wanted to find out whether there was any gender bias within the commentaries, for example whether the male tennis players were perceived as powerful and important, whereas female players were seen as subordinate. The coding grid that they used is shown in Figure 10.2.

GENDER AND ETHNICITY PORTRAYALS ON ESPN'S *SPORTSCENTER*, 1999–2009

SportsCenter is ESPN's flagship sports programme, and as a result it is a dominant force in sport broadcasting, influencing, for example, how people view female athletes and athletes from ethnic minorities. Using a longitudinal research design, Jacob Turner (2013) examined representations of gender and ethnicity on the programme to explore the extent to which hegemonic white masculinity was perpetuated and to identify any changes over a ten-year period. To do this, 42 episodes were used as a sample, 21 from 1999 and 21 from 2009. A number of basic variables were recorded for each story aired, these being its length, the level of competition to which the story referred and the specific sport. This was followed by an analysis of the type of story, such as human interest, score reportage or news update, and whether the story was 'episodic' (without broader context being provided) or thematic (with broader context). This was followed by an analysis of the newsworthiness of the story, based on its prominence, singularity, timeliness, impact and controversy. Finally, the sex and ethnicity of those involved in the programme (athletes, reporters, hosts and so on) were recorded. Overall data were collected from 746 stories. This allowed Turner to determine that, over the ten-year period, coverage of women's sport actually dropped (although not significantly so), and women remained largely invisible. When women's sport was covered, it was generally covered in an episodic way, compared to coverage of male sport, which was more thematic, and the majority involved score reportage. Men's stories also lasted about twice as long as stories about women. In contrast, African-American athletes were generally overrepresented on the programme, whereas white people remained overrepresented in terms of positions of power, such as head coaches and owners. As Turner concluded, such results about the coverage of women's and ethnic sport, 'when taken together, point to the perpetuation of normative hegemonic white masculinity in mediated sports' (p. 1). There are great opportunities to replicate and extend Turner's study in a range of different contexts, and this is an area with great research potential if you are interested in issues of power and the method of content analysis.

As well as frequencies of occurrence, you can measure a number of other variables as part of a content analysis. You may wish to measure the prominence of a particular concept; for example, where does the concept appear? Does it appear early or later within a text? How much space in the text is devoted to the concept? In what context does the concept appear? What you choose to measure should, of course, achieve your research objectives. Some sources available to you include:

The media

The media can be a useful source of data; however you should be aware of the following issues:

- The intended audience. You need to assess who the report was written for and how the intended audience may influence the report.

Men/women:		
Match:		
Round:		
Comments	Male commentator	Female commentator
• Positive		
Fitness/athleticism		
Play		
Misc.		
• Negative		
Fitness/athleticism		
Play		
Misc.		
• Victories		
• Defeats		
• First name calling		
• Emotions		
• Character flaws		
• Beauty and fashion		
• Patronising		

Figure 10.2 Sample coding grid for content analysis

- Accuracy. It is generally difficult to check the accuracy of newspaper reports. If you use one particular newspaper, it is useful to crosscheck reports with another as far as is practically possible.
- Distortion. The reporting of news follows a complex path, along which it is highly possible for distortion to take place. Occurrences may be distorted by witnesses who misreport incidents, journalists who try to make a story 'newsworthy', editors and so on. Again, cross-checking is important here.

Social media

Various forms of social media (blogs, Twitter, Instagram and so on) are potentially rich sources of data for sport-related research. Their immediacy, accessibility and interactivity provide valuable opportunities for the researcher. Social media sources may provide visual and audio (as well as written) data, and their potential for providing a rich and varied understanding about sport should not be underestimated. Chapter 12 explores the issues surrounding such research in more depth.

Advertisements

Advertisements can provide extremely useful data, not only in terms of the words used but also the imagery presented. Lucas (2000), for example, examined three television commercials produced by Nike demonstrating how Nike portrayed itself as being actively involved in the decision of women to participate in sport, yet at the same time the company could be seen to be constraining such participation by directing them towards certain types of sporting activity. In this research it was not just the words or the imagery, but a combination of the two, that was analysed to allow the author to conclude that such advertising disempowers sportswomen by telling them the 'right' way to play sport. Company brochures may also provide a wealth of useful data.

Private papers/diaries/letters

These can be extremely difficult to obtain, and there may be ethical considerations in using such documents. In reality, private papers are generally only an option if you have clear and agreed access to such documents before the research commences – you should not commence a research project and hope to gain access to such papers. Diaries have the added advantage of recording information significant to the diarist at, or very close to, the time that events took place.

Autobiographies and biographies

Accounts of the lives of many well-known sportsmen and women are freely available. They can provide an insightful account of an individual's sporting experiences and give an understanding into differing areas; although be careful, as most will be ghost written. Biographies tend to be less reliable, but they may still provide some useful information. As with analysing media reports, you need to take into account issues of audience, accuracy and distortion when assessing your sources.

Photographs, films and video

It is not just words that can be analysed. Pictures can provide a wealth of descriptive data and may be used in a similar manner to non-participant observation.

You should be aware of a number of issues before you decide to undertake documentary or archive research. If you require permission to access official documents, the timescale may also be inappropriate – gaining permission to use government documents may take a number of months, therefore if you are constrained by time, you should reconsider your approach. You may also have to gain permission even to photocopy material. Retrieving the documents also takes time – often you will have to spend considerable time identifying and locating the appropriate source. On many occasions, what you think is appropriate will turn out to lack relevance for your research, hence such research can be extremely time-consuming.

Public records

These are generally produced by local or central government. Although records such as the census may seem to be objective sources of data, care still needs to be taken to assess such sources. The census, for example, may under-record certain groups in society. Other sources that may be of interest include summaries of information such as Social Trends or the Annual Abstract of Statistics.

You may come across the term *big data*. In reality this is a difficult term to define, and big data itself may come from sources mentioned earlier, especially social media and public records. Essentially big data are large datasets that can be analysed to identify statistics, patterns, trends and relationships. Given the size of the data sets, such analysis needs to be done using computer analysis. Although sometimes seen as 'the next big thing' in research, as with all data, big data still has strengths and weaknesses, and it's worth a read of Spaaij and Thiel (2017) if you plan to use big data.

USING AUTOBIOGRAPHIES TO EXPLORE STRESSORS ENCOUNTERED BY INTERNATIONAL CRICKET CAPTAINS

Smith *et al.* (2018) wanted to find out the causes of stress in elite sport captains, normally a difficult group to access. Using the insights gained from an analysis of 12 autobiographies, they were able to identify seven broad themes: dealing with multiple roles, team stressors, interactions with players, dealing with selection issues, interactions with other personnel, scrutiny and criticism from the media, and extreme situations.

Summary

- Unobtrusive methods are those where the researcher does not interact with the subjects or environment under investigation. Such methods are advantageous in that they may be stronger in measuring actual, rather than reported, behaviour. They are also generally much easier to undertake.

- The lack of interaction may make it difficult for the researcher to be able to clearly interpret the phenomenon being investigated.
- The two main forms of unobtrusive investigation are those of observation and content analysis.
- Observation can be used to collect qualitative and quantitative data from subjects in their natural environment.
- Content analysis is used to collect data from texts, such as newspapers, television, photographs and so on.

Activity
Observation

Identify a research question for which observational data is appropriate. Undertake a brief observational study, paying particular attention to the following points:

1 Sampling. What is the best location? Who or what will you observe?
2 Data collection and analysis. How will you record your data? How will you analyse the data you do collect? (You may want to read Chapters 13 and 14 before you do this.)
3 What other additional means could you use to strengthen the reliability and validity of your findings?

Content analysis

Choose a high-profile athlete and locate them on Twitter or Instagram. Undertake a content analysis to explore how they present themselves on social media, trying to identify the key themes and messages that are presented.

ABOUT YOUR RESEARCH PROJECT

If you are using unobtrusive methods for your research project, consider the following points:

- If you have chosen one of the methods described in this chapter, then can you justify why the method you have chosen is the most appropriate one for your research project?
- Consider the issues of validity and reliability. How will you ensure that your observational or content analysis study is both reliable and valid? What are the threats to reliability and validity?

Further reading

Again, there are a wealth of resources available here, a broad range of which include:

Kellehear, A. (1993) *The Unobtrusive Researcher*, St Leonards, NSW: Allen and Unwin.

Neuendorf, K. (2001) *The Content Analysis Guidebook*, London: Sage.

Riff, D., Lacy, S., Fico, F, and Watson, B. (2019) *Analyzing Media Messages: Using Quantitative Content Analysis in Research*, New York: Routledge.

Schreier, M. (2012) *Qualitative Content Analysis in Practice*, London: Sage.

Chapter 11
Collecting data IV: Ethnographic research in sport

Collecting data IV: Ethnographic research in sport

This chapter will:

- Outline what is meant by an ethnographic approach to sport research.
- Describe the characteristics of an ethnographic approach.
- Describe the stages of undertaking a sport-related ethnography.
- Discuss some of the issues of writing up an ethnographic research project.

Introduction

In many ways, we are always – whether we know it or not – taking part in ethnographic research. If you play for a sport team, if you go to the gym, if you watch a sport team, then you get to know about what it is like to take part in those activities, how to behave, the social structures that exist and so on. This knowledge will have been gained not only through taking part, but by watching, talking to and interacting with other participants in their 'natural' setting. This is, essentially, ethnographic research. Ethnographies are generally characterised by their focus on a particular group or subculture (such as members of a particular gym) and the inseparable relationship between individuals and their social context. They involve the collection and use of extremely 'rich' data, and depth of information, often using several data collection methods, most notably observation, participant observation and in-depth interviews with key informants, focusing not only on what is said and what is observed, but the approach may also explore what is heard, smelt, touched or tasted. Atkinson and Hammersley (1994, p. 1) suggest that:

> We see the term as referring primarily to a particular method or set of methods. In its most characteristic form, it involves the ethnographer participating, overtly or covertly, in people's daily lives for an extended period of time, watching what happens, listening to what is said, asking questions – in fact, collecting whatever data are available to throw light on the issues that are the focus of the research.

Thus, ethnography investigates a group through collecting data, often (though not always) over a substantial period of time while being immersed within the day-to-day activities of the group. Although it is common to hear the defining feature of ethnographic research as being that of long-term immersion, Holt and Sparkes (2001) approach their definition from a slightly different angle and suggest that the defining feature of ethnography is its purpose. This purpose is the study of a group of people and their culture, where understanding of the group is obtained through examining behaviour from the group's, rather than the researcher's, perspective. To achieve this, the researcher has to take on the role of 'insider'.

AN ETHNOGRAPHIC INVESTIGATION INTO BOXING SUBCULTURES

The aim of the researcher undertaking an ethnographic approach is that of immersion within the group. As Sugden (1996, p. 201) remarks:

> It is only through total immersion that he or she can become sufficiently conversant with the formal and informal rules governing the webbing of the human interaction under investigation so that its innermost secrets can be revealed.

Sugden's own research into various boxing subcultures required him to become part of each subculture himself, so that the values, norms and behaviours otherwise hidden from the researcher could be uncovered (pp. 2–3):

> The essence of good sociology is making sense of the mysterious. Here was a social universe which was buried deep within a subcultural envelope about which I knew next to nothing and about which there was virtually nothing written.

To 'make sense of the mysterious', Sugden became immersed within the group over an extended period of time (p. 3):

> *For the next two years I led a dual existence: in the semi-rural idyll of the University campus as John Sugden, the anonymous college postgraduate student; and in Hartford's ghetto and in the basement gym as 'Doctor John', the idiosyncratic English ethnographer and the boxing club's odd-job man.*

By becoming part of the subculture – albeit not completely immersed as a boxer, but rather as observer – Sugden was able to uncover many of the otherwise hidden values held by the group. During one bout in Havana, for example, it was noted (p. 162) that:

> *Despite the fact that there is a lot at stake and that the fights themselves are conducted with furious intensity, the young boxers show incredible self-discipline and emotional restraint. There is little overt sign of anger, even in the most bruising encounter. After the fight the two boxers hug one another, thank the referee and the opposite corner men and skip out of the ring without further ado.*

Such a scene may prove difficult for the non-ethnographic researcher to understand, yet through immersion into the group, Sugden was able to explain (p. 162) that Ajo (their coach):

> *tells me that while winning and losing have some significance, at this level he is more interested in combinations of technique and temperament, believing that if the balance between these can be established early in a fighter's career, then the victories will automatically follow later.*

Thus, by a combination of immersion within the group for an extended period of time, and the use of different data collection methods while immersed, Sugden was able to both describe, and, more importantly, explain the behaviours of members of the particular boxing subculture by collecting data that would – in all likelihood – be unavailable to the non-ethnographer.

The characteristics of ethnography

Ethnographies generally have a number of common characteristics:

- They investigate human behaviour and how such behaviour is related to the values and attitudes of the particular group under investigation. These 'cultural patterns' can then be used to explain the behaviour of members of the group.
- The ethnographer studies the group on its 'own ground', observing natural behaviours in a natural setting.
- The ethnographer will often use a range of methods to collect data.
- Often these methods will be flexible, and data are collected from whatever sources are available or appropriate at the time.

- The ethnographer is often more interested in taking a holistic perspective than in focusing on individual aspects of group behaviour. It is the complex networks of interdependencies rather than isolated areas that are of interest to the ethnographer. Thus, it may be that the normal, mundane behaviours are more important than the extraordinary or unexpected behaviours.
- Ethnographies focus on the emic perspective. The emic perspective is that of taking the point of view of the people being studied, rather than the etic, or researcher's perspective.
- To gain understanding of the complex relationships within a culture, immersion is often necessary for a considerable period of time. Time is needed to gain access, to develop trust with those being studied and to develop an understanding of what is actually going on within the group.

 KEY TERM

EMIC AND ETIC PERSPECTIVES

You will come across the terms *emic* and *etic*. Essentially, they are differing ways of examining something. An etic approach is one that takes the viewpoint of the researcher, and it describes and interprets things from that 'outsider' perspective. An emic approach, on the other hand, seeks to understand and describe from the perspective of those being researched and to produce an account that is meaningful to those being researched.

The 'short-term ethnography'

Even if you have a relatively short window for fieldwork, ethnography is still entirely feasible as a research design. Indeed, some settings (for example a sport tournament) have relatively short lifespans, which would preclude long-term ethnography. Although ethnographic research is often characterised by long-term immersion into the field, rich and detailed data can also be collected through shorter periods of immersion – such as, for example, Sugden's (2021) short-term ethnography of the role of soccer and rugby in Fijian Intergroup relations – and as such, the approach becomes much more accessible to the researcher with a limited timescale (such as a dissertation student). Pink and Morgan (2013) describe this as short-term ethnography, an approach characterised by the following features:

1 *Intensity.* Rather than spending time "hanging around" and passively observing, the short-term ethnographer takes a more active role, guiding

participants to engage with relevant behaviours (for example asking them to carry out a particular action, rather than waiting for them to do so).

2   *Focus on detail.* Specifically, link the details of participants' behaviours to the researcher's own experiences to create "bridges" between participant and observer to develop greater understanding.

3   *The ethnographic-theoretical dialogue.* The role and use of theory needs to be more focused from the outset, and analysis should take place during the ethnography to allow a continual, intense dialogue between observation and theory, which can then shape and focus the remainder of the ethnography.

4   *The use of audio-visual and other traces of ethnographic encounters.* Revisiting data in the form of videos, photographs, audio recordings or artefacts can allow continual analysis after the fieldwork has ended.

In addition, short-term ethnography also has a focus upon a particular problem or question, rather than a broader focus on exploring the culture as a whole. Hence it provides a useful alternative to longer periods of immersion and is useful where timescales make longer-term immersion difficult. It is important to consider these characteristics though, rather than simply try to condense a more "traditional" ethnographic approach into a shorter timescale.

Undertaking a sport ethnography

A sport-related ethnography is a very flexible methodology, in that data collection is often unstructured, unplanned and even unexpected! Thus, unlike an experimental study, for example, it is difficult to provide a precise framework with which to approach such an undertaking. The following provides a generalised series of stages for undertaking an ethnographic piece of sport research.

1 Identifying the question

The researcher normally would not enter the field without having some sort of idea what the research question is. Although a characteristic of these types of study is their inductive nature – that is, where the theory emerges from or is grounded in the data (see Chapter 2) – some concept of the overall objective of the study has to exist so that the researcher will know what to observe in the field. What they should not do, however, is impose a fixed theoretical framework upon the research prior to data collection. As Holt and Sparkes (2001, p. 242) suggest:

> An important requirement of ethnography is that researchers suspend a wide range of common-sense and theoretical knowledge in order to

minimise the danger of taking on misleading preconceptions about the setting and the people in it. . . . In researching settings that are more familiar, it can be much more difficult to suspend one's preconceptions, whether these derive from social science or from everyday knowledge. One reason for this is that one finds it so obvious. . . . Therefore, while the ethnographic insider has the problem of making the strange seem familiar, the ethnographic insider has the task of making the familiar seem strange in order to maintain analytical distance.

2 Deciding upon an ethnographic approach

The next stage is to determine whether an ethnography is actually a suitable research design. If a rich understanding of a group or subculture is your objective, then an ethnography may be appropriate. If you require more descriptive data, or wish to assess a large population using statistical techniques, then other methods are more appropriate. Given the available resources timescale, as well as the nature of the research question, you also need to consider whether a short- or long-term ethnography would be more suitable.

3 Considering your personal characteristics

Your own characteristics will be an important consideration. Your age, gender and even sporting experience or ability may all have a potential impact on your choice of ethnography and how you experience the ethnographic process. Richards (2015), for example, provides an illuminating example of the issues that faced her as a female ethnographer in men's football. You may wish to allow your personal characteristics to dictate your choice of sample. For example, if you are already a member of a group such as a football team, then consider using this opportunity to undertake an ethnographic study of your team. It is not always the case that your research question should determine the sample. In certain cases, the sample may determine the choice of research question!

4 Selecting the setting

You need to be able to answer the question, 'What am I doing an ethnography of?'. As stage 3 suggested, although the setting is often chosen after the research question has been determined, it may also be the case that the setting is chosen first, maybe because it is familiar or accessible to the researcher. The important issue is that the choice of the setting and the research question are compatible. Some settings, such as a sport organisation, may have clearly defined boundaries. Others, for example those encountered when undertaking an ethnographic study into a particular sporting community, have much less clearly defined boundaries. It is relatively easy for the researcher undertaking an ethnography into a sport organisation to identify the setting in terms of both the physical location and the members of the group being studied. In other cases this can be more problematic, and this needs to be considered so that the boundaries of the ethnography do not become too broad and unmanageable.

5 Considering the timeframe

As already noted, ethnography can be both long- and short-term. Unlimited time and resources are not generally available, however, and you need to consider the time to be spent on the study. The timeframe needs to be evaluated against the objectives of the study – will there be sufficient time for you to collect the data you need to achieve your research objectives?

6 Gaining entry to the setting

Gaining entry to the group from which you want to collect data is a key stage in ethnography. The method of entry has implications for the subsequent reliability and validity of data obtained, and thus it must be approached with care. One method, as used by Giulianotti (1995; see also the case study 'An ethnography of sport fans'), is to find a 'gatekeeper', trusted by group members, who can then introduce you to other members. Other methods may be more fortuitous, such as Gallmeier (1988), who was able to use his father's position as sport editor of the local paper and associate of the owner of the local team to gain access to the otherwise inaccessible players of a professional ice hockey team. You need to consider how you enter the setting and the information you provide to members when you do enter. As Grills (1998) suggests, your access to informants, and thus data, will influence how those in the group interpret your motives and interests as a researcher. Entry is a crucial stage in ethnography, and one you should consider at length. Ultimately, there is no one 'best practice' that we can recommend; it is dependent upon a number of variables related to the characteristics of the group, and you as a researcher.

7 Considering your participants

A group may have many members, many behaviours, values, artefacts and so on. The researcher – especially if constrained by a limited timeframe – simply cannot record all the potential data, and thus choices need to be made about what data to measure. In terms of who you should collect data from, Atkinson and Hammersley (1994) suggest two categories. First, there are those that you, in your initial fieldwork, identify as suitable informants. Second, there are those who volunteer themselves, or are volunteered by other members of the group. It is one of your roles, as ethnographer, to assess the most appropriate sample. Unlike methods such as questionnaire surveys or in-depth interviews, the choice also needs to be made about what data to collect, as well as who to collect it from. The types of things you should be observing will vary, depending upon the research objective, but they can include:

- The history and context of the setting. What background information will be useful to explain the data you collect? What is the history of the group? Are there any idiosyncratic features that may influence your observations? Do similar groups exist elsewhere?
- The physical environment. You should note the location and its appearance. You can also note the other physical factors, such as the smell, the noise and so on. You should aim to gather as much data as possible to allow the reader of your ethnography the sense of what it is actually like to be within that setting.
- Artefacts within the setting. Artefacts such as pictures, posters, décor and so on can all provide useful data in an ethnography. Where are they located? What is their purpose? Asking questions such as these can be extremely useful to the ethnographer.
- The people within the setting. Be descriptive! How many people are there? What do they look like? What are their characteristics?
- The relationships between people. How are people interacting? What norms and values are governing their behaviour? Does their behaviour seem to follow any patterns or rules? Why are they behaving in the way that they do?
- As well as listening to what people say, perhaps through interviewing them, observe what they do and how they are doing it.

8 'Learning the ropes'

This refers to being able to fit in with the group without arousing suspicion, standing out or antagonising those within the group in any way. As Gallmeier (1988) notes, there are no explicit guidelines for this; however, it is an 'absolute necessity' (p. 220) to establish trust and rapport with those being investigated. This will enhance both the amount and the quality of the data that you collect. Without establishing such trust and rapport, you will find collecting useful data a difficult task indeed.

9 Collecting the data

A range of data collection methods is often employed, with observation and participant observation extensively used, as well as key informant interviews. Data are generally written in the form of field notes, although you may – with the participants' consent – wish to use smartphones or cameras to make audio and video recordings. If you rely on recording equipment, always back up against possible technological failures by making written notes as well. Detailed write ups of your fieldwork should be made using your field notes as soon as possible (preferably while you are in the field, unless circumstances dictate otherwise). At the beginning, don't restrict yourself in the data that you collect – quite often it is a case of collecting as much data as you can. As your analysis of the data proceeds, you can become more selective in what you record.

10 Analysing the data

Although this stage is placed as the final stage, data analysis in reality is a continual process and takes place during, rather than at the end of, the ethnography. Interpretation emerges from the data, and then further data can be collected to support or refute the interpretations. Thus, explanations can be continually developed, tested and refined.

AN ETHNOGRAPHIC STUDY OF SPORT OPPORTUNITIES IN A CANADIAN INNER CITY

Holt *et al.* (2013) wanted to examine the issues related to the provision of sporting opportunities to young men in a Canadian inner city. To do this, one member of the research team spent a total of 15 months undertaking participant observation within a range of sport programmes targeted at the homeless or those living in subsidised housing. Throughout that time he was able to identify and develop relationships with relevant gatekeepers who were then able to introduce him to 12 youth workers involved in the delivery of such programmes. The process was emergent, in that the research team met regularly to discuss findings and identify the future directions of the research as the data collection progressed. The interviews, combined with field notes taken during the participant observation (a total of 54 entries), led them to conclude that, at a personal level, sport allowed participants to overcome boredom and provided an escape from day-to-day existence. Socially it allowed them to develop positive relationships with others. Such opportunities, however, were limited by structural constraints such as those relating to money and the structure of the programmes offered.

Ethnographic methods

Although there are a number of methods traditionally associated with ethnography, it is not possible simply to say which methods should be used. The choice should, as always, be made in terms of which method, or methods, will provide the richest data to investigate the research problem. The following methods are the most commonly used within ethnographic research:

- Observation. Simply watching the group can provide a wealth of information, especially if you can observe different members of the group within their 'natural' environment. This is often an appropriate method during the early stages of an ethnography. As well as observation, think about things such as what you hear, what you can smell and so on, as these data may be extremely useful.
- Participant observation. In most cases, participant observation will be an essential element of ethnographic research in gaining an empathetic understanding of the group's behaviours that you may observe.
- Structured and unstructured interviews. You should consider the use of both forms. Structured interviews will allow you to collect predetermined data; yet you should not limit yourself – you should allow new and important data to emerge from your informants through unstructured interviews.
- Life histories. Essentially this is the informant narrating their experiences to the ethnographer, so that a detailed picture of the culture or group can be developed. Life histories are an excellent method of understanding the group and changes within the group. You should, however, be aware of the possibilities of forgetfulness, biased recall, exaggeration and so on.
- Unobtrusive methods. I have examined the use of unobtrusive methods in Chapter 10, and such methods can help enhance understanding of a group or culture as part of an ethnographic approach, for example through undertaking a content analysis of any documents or texts produced by members of the group, or analysing relevant blogs or social media.

You should also be flexible in how you collect your data and be prepared to collect data at any time. Sands (2002) has noted how, as an ethnographer, he interviewed a sprinter almost immediately after a race. Sands recalls that 'in that brief five minutes, what he told me was more succinct and from the heart than what I could have received in a two-hour interview' (p. 67). As the quote from Sands suggests, you must, as an ethnographer, be prepared to be flexible and to grasp opportunities as they arise. Always carry something to record data when you are in the field, to take advantage of unexpected data collection opportunities.

Ethical issues in sport ethnography
By its very nature, specifically that of immersion within a group, the sport ethnographer will face a number of ethical issues about their role within the

group. Palmer (2000) summarises a common ethnographic issue that she faced when researching La Société du Tour de France. The issue was that of gaining access – access was only available to accredited journalists, and not to researchers. Palmer was able to use her contacts with an Australian television network to obtain a press pass, and thus fraudulently gain access, raising key ethical issues regarding deception. As she notes, 'The researcher needs to be able to work with whatever is available' (p. 371), and she justified her approach on the grounds that the accounts she would have obtained otherwise would have been 'nothing short of fraudulent'. By posing as a journalist she gained access to situations where the influence of La Société was visible. Unfortunately, by posing as a journalist, she was unable to use many of the tools of ethnography, such as participant observation or detailed interviews, as to do so would have been inconsistent with her role as journalist. This is a good example of an ethnography where it is simply not possible to use the full range of ethnographic methods, and the researcher must weigh up the issues involved and make the decision that would provide the best data. In this case, the justification was made on the basis of the validity of the data obtained.

ISSUES WITH ETHNOGRAPHIC RESEARCH: AN ETHNOGRAPHY OF SPORT FANS

Giulianotti (1995) carried out participant observation with two groups of rival football hooligans in Scotland. Some of the issues that he faced were as follows:

Gaining access. Gaining entry to these groups was difficult in that they were cautious of 'unsympathetic reporting', that is the possibility of condemnation by the researcher. Giulianotti struck a 'research bargain' to gain entry by providing limited information on the opposing group to develop trust with the groups. Further entry was gained by the technique of 'snowballing', whereby one individual will provide access to another, who will then provide access to another and so on. This method is useful, as trust can be further enhanced if an existing member of the group introduces the researcher.

Risks while conducting research. Giulianotti encountered some initial hostility. However, the use of snowballing as a means of gaining access was instrumental in reducing risk – it is likely that a researcher obtaining an entrée to the group by other means would have been much more at risk. Giulianotti also notes that the researcher needs to be aware of the difference between threat and banter.

Validity of data. Giulianotti's research posed a number of questions with regard to its validity. As he notes, each group were keen to portray themselves as the 'hardest' fans in Scotland, thus providing motivations for each group to over- or misrepresent their activities to the researcher.

Experiential ethnography

Blurring the boundaries between ethnography and autoethnography, Sands (2002) views experiential ethnography as an approach in terms of the researcher becoming a complete participant within the study. To do this, the researcher has to go through a number of stages: Learning about the group (anticipatory socialisation); becoming a member (recruitment); learning about the norms, values and behaviours of the group (socialisation); and finally acceptance as one of the group. Each of these stages, in itself, may provide understanding about the group. Experiential ethnography may allow the researcher to collect otherwise 'hidden' or inaccessible data. As Sands (2002, p. 131) suggests:

> In my research with sprinters and football players, I experienced sensations and feelings through participation that would have lain outside the non-experiential ethnographer's boundaries of observation. In effect, my body's lived experience of performance and competition not only allowed me access to sensations of pain, elation, adrenaline rushes, and wild swings of emotion generated through cognitive appraisal of performance but also brought me closer to the cultural experiences of my teammates and other like athletes.

Thus, experiential ethnography would seem to have strengths in uncovering sport experiences. However, you must approach this methodology – as with any methodology – with some caution in terms of assessing its potential weaknesses as well as its strengths. It can be easy to simply become autobiographical in your write-up, with no real theoretical or explanatory framework within which to place your own experiences. Second, the danger of 'going native', or taking on the beliefs and values of the group, may be an issue. Giulianotti (1995), for example, noted that each of the groups of football hooligans he investigated was keen to be presented as the 'hardest' in Scottish football. In the unlikely event of Giulianotti going native, then the value of his findings could have been questioned in terms of his own subjectivity, in perhaps selecting evidence to show that 'his group' was 'harder' than other groups. Perhaps the key for the researcher is to be 'objectively subjective' in being able to assess conflicts between his or her roles as participant and researcher.

Writing the ethnography

During your fieldwork, you may collect large amounts of data in the form of written field notes, recorded interviews, photographs, videos, analyses of documents and so on. It is now that you need to make the move from viewing ethnography as a methodology to that of the written report. The process of producing a meaningful report – often restricted by time and word counts – can be, at the beginning, an extremely daunting task. Unfortunately, there is no set procedure that exists to guarantee success!

The first stage of reporting is that of making sense of the data. The best way to do this is through the process of coding. You should read Chapter 15, which deals with the issue of making sense of qualitative data. Through a systematic process of coding and analysis, you will soon begin to make some sort of sense of the data. (You should, ideally, begin this process during the fieldwork.) By being systematic in your coding, you can soon make the task seem less daunting than it initially appears.

Although there is no one correct way to present your findings in an ethnographic report, as a general guideline your write-up should include the following:

- Statement and justification of the research problem (making it clear how the research question has emerged).
- A literature review that summarises both existing knowledge and understanding, but also any gaps in such knowledge, and how your study relates to those gaps.
- A detailed description of the study design, including the setting.
- Presentation of the data.
- Explanation of the findings.
- A summary of the key contribution of the ethnography, as well as any recommendations for further research.

Gall *et al.* (1996, p. 607) provide a statement that should guide you in your writing-up: 'If an ethnography has been done well, readers of the final report should be able to understand the culture even though they may not have directly experienced it'. This is excellent advice.

Summary
- Ethnography involves the study of a group, whereby the researcher becomes 'immersed' within the group's natural environment for an extended period of time.
- Data collection is generally flexible and varied, being undertaken at whatever times are appropriate, often using a variety of methods.
- The researcher needs to be aware of certain issues (such as entry to the group and their particular role within the group), as these may have implications for the validity of the findings.
- Ethnography may be an appropriate research design in certain cases, but where time and resources are limited – for example, in the case of a student research project – it needs to be carefully considered.

Activity

Locate a sport-related ethnography. Critically evaluate the ethnography, and try to determine why the ethnographic method was chosen and how such an approach allowed the researcher to gain understanding of the group. Try to answer the following questions:

- Would the use of a different methodology have allowed the same understanding to be developed?
- What was the chosen setting? How and why was it chosen?
- How did the researcher gain access to the setting?
- What methods were used to collect data?
- What were the main conclusions of the study?
- Do you feel that you know what it would be like to be a member of that group from reading the paper?

ABOUT YOUR RESEARCH PROJECT

If you are undertaking an ethnography, consider the following points:

- Can you justify the use of an ethnographic approach? What will the ethnographic approach provide that other research designs will not?
- If you are undertaking a short-term ethnography, how will you adapt your approach from a more traditional longer-term ethnography?
- What is the justification for your choice of setting? Can you justify the choice in academic terms?
- How could your personal characteristics influence the data collection process? How will you take this into account when undertaking your research?

Further reading

If you intend undertaking ethnographic research, it is also worth locating and reading as many ethnographic studies as you can, even if they do not relate directly to your own subject area, although there are an increasing number of high-quality ethnographies that have been published within sport journals over recent years. You can also have a look at:

Brewer, J. (2000) *Ethnography*, Buckingham: Open University Press.

Brownell, S. (2006) 'Sport ethnography; A personal account', in Hobbs, D. and Wright, R. (eds), *The Sage Handbook of Field Research*, London: Sage, pp. 243–54.

Hammersley, M. and Atkinson, P. (2007) *Ethnography: Principles in Practice*, London: Routledge.

Sands, R. (2002) *Sport Ethnography*, Champaign, IL: Human Kinetics.

Silk, M. (2005) 'Sporting ethnography: Philosophy, methodology and reflection', in Andrews, D., Mason, D. and Silk, M. (eds) *Qualitative Methods in Sports Studies*, Oxford: Berg, pp. 65–103.

Sparkes, A. (2002) *Telling Tales in Sport and Physical Activity*, Champaign, IL: Human Kinetics.

Chapter 12
Online sport research

Online sport research

This chapter will:

- Discuss the sources of online data.
- Explain the process of undertaking netnographic research.
- Outline some of the key ethical issues specific to online research.

Introduction

Sport is now as much a virtual phenomenon as a face-to-face one, and this rise in both the quantity and diversity of online sport provides a rich possibility for the sport researcher, something that has accelerated as a consequence of the COVID-19 pandemic, which forced many researchers to re-evaluate the apparent inauthentic and ephemeral nature of the internet as compared to the 'authenticity' of "real-world" research. This chapter will outline some of the key issues surrounding online research in terms of the range of opportunities open to you, the process of undertaking online research and the associated ethical issues that you will face as an online researcher. The chapter focuses more upon the 'naturally occurring' data that is present on the internet and the use of the netnographic approach, rather than the use of the internet for conducting 'traditional' methods of data collection such as online surveys or asynchronous interviews, the principles of which are outlined in Chapters 8 and 9.

Sources of data

There is a wide variety of material on the internet that can be used to provide data. Some sites, such as online newspapers, provide useful sources of

DOI: 10.4324/9781003195467-12

data and can be analysed in the same way as any text, through content analysis (see Chapter 10). As well as the analysis of texts, however, the internet provides a valuable tool for researching people through their use of, involvement with and behaviour in various online environments such as:

- Blogs and microblogs such as Twitter or Instagram.
- Social news networking sites such as Reddit.
- Content communities such as YouTube.
- Social networking sites such as Facebook.
- Specialist forums such as SportForum.net.
- Fan forums such as forums.footballsfuture.com

Each online environment is rich in a variety of material, such as text, photographs and videos, all of which can provide valuable data, which is continually being updated and is highly interactive. The data can be collected through various levels of researcher immersion within the chosen site. In its most basic form, this could simply be through a content analysis of data from various sites, such as an analysis of athlete maltreatment through Twitter (Kavanagh *et al.* 2016), fan tweets following a team scandal (Brown and Billings 2013) or female athletes' self-presentation on Instagram (Li *et al.* 2021). At the other end of the continuum, this could involve the researcher immersing themselves within an online community to develop a rich, descriptive and explanatory account of online behaviour in the form of a 'netnography' such as Kerrigan *et al.*'s (2014) study of the role of mobile music technologies to enhance the running experience, or even augmenting the online analysis with other methods, such as interviewing users/creators of content, for example Ehrlén and Villis's (2020) analysis of photo-sharing as social support for climbers and runners on Instagram.

A CONTENT ANALYSIS OF FAN REACTIONS TO ALCOHOL-RELATED PLAYER TRANSGRESSIONS

Smith *et al.* (2014) were interested in how sport fans reacted to reports of alcohol-related player transgressions within the Australian National Rugby League and the Australian Football League. To do this, they undertook a content analysis, studying 11 different fan forums, including specialist forums for each league, general sport discussion forums and several newspaper sites. This allowed them to collect over 7,000 pieces of archival data in the form of fan comments. From this data they concluded that the club or league's response to the transgression was more concerning to fans than the actual transgression itself, and the tension between needing to protect a club's image and brand equity and the social and moral expectations of players was problematic, with the key desire of fans to be that of parity across cases.

Undertaking a 'netnography'

The term *netnography* (Kozinets 2010) applies the principles of both traditional and/or short-term ethnography and applies them to online activity, with the same intended outcome, that of developing an understanding of a group or community through an approach that is naturalistic and immersive, and through the flexible use of a variety of methods. (If you are considering a netnographic approach, make sure you read Chapter 10.) Kozinets outlines a number of steps to undertaking a netnography.

1   Defining your research question. As I noted in Chapter 7, there has to be a clear and coherent link between your ontological and epistemological standpoint, your research question and your research design. Is a netnographic design an appropriate one for your study? Can you justify its use, or would alternative designs be better to answer the question? You also need to assess whether there is an adequate online presence; for some groups or communities, online interaction and engagement may be sparse.

2   Identifying your site. Which community are you going to choose? As Kozinets (2010) outlines, your site needs to be relevant, active, interactive, substantial, heterogeneous (that is, have a variety of different participants) and data-rich. Take time to get to know the community before you attempt to gain entry, however.

3   Considering ethics. You must get ethical clearance before the research starts.

4   Gaining entry. How are you going to enter the online culture? Are you going to lurk anonymously, in which case your ethical stance will need to be justified, or become part of the community? If the latter, then how will you introduce yourself and provide full details about your study so that informed consent may be provided by all of your participants? How will members react to an outsider entering their social world, and how will you react with the negative reactions that may result? How will you ensure that you are not seen as 'intruder' into a private world? How will you allow participants to get further information about the project, its aims and your objectives? You shouldn't overload participants with information at the very beginning, so make sure that only the essential information is provided, but also make it clear where further information can be located.

5   Collecting data. As soon as you begin to gain entry, collect data from all sources, such as emails, postings, blog entries, videos and so on. Remember that social media sites are ephemeral; site and links change often. URLs disappear, content changes and pictures are removed. Also keep your field notes up to date on a regular basis, making notes of everything that happens. Data may be:

   ●   Archival data – existing data that the researcher has had no role in creating or prompting. This can be downloaded through a variety of ways, ranging from manual searching to the use of more advanced data mining software, such as the use of Radian 6 to extract data from social media sites.

- Elicited data – created through interaction with group members, for example through posting a comment on a blog and recording the subsequent comments and reactions of group members.
- Field note data – your own records of the research; your own reflections of the group, their behaviours and interactions; and your own place as a member of the group. Field notes are used not to record data, but to write down your thoughts on why things are happening and to record your own experiences and reflections on the process. You can also record the key decisions you made during data collection and the critical incidents encountered as netnographer.

6   Analysing data. As with any qualitative research, data analysis can be done manually or through appropriate software. One thing to be aware of, however, is that the potential volume of data that might be easily obtained from larger, more active sites, may well make manual analysis difficult, if not impossible. Don't fall into the trap of collecting an unmanageable volume of data, as this will only impact negatively upon the quality of your analysis.

7   Exiting from the group. One further aspect that is widely overlooked is that of how you exit the community. The nature of netnography means that it is all too easy to exit too quickly and to suddenly 'disappear' without any comment or acknowledgement, which isn't an ethical practice. You need to ensure that your exit from the group is appropriate, and that any promises made, such as to share the key conclusions from your netnography, are kept. This is important not only for your own responsibilities as a researcher, but also to ensure that any future approaches by others wishing to undertake research are met positively.

Netnographic methods

A variety of methods are available to the netnographer. One characteristic of the netnographic approach is that of the eclectic, flexible approach to data collection, and the opportunity to collect a variety of data using various methods is a strength in allowing a rich, descriptive and analytical picture of the online community to be presented. Hooley *et al.* (2012) have outlined some of the methods that you might consider, which include:

- Participant observation – become involved in the community, take part in the activities, post articles and so on. Think about your experiences, and the rituals and behaviours that you notice.

- Interviews and focus groups – these can provide rich data beyond that of analysing the content of the sites, and they allow rich descriptions and explanations to emerge. Often these will take place after a period of observation.
- Online surveys – these can be useful to collect quantitative data, and occasionally qualitative data, or to stimulate discussion, such as the brief surveys used by Siuda (2021) in his study of subversiveness in online sport gaming to develop important topics that otherwise received limited discussion.
- Examination of documents and written and visual culture online – for example Lizzo and Liechty's (2020) strategy of analysing photos, videos and web links when they 'added notable context or additional insight to the text' (p. 8).

The key, however, is to immerse yourself within the community and use whatever sources are appropriate to your research.

A NETNOGRAPHY OF THE SELF-MANAGEMENT OF SOUTH KOREAN SPORT STARS ON SOCIAL MEDIA

The almost immediate, largely unregulated nature of social media means that those in the public eye – such as athletes – have to exercise self-management in posting online, otherwise the potential risks of inappropriate posts are high. Yoo (2021) undertook netnographic research to explore such self-management of South Korean athletes operating within an increasing trend of neo-liberalism, where the need to develop physical capital through online activity was seen as crucial, yet the dangers of doing so were always apparent. As well as immersing herself within the accounts of ten successful athletes, she also interviewed each athlete in depth. Through both sources of data, she was able to identify that online activity had made athletes a "self-living commercial" that had to be carefully self-managed as "a prerequisite for survival".

Assessing your data

The use of online data adds an additional set of questions for the researcher who is interested in assessing the quality of the data they obtain. The key issue is that of anonymity of your sources of data. Online, people have the opportunity to present themselves as something they are not, provide false information and behave in ways that they would not be able to, or want to, in day-to-day life. (Before undertaking any nethnographic research, it is certainly worth reading Suler's [2004] discussion of why people behave differently online.) Don't be put off by this – in reality, any method is open to such issues, and what you need to do, instead, is to try to assess the quality of the data that you do obtain. You may, for example, be undertaking a netnographic study of a fan community and obtain a lot of data from a fan who is clearly unhappy with the team management. They might be a concerned fan, or they might be a 'troll' trying to inflame other fans. In this case you can have a look at things like when they joined the community, how many posts they have made, whether they have posted about other matters, whether they seem knowledgeable about the team and so on. Otherwise, the criteria with which you assess your data are the same as those with which you would assess any other piece of qualitative research, such as trustworthiness, credibility and so on (see Chapter 7). The more immersed you get within the online community, the easier assessing your data becomes.

CASE STUDY

A NETNOGRAPHY OF HOW AMERICAN AND CHINESE ATHLETES USED TIKTOK AS A FAN-ENGAGEMENT TOOL DURING THE PANDEMIC

BY DR YIRAN SU, UNIVERSITY OF GEORGIA

Our paper (Su *et al.* 2020) focused on how American and Chinese athletes used TikTok as a fan-engagement tool during the pandemic. As a new media platform, TikTok hasn't been studied in sport management, and there are few articles that provide theoretical and methodological guidelines to netnographic research involving video-centric platforms. The project started with a discussion of the multi-modality of the TikTok videos, which included the audio, video, textual aspects of each video, and the affordances and algorithmic culture provided by the platform. We also referred to work in video ethnography, where researchers view the video-recorded material and reflexively discuss the content. After several round-table discussions among the authors, our coding process was guided by two central questions:

1   What is the connection between the videos and the athletes?
2   How does the external environment influence the presentation of the video, including the social impact of the pandemic and the nature of TikTok?

An essential feature of social media, video is the rich interaction between various "actors" that cannot fully be captured by still images alone. Taking into account the social distance during a pandemic, this research highlights the importance of personal relationships for any athlete in their "backstage" lives.

Among the methodological concerns that caught my attention was the subjectivity of the researchers. Peshkin (1988) describes subjectivity as the qualities of individuals that can alter or affect the outcome of a research project by filtering, skewing, shaping, transforming, or construing and misconstruing what occurs from the beginning of the project. Our research teams consisted of two Chinese researchers, fluent in both Chinese and English, and also familiar with TikTok – one American, and one Australian who were relative newcomers to both TikTok and Chinese sport contexts. Acknowledging and accepting our own bias and limitations when conducting this netnography project contributed significantly to the balance and richness of our findings. At each step, we sought to take both an insider position (e.g. being better able to obtain relevant data and utilizing the knowledge and experience of a researcher) and an outsider position (e.g. maintaining an unbiased analytical point of view).

The ethics of online research

Social media research provides a number of ethical challenges and dilemmas, to which there is often no clear-cut answer, especially within the areas of informed consent and maintaining anonymity. The differing models of online research do have differing ethical concerns, and it is important that the nature of the research, whether it is a simple content analysis of archival data or a more interactive netnographic approach involving interaction between researcher and participants, guides your ethical considerations. The ethical issues that go beyond those discussed in Chapter 7 are as follows.

Public versus private data and issues of informed consent

As I noted in Chapter 7, gaining informed consent is an essential aspect of any research project; however, the challenges of internet research don't always make this possible, and there are debates as to whether it is always necessary. The area that seems most clear is that of data posted on closed sites, that is those that require some form of registration or logging in to access. Here, it is essential that informed consent is obtained. Archival data that are posted in 'public spaces' without any need for registration or logging on, however, could, it is argued, be seen as being in the public domain and thus available to the researcher. The critical issue is that participants may have had no expectation that their comments or posting would be read by those outside of the online community when they were originally made. Kozinets (2010), however, clarifies the dilemma faced by the researcher when he argues that 'if the researcher does not record the identity of the communicators and if the researcher can legally and easily gain access to these communications or archives' (p. 142), then their analysis should not come under traditional models of human-subject research. If in doubt, however, you should respect the expectations of the subject in terms of their privacy.

Elicited data, on the other hand, do follow a human-subject model of research, and here it is important that informed consent is obtained.

This could be done via email or other written communication. The issue remains, however, of who is providing the consent, and the anonymity afforded by the internet does mean that the comprehension, competency or the age of the person providing consent cannot be ascertained with complete confidence. If there are doubts about the individual's ability to provide informed consent (for example you are unsure of their age), then you may well be better advised to undertake an alternative approach whereby the information can be ascertained. As with all ethical issues, if doubts remain, then you need to reconsider your approach.

Anonymity

Anonymity presents a number of challenges. Even if participant names or user names are omitted, then a Google search will quickly identify users either through a search of their user names or if you report quotes verbatim within the research report. You may also find, however, that some users may wish to be identified or given credit within the report; for example, the creator of a blog may want to be given recognition. I would advise you to treat online pseudonyms as real names, and in the same way that you would not report real names within a research project, then you should assign alternative pseudonyms to the names adopted by online participants.

ETHICAL CONSIDERATIONS FOR THE ONLINE RESEARCHER

Eysenbach and Till (2001) provide an outline of the ethical considerations that you need to be making before starting your online research. These are as follows:

- Intrusiveness – Discuss to what degree the research conducted would be considered 'intrusive' by members of the community.
- Perceived privacy – Discuss (preferably in consultation with members of the community) the level of perceived privacy of the community. (Is it a closed group requiring registration, for example?)
- Vulnerability – Discuss how vulnerable the community is: For example, a forum for those experiencing sport gambling issues is more vulnerable than one discussing training techniques.
- Potential harm – As a result of these considerations, discuss whether the intrusion of the researcher or the publication of results has the potential to harm individuals or the community as a whole.
- Informed consent – Discuss whether informed consent is required or can be waived. (If it is required, how will it be obtained?)
- Confidentiality – How can the anonymity of participants be protected?
- Intellectual property rights – In some cases, participants may seek not anonymity but publicity, so that use of postings without attribution may not be appropriate.

The lack of clarity overall in terms of online ethics means that there is rarely a simple answer. The essential requirement for you, as a researcher, is to ensure that you fully consider all of the ethical issues associated with your project and to ensure that you have full institutional ethical clearance before you start the research process.

Summary

- There are a variety of online data sources available for you to use in your research.
- The use of online sources of data may range from a simple content analysis to a more immersed, in-depth netnography.
- There are, however, a number of specific ethical issues of which you need to be aware before undertaking any online research.

Activity

Think about the online communities of which you are a member. Do any of them provide potential research opportunities, and if so, in what way? What sort of data would you collect from such communities?

ABOUT YOUR RESEARCH PROJECT

- Consider whether the use of an online research design would be appropriate for your study. If you were to undertake research into an online community, how would you negotiate access? Identify your strategy for entering the field.
- Identify the key ethical issues you would face, and explain how these issues would be addressed for this piece of research.

Further reading

The recent text by Cleland et al. (Cleland, J., Dixon, K. and Kilvington, D. (2020) *Online Research Methods in Sport Studies*, London: Routledge) is a really useful and up-to-date, subject-specific resource for those considering online sport research. You may also want to have a look at:

Hooley, T., Marriott, J. and Wellens, J. (2012) *What is Online Research*, London: Bloomsbury.
Kozinets, R. (2010) *Netnography: Doing Ethnographic Research Online*, Los Angeles: Sage.
Poynter, R. (2010) *The Handbook of Online and Social Media Research*, Chichester: Wiley.

Chapter 13
Analysing data I: Quantitative data analysis

Analysing data I: Quantitative data analysis

> **This chapter will:**
> - Describe how to prepare your quantitative data for analysis.
> - Introduce a data analysis software package – JASP – and briefly run through its use.
> - Introduce the concept of inferential statistics, and describe how such statistics allow you to make conclusions from your findings.
> - Outline the idea and meaning of the concept of statistical significance.

Introduction

The quantitative data you collect needs to be organised, analysed and interpreted. For non-statisticians this can be challenging, both in identifying what to do with the data and what the subsequent results mean. Provided you approach things systematically, it may well be easier than you think, especially if you have good, focused objectives and a clear idea of exactly what you need to find out. The field of statistics is a large and complicated one, and a book of this type can only provide you with a broad overview. I would strongly recommend that, if your research involves any level of statistical analysis, you should also read one of the many available specialist texts such as Field's (2017) excellent *Discovering Statistics Using SPSS* or O'Donoghue's (2012) *Statistics for Sport and Exercise Studies*, ideally before you start thinking about your research design, rather than waiting until you get round to the analysis. If you're really unsure about statistics, then reading the early chapters of Spiegelhalter's (2019) book *The Art of Statistics* is a really good introduction for the nervous statistician.

Statistical analysis can be broadly separated into two forms: Descriptive and inferential. Descriptive statistics organise your data, normally analysing one variable at a time, for example in terms of producing frequency counts of participation in sport or calculating the mean points scored per game by a team. As their name suggests, they *describe* data. Inferential statistics go further than this and allow you to *infer* relationships or differences that exist between two or more variables, such as calculating a relationship between experience and ability at a particular sporting task, or identifying gender differences in sport preferences, and to draw conclusions about the overall population under investigation.

There are a couple of points to note at this stage. The first is that statistics in themselves have no real meaning. They are simply tools with which to help you make sense of the data. Thus, simply to report the results of a statistical test is only the first stage. The importance lies in how such statistics are interpreted and how that interpretation is related to your research objectives. The second point is that statistics can only interpret the data that you have collected, and if your data lack reliability, validity or relevance, then no amount of statistical testing can rescue that.

The use of computer software in quantitative analysis

A number of computer packages are available to assist you with quantitative data analysis. Previous editions of this book have focused on *SPSS for Windows*; however, this time round I'm suggesting that you consider using an alternative – *JASP*. JASP is a free, open-source programme available for you to download at jasp-stats.org/download. I'm suggesting JASP, as:

- It is free and will remain so. In your future careers, you will thus always have access to the required software to do your own analysis, which may not be the case with paid-for programmes such as SPSS.
- It is very simple, operating on a "point and click" principle that is more intuitive than SPSS. I'd suggest that you could pick up the basics in half an hour.
- It uses a single window to generate and analyse data, rather than the separate "data view" and "variable view" in SPSS.
- The way output is generated in SPSS is, to me at least, a little clumsy, created in a separate window. JASP output appears in the same window and is more focused on the required information, rather than having extraneous information presented, as is the case with SPSS.
- Tables and charts created in JASP will be APA formatted by default.
- There are a number of high-quality support tutorials available on YouTube.

You may still wish to use SPSS, and there is nothing wrong with this at all. If this is the case, you might want to refer to earlier editions of this book. Alternatively, you might prefer other software packages that aren't covered within this text but that are becoming increasingly used (such as "R"). Whichever one you end up using may be down to personal preference; as I've said before, it's what you do with the results that are more important than just generating them.

Using JASP

Before you use JASP for the first time, make sure you locate the JASP statistics channel on YouTube. You will find a range of tutorials to guide you through all aspects of the programme. When you do open up JASP for the first time yourself, you'll be presented with a fairly simple screen (Figure 13.1).

You can access the main menu by clicking on the three bars at the top left of the screen. The menu items are generally self-explanatory and allow to you to save your work, export data and results, and change preferences (most notably how p-values are reported and the number of decimal places).

To do any analysis, JASP needs to access your results, and to do this, you need to create a data file, where all of this data are available. Although JASP has its own format (.jasp), you'll probably be better off using formats such as .csv (through Excel) or .sav (from SPSS). If you've used an online survey package, you'll probably find that the results are downloaded in .csv format anyway. The data should be presented in "long" format, so each question (or variable) has its own column and each respondent has its own row. The first row, however, needs to be the variable name (see Figure 13.2).

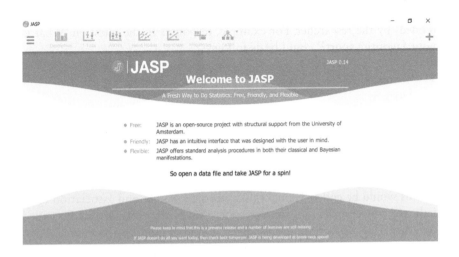

Figure 13.1 JASP home screen

A	B	C
level	self-confidence	performance
2	67	3
2	79	5
1	58	5
2	65	4
1	68	3
2	67	4
1	53	2
2	73	5
2	77	3
1	65	5

Figure 13.2 A data file for JASP

Creating your data file

1 Coding data

Coding refers to translating the responses into numerical values. You might already have done much of this when, for example, creating an online questionnaire. Coding can be relatively straightforward; for example, an open question on age worded 'How old are you?' is already numerical and does not need to be coded. All responses should be assigned numerical values if they are to be quantitatively analysed; for example, responses to a closed question on an individual's job role within a sport organisation could be coded so that answers of "marketing" are coded as 1, and "sales" coded as 2, "operations" as 3 and so on. Open questions should be grouped together (coded) by the researcher. For example, responses to the question 'What is your favourite sport?' could be as follows:

- Tennis.
- Hockey.
- Soccer.
- Basketball.
- Association football.

Each group of common answers would then be assigned a numerical value. Tennis would be coded 1, hockey 2 and so on. Soccer and association football are conceptually the same response, and they would thus be coded together. Thus, each response is converted into a number. Occasionally you may encounter difficulties in deciding whether to code differing responses together or separately. The answer to this is dependent upon whether they are conceptually similar in terms of your research question. If in doubt, code the responses differently, as you can always combine different codes together as one afterwards, which is a lot easier than separating one code into two.

Responses from the other types of questions should be relatively straight-forward in terms of converting to numerical values. If you are using scales, then each potential response is allocated a number. Have a look at the following ordinal scale for example:

I take a positive attitude towards myself as an athlete

Never	Seldom	Sometimes	Often	Almost always
❏	❏	❏	❏	❏

Each response can be allocated a logical numerical value. Thus, a response of 'never' is coded as 1, 'seldom' as 2, 'sometimes' as 3 and so on. Therefore, in this example, the response would be coded as 4. Occasionally a question may be 'reversed', that is asked in the opposite way; for example, this question may be asked as 'I take a negative attitude towards myself as a sportsman or woman'. The scoring for this would also be reversed, thus 'never' is scored 5, 'seldom' as 4 and so on.

2 Inputting data

Choose a variable name for each variable and insert that in row one. The numbers produced from step one should then be input into the spreadsheet starting at row two. Let's take a simple hypothetical study about sport refereeing, with a sample of ten referees (this would not be enough for this type of study, obviously, but I've used a small sample for simplicity here) exploring the relationships between:

- Level (amateur or professional, with amateur coded as '1' and professional coded as '2').
- Self-confidence (scored as a percentage).
- How highly each referee rated their own performance in a game (on a scale of 1–5).

The data file could look as already shown in Figure 13.2. (Notice the first row is the variable name; each subsequent row is a respondent.)

3 Checking data

Once data entry has been completed, then a careful check should be made for accuracy. It is easy to make inputting errors, for example making a double keystroke by accident and entering '11' rather than '1'. The data set should be checked beforehand as far as possible to minimise the effect of such errors, and any unusual or unexpected results that occur after the analysis should also be checked in case of mistakes in data entry. Once you've imported the data into JASP, I'd also recommend using boxplots to check for any outliers, or values that differ significantly from other values within the data, once you've imported your data. If you have any such outliers, then firstly check that they aren't due to inputting errors. If not, then you have to make a decision about whether to keep them, remove them (trimming) or convert them to the highest or lowest (as appropriate) value that would not be considered an outlier, a process known as Winsorization. Whichever approach you take, you must explain and most importantly justify your choice.

Make sure the file is saved in an appropriate format (here as a .csv file). It is now ready to import into JASP. We do this through clicking on *Open* in the JASP menu, then following the links until you locate your file. The data set will now appear in the main JASP window. You'll notice that next to the variable name, JASP will automatically assign the variable to one of four types (it's not always infallible though, so do check carefully). These four types are similar to those we covered earlier in the book:

1   Nominal text – These are variables without numerical value. You might, for example, have some short qualitative responses that you may want to analyse qualitatively later.
2   Nominal – This is data that has no natural order or ranking, although we tend to assign arbitrary numerical values to allow for analysis – for example assigning favourite sports as 1 = soccer, 2 = basketball, 3 = tennis and so on.
3   Ordinal – This refers to variables with an inherent order; for example, we often use scales in questionnaires that might range from 1 ("not at all") to 5 ("very much so"). The distance between each score isn't meaningful (for example, we can't say that a score of 2 is twice as high as a score of 1), the only thing we can say is that there is an order in that 2 is more than 1, but we don't know by how much (this is an important point later; many people will treat such scales as continuous and analyse the data accordingly, but you should see them as ordinal data).
4   Continuous – These are "true" numbers, with equal distance between measures and a true zero, for example age in years or height in cm.

The data will appear in JASP as seen in Figure 13.3.

We can now add a little bit of meaning to the numbers where appropriate (for example, looking at the data, level being either '1' or '2' doesn't really mean that much). So now you can now label the values for each variable as necessary. Click on the variable name (in this case "Level"), and a window appears above the data (Figure 13.4).

Figure 13.3 Data presented in JASP

Figure 13.4 Labelling variables in JASP

Under "Label", replace 1 with "Amateur" and 2 with "Semi-Professional", and you'll see the labels appear in your spreadsheet (see Figure 13.5).

We can now check the data for outliers, as suggested in step 3. We do this by clicking on "Descriptives" then "Descriptive statistics". We move the variable to be explored into the variable box. Then under "Plots", click "Boxplot element" and "Label outliers". You'll see a boxplot produced in the right-hand window as shown in Figure 13.6.

This highlights one outlier (underneath the boxplot) and tells me that it's in row 7. I can now check that it wasn't an inputting error and make a judgement about what to do with it. In such a small sample as this, there's

Figure 13.5 Values labelled in JASP

Figure 13.6 A boxplot in JASP

a very strong possibility that valid data will appear as an outlier, and it's a value that's not unexpected, so I would keep it unchanged.

Finally, I could enter the value for any missing values, if any were to occur. I'd do this through "Preferences", and then "Data preferences". Under the missing value list, enter the value for missing values (e.g. "999") and click on the + sign. Whilst you are on the "Preferences" menu, I'd also take this opportunity to go down to "Results preferences" and tick the boxes for "Display exact p-values" and "Fix the number of decimals", and change to two decimal places.

You are now ready to analyse your data. Before you do this though, remember two key points:

1 Analysis isn't about analysing every single combination of variables – spend some time identifying what information you need from your analyses before you start (e.g. which variables need reporting, which variables need to be analysed together to identify differences and relationships, and so on). What you must not do is simply fall into the trap of analysing everything you can. Analysing a large number of variables in the hope that something significant will emerge is called "p hacking" and is bad research practice, highly likely to identify false positives. A second questionable practice is to find significant results and develop a hypothesis afterwards. This is known as HARKing (hypothesising after the results are known) and again must be avoided.

2 You are looking to present the results as they exist, so don't get disappointed if you don't find anything significant. There are no "good" or "bad" results. A non-significant or an unexpected finding is just as valuable. The fact that the vast majority of studies that you read in journals have a significant finding is due to publication bias, with significant results somehow being seen as "better". This isn't the case, and non-significant findings can have equal value.

Descriptive analysis

Descriptive analysis explores a single variable at a time to describe or summarise the findings from that variable. This is often useful, for example, when summarising the demographics of a sample, where variables such as age and gender can be described.

Measures of central tendency

A measure of central tendency is a value that describes a particular characteristic of a set of scores by ascertaining a point that is "central" to your data for that variable. The most commonly used measures are those of *mean*, *mode* and *median*. The *mean* is the average score of all observations of a variable. You may, for example, be interested in the attendances of a particular sport team. Rather than select one attendance figure (which may be misleading), a better approach would be to average out the attendance figures over a period of time, for example a single season. A second measure of central tendency is the *mode*. You may be interested to find out the most common age for individuals to drop out from competitive sport. In this type of research, a modal score can often be more useful than a mean score. The mode refers to the category with the largest number of observations. Finally, the *median* is the point that divides the observations, once ordered, into two equal parts. If the weekly hours spent training for a sport were measured as 2, 2, 4, 5, 6, 10, 10, 11, 15 then the median would be 6, as there are four values above this value and four below. A median split can be used to split one group into two subgroups for the purposes of comparison. It may be that the researcher is interested in the relationship between the time spent training and self-efficacy while competing. In this case, a median split could be used to divide the group into 'low' trainers (those scoring below the median) and 'high' trainers (those scoring above the median).

 KEY TERM

CONFIDENCE INTERVALS

There is always the question of how well does any statistic (for example, the mean) obtained from the sample reflect the population itself? Here the idea of confidence intervals is important. A confidence interval is a range of values that you can be confident contains the true value of the population. These are normally set at either 99 per cent or 95 per cent. We can illustrate this with an example. Let's say we have calculated the mean height of a basketball player at 200 cm from our sample. Through calculating our 95 per cent confidence intervals (there are a wealth of online resources to show you how to do this), we get a range of values (for example 180–220 cm) that we are 95 per cent confident contains the true value of the mean.

Measures of dispersion

Measures of dispersion indicate the spread of the data around the mean or other measure of central tendency. The most commonly reported measure is the *standard deviation*. The standard deviation (SD) measures the extent to which scores deviate from the mean. Thus, two samples may have identical means but differing standard deviations. The researcher is then aware that the measures from the sample with the larger standard deviation are likely to deviate from the mean score to a greater extent; that is, they will be more spread out. A smaller standard deviation means they are more concentrated about the mean. A further, although less commonly used, measure of dispersion is that of the *range*. The range is simply the difference between the lowest and highest score in the distribution.

We can explore descriptive statistics in JASP through clicking on "Descriptives" and dragging the relevant variable into the "Variables" box. Clicking on "Statistics" underneath opens up a menu, and we can choose a range of options as seen in Figure 13.7. This will create an output table as seen to the right in the figure (which can then be copied and inserted into a Microsoft Word file).

Relational measures

A *rate* measures the frequency with which a value occurs compared to a maximum frequency with which it could occur. An example would be that the rate of regular participation in sport in the UK may be 0.15 (that is, 15 people from every 100 participants), whereas the rate in the USA may be 0.18 (or 18 in every 100). Rates can be useful in comparing different populations. For example, you may want to find out differences in sport participation between two countries with significantly different populations. Rather than simply provide figures as to overall participation (which would effectively be meaningless), a rate would provide a more useful comparison. A *ratio* compares the relative sizes of two numerical values; for example, it

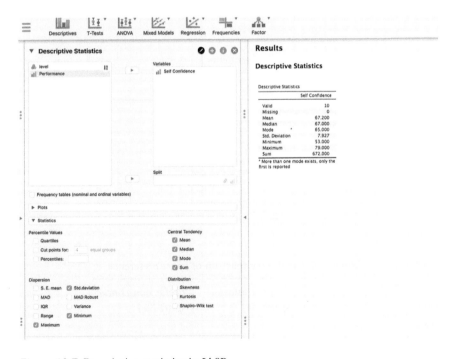

Figure 13.7 Descriptive statistics in JASP

could describe the numbers of males compared to females in a sport crowd. Finally a *percentage* is a ratio expressed as a fraction of 100, for example, using the earlier scenario, the percentage of male fans in the entire crowd may be 15 per cent or 15 per 100. When comparing groups, we tend to use percentages as they allow groups of different sizes to be compared.

Presenting descriptive statistics

Descriptive statistics are generally presented within the text (when it's a small amount of data) or in the form of tables and graphs. Tables should be included where the information is appropriate to the research question. (You should not include every single result unless it is relevant.) Tables should include percentages as well as raw scores – this allows easier comparison between groups of different sizes. (You should also include the raw scores and an indication of the total number of responses.) You must also label each table accordingly. The format of your table should be similar to that presented in Table 13.1.

Cross-tabulation involves producing a table with the responses from the dependent variable across the top and the responses from the independent variable down the side, as demonstrated in Table 13.2.

You should always tabulate your results and only use graphical means when it actually illustrates a point or reveals a trend or relationship between variables. So, for example, a response of 50 per cent male and 50 per cent

Table 13.1 Age of respondents

Age category	Per cent	n
0–10	18.1	17
11–20	26.6	25
21–30	29.8	28
31–40	14.9	14
41–50	6.4	6
Over 50	4.3	4
	100	94

Table 13.2 Gender comparison of sport preference

	Prefer contact sport (%)	Prefer non-contact sport (%)
Male	79	21
Female	22	78

female would not merit any graphical output, but a response of 10 per cent male and 90 per cent female would be worth considering. Do be careful not to make charts over-elaborate, and be careful with the overuse of bright colours or complex patterns. Bar charts and histograms can be useful, pie charts very rarely so. Charts can be created in JASP very simply by going to the "Plots" menu and ticking the appropriate box.

Inferential statistics

The measures discussed here investigate single variables, such as team scores, hours spent training in a week and so on. Often, however, we are more interested in the relationship or differences between two or more variables; for example, think about how we could answer the following questions:

- Is there a relationship between competitiveness and willingness to engage in gamesmanship?
- Did the COVID-19 pandemic lead to a decrease in physical activity?

These are questions that can't be answered by descriptive statistics and instead fall into the realm of inferential statistics. Inferential statistics assess the association between independent and dependent variables (go back to Chapter 6 if you are not clear about these terms). These may be bivariate (measuring the effect of a single independent variable upon a single dependent variable) or multivariate (involving more than two variables). Within this chapter, the focus will be on bivariate tests. There are two categories of inferential test, chosen on the nature of the data that you have: Parametric and non-parametric tests.

Parametric tests

These tests use interval or ratio data (see Chapter 6 for a reminder), or what JASP classifies as continuous data. Parametric tests assume that the data is drawn from a normally distributed population (i.e. the data is not skewed) and have the same variance (or spread) on the variables being measured.

Non-parametric tests

These are used with ordinal or nominal data and do not make any assumptions about the characteristics of the sample in terms of its distribution.

Inferential statistics require you to test a hypothesis or, more accurately, a null hypothesis. A null hypothesis suggests that there is no relationship between your variables. Thus, you are assuming no association, and it is the role of the test to contradict this hypothesis. As a researcher, you assume the null hypothesis is true until the evidence strongly suggests otherwise. This evidence comes from the appropriate statistical test.

Interpreting your results

Inferential statistics do not tell us unequivocally whether there is a relationship between two or more variables. Instead, they calculate the likelihood of whether an apparent relationship or difference between two or more groups is down to chance or not. You could measure the heights of female basketball players from the UK and the Netherlands. If the difference in average heights was 15 cm, then you would probably see that as a significant difference. What, however, if the difference was 1 cm? You'd probably say that there was no real difference. So, at what stage can we say that there is what we call a *statistically significant* difference between the two groups? Fortunately, this uncertainty is largely (but not completely) removed using inferential statistics. Inferential statistics provide a 'p-value'. A simple way to think about the p-value is that it indicates the compatibility between your findings and the null hypothesis, with the lower the p-value (which ranges from 0 to 1), the less the compatibility. We can define a p-value as the probability of a result equally, or more extreme than you got if the null hypothesis were true. Let's take our example. We run a test and find out that the difference in heights is 3 cm, and we get a p-value of 0.04. So, if our null hypothesis (that there's no difference in heights) is true, there's only a 4 per cent chance we would see a 3 cm (or greater) difference between the two groups due to random variation. A value of 0.05 is the generally accepted level of significance, thus a p-value of 0.05 or less strongly suggests that you have a relationship that is not due to chance. So in this case, we would reject the null hypothesis of there being no difference in height and conclude that there is a difference in the heights of basketball players from the UK and the Netherlands. If you have a larger p-value, then you could not really be confident enough that the results do show an actual difference or relationship. Do remember three key things though:

- This value, however, is completely arbitrary, decided upon almost 100 years ago, so it's actually better practice to report and interpret the exact p-value.
- The p-value doesn't tell you the size of any effect. A small effect can be statistically significant, so do make sure you explore the effect size as well.
- Be alert to the possibilities of false positives and false negatives as a result of unquestioningly accepting the p-value (especially if it is close to the threshold that you set). Such errors (type 1 and type 2 errors) are outlined later in the chapter.

SIGNIFICANT AND NON-SIGNIFICANT RESULTS

You will often find that your results are not statistically significant, which might seem disappointing; however, it is important to realise that the aim of quantitative research is not simply to find significant results. The whole point of your statistical analysis is to provide empirical data to answer a research question or test a null hypothesis, and if that evidence suggests no significance, then this is equally as valid as identifying a strong significant value. So do not be discouraged by results that are not significant. They are not 'wrong' as such. The reasons for the non-significant findings will provide you with some valuable material for when you come to discuss your results.

Which test to use

We gain the p-value from carrying out statistical tests. It's thus very important to choose the right test. A guide to some of the more common tests can be seen in Figure 13.8. The two key questions to ask at this stage are: (1) Am I looking to do a test of association, or a test of difference? and (2) Is my data parametric or non-parametric?

Tests of association

Tests of association refer to those tests that measure whether two or more variables are related; that is, as the independent variable changes, then the dependent variable alters accordingly. Thus, you may be interested to examine whether there is a relationship between participation in sport and income. Correlations are the most common tests of association between variables.

Testing differences

Tests of difference generally assess whether differences between two or more groups are likely to have occurred by chance, or whether they are the result of the effect of a particular variable. Thus, questions such as whether males differ from females in terms of amount spent on sport-related merchandise, or whether undergoing a six-week period of relaxation techniques lowers pre-competitive anxiety among young golfers, would be answered through testing differences. Commonly used tests of difference include t-tests and ANOVAs.

Is my data parametric?

Firstly, check that your data is ratio or continuous data. If not, then your data will be non-parametric. Then you can do a check for normality, again

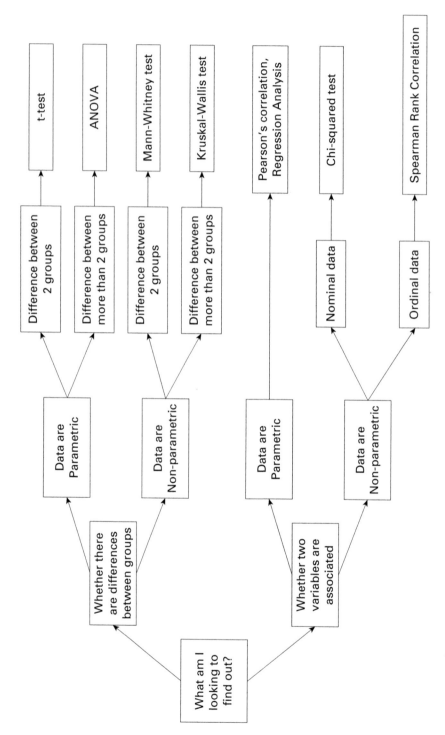

Figure 13.8 Choosing a statistical test

a requirement for parametric tests. You can do this visually, by creating a histogram of the data, or by a test such as a *Shapiro-Wilk Test* (available under "Descriptives" in JASP), which tests the null hypothesis that your dataset is normally distributed. One note of caution, however. Parametric tests only require your data to be approximately – not perfectly – normally distributed. For large datasets (a minimum of 50 per group) I would be more confident in assuming a normal distribution, especially as tests such as t-tests and ANOVA's aren't overly sensitive if they violate normality. If you have a smaller sample, then more caution will be necessary. If data isn't normally distributed and you really aren't happy, then you may want to think about transforming the data, meaning we apply a mathematical function (such as applying a square root to all values) to push the data closer to a normal distribution.

Testing relationships between variables

Correlation

Correlations investigate the relationship between two variables, for example the relationship between advertising spend and sales of a particular sport product. We use a Pearson's correlation for parametric data and a Spearman Rank correlation for non-parametric data. A correlation can indicate:

- Whether there is a relationship between the two variables.
- The direction of the relationship (i.e. whether it is positive or negative).
- The strength or magnitude of the relationship.

A positive correlation exists where higher scores on one variable correspond with high scores on another; for example, performance may increase as self-efficacy increases. A negative correlation is where higher scores on one variable correspond with lower scores on another; for example, performance in a complex sporting task may decrease with increasing levels of anxiety. The size of a correlation will range from -1.00 to $+1.00$. A score of -1.00 represents a correlation that is a perfect negative correlation; that is, as the score on one variable decreases, then the score on the other variable increases. A score of 0.00 represents variables that are not correlated, or have no relationship with each other, and a correlation of $+1.00$ represents a perfect positive correlation, that is the variables increase or decrease together.

While correlations are useful to identify relationships, they are unable to determine causality, that is the extent to which variable X causes variable Y. This is because it is often unclear whether it is actually X causing Y; for example, does increasing anxiety lead to a reduction in performance, or does Y cause X? Could it be that decreasing performance leads to increasing anxiety? A further possibility is that they are interrelated. Finally, there may be an unidentified variable that is leading to an increase in both X and Y. Thus you should be extremely cautious in assuming causal relationships from correlations (your use of theory and previous work is very important in making this assumption). If you do, you have to be clear that you have correctly interpreted the independent and the dependent variables.

CORRELATIONS USING JASP

- Select "Regression" from the menu.
- Select "Correlate" from the options (classic rather than Bayesian).
- Move the variables you want to analyse into the "Variables" box.
- Decide what type of correlation you need to use, for example a Pearson's or Spearman's correlation.
- Click "Report significance", "Flag significant correlations" and for simple correlations "Display pairwise".

The result will be, as I noted earlier, a score between -1.0 and $+1.0$. You can interpret the size of the effect under investigation using this score, with a correlation coefficient of < 0.1 being a small effect, 0.3 a medium effect and a score of 0.5 or higher a large effect.

 KEY TERM

ONE-TAILED AND TWO-TAILED TESTS

Your test will explore a specific prediction (your hypothesis) that may be directional or non-directional in nature. A hypothesis such as 'A reduction in disposable income will result in lower spending on sport goods' is directional; that is, we are explicit about the direction of the relationship. On the other hand, you may be testing the hypothesis that 'The introduction of a new manager will affect output in a sport manufacturing organisation'. This is non-directional, in that you cannot predict whether the change will be positive or negative. If this is the case, you need to select a two-tailed test. If you have a directional hypothesis, then you need to select a one-tailed test; otherwise you increase your chance of making a type II error.

Regression analysis

Although a correlation may indicate a relationship between two variables, it does not provide any indicator of the magnitude of effect, for example what a likely outcome would be of an increase in the independent variable upon the dependent variable. Regression analysis between two variables effectively calculates a 'best fit line'. This line will subsequently predict the effect of one variable upon the other. Regression is undertaken through selecting "Regression" then "Linear regression" on the JASP menu. This will report first an 'ANOVA' which, essentially, will tell you the extent to which regression analysis predicts the effect of the independent variable on the dependent variable. If this is significant, then the regression model is a better predictor than simply using mean scores, and the subsequent coefficients (identified by B) allow you to identify the effect of a change in the independent variable upon the dependent variable. For more detail on this test, see Goss-Sampson (2020).

Chi-squared test

The Chi-squared test is a useful test to explore relationships between nominal or ordinal variables. The Chi-squared test compares the frequencies of a given variable with the frequencies that would be expected if there were no relationships between groups. As an example, you may be interested in whether those who play team sport are more likely to have suffered injury than those who play individual sport. We can produce a simple cross-tabulation using JASP firstly by entering the data in a .csv file where in the injury column, '1' refers to an injury, and '2' to no injury, and in the sport column, '1' refers to individual and '2' to team sport (Figure 13.9).

	A	B
1	injury	sport
2	1	2
3	2	2
4	1	1
5	1	1
6	2	1
7	2	1
8	1	1
9	2	2
10	2	2
11	1	2
12	1	1
13	2	1
14	1	2
15	1	2

Figure 13.9 Data file for a Chi-squared test

After opening the file up in JASP. We can go to "Frequencies" and then "Contingency tables". By putting "injury" into rows and "sport" into columns, we can create a cross-tabulation (Figure 13.10).

Straight away we get some idea that there is a relationship, in that those playing team sport were more likely to get injured; but to test the significance of the relationship, we do a Chi-squared analysis (see Figure 13.11). Under the "Statistic" bar, click on the X^2 box, and under "Cells", click on expected row and column percentages. This now gives us a p-value of 0.02, confirming a significant relationship.

Contingency Tables

Injury	sport Individual	Team	Total
Injury	6	22	28
No Injury	12	10	22
Total	18	32	50

Figure 13.10 Cross-tabulation of injury v sport

Contingency Tables ▼

Injury		sport Individual	Team	Total
Injury	Count	6.00	22.00	28.00
	% within row	21.43%	78.57%	100.00%
	% within column	33.33%	68.75%	56.00%
No Injury	Count	12.00	10.00	22.00
	% within row	54.55%	45.45%	100.00%
	% within column	66.67%	31.25%	44.00%
Total	Count	18.00	32.00	50.00
	% within row	36.00%	64.00%	100.00%
	% within column	100.00%	100.00%	100.00%

Chi-squared tests

	Value	df	P
x^2	5.86	1	0.02
N	50		

Figure 13.11 Chi-squared analysis of sport v injury

You do need a good sample size to do a Chi-squared analysis, however, as it requires most (80 per cent) of your cells to have a count of at least 5, and all cells to have a count of at least 1. This is generally feasible if you have a 2 × 2 cross-tabulation, but as soon as you have more categories (for example a 3 × 3 cross-tabulation) it gets more difficult.

Testing differences between groups – Parametric tests

The independent-samples t-test

The independent-samples *t*-test examines whether the mean scores of two different groups can be considered as being significantly different. For example, you may be interested to compare the effects of mental rehearsal on putting performance in golf. You randomly assign your participants to either the rehearsal or non-rehearsal group and compare their scores to see if there is a significant difference. It can be used when:

- The data are interval or ratio in nature.
- The groups are randomly assigned (hence, you should use an ANOVA test, outlined in the next section, rather than a *t*-test to compare differences between males and females, as gender is not randomly determined when you come to assign your groups).
- The two groups are independent of each other.
- The variance, or spread, in the two groups is approximately equal.

The paired-samples t-test

Whereas an independent *t*-test measures differences between two groups, the paired *t*-test measures whether the mean of a single group is different when measured at different times, for example, whether the performance of a group on the putting task after mental rehearsal was significantly different from that before the rehearsal.

T-TESTS USING JASP

- Select "T-Tests" from the menu, (classical rather than Bayesian) and choose either "Independent" or "Paired sample" *t*-test.
- Select "Compare means".
- For an independent-samples *t*-test, move the independent variable into the Grouping Variable box, and the dependent variable into the Variables box.
- For a paired samples *t*-test, move both variables into the Variable Pairs box.
- For both tests, tick "Effect size" (we would normally use Cohen's *d* for the independent samples *t*-test).

Analysis of variance

An analysis of variance (ANOVA) is similar in nature to the independent *t*-test; however, it allows you to ascertain differences between more than two groups. If you are looking to explore gender differences, then this is a more appropriate test to use than an independent *t*-test, as it doesn't assume that participants have been randomly assigned to each group.

ANOVA USING JASP

- Select "ANOVA" from the menu (classical rather than Bayesian).
- Move the independent variable into the Fixed Factors box
- Move your dependent variable into the Dependent Variable box
- Tick "Descriptive statistics" and "Effect size".
- Under "Assumption checks", tick "Homogeneity tests". (The result from this should be non-significant, that is $p<0.05$. If you get a significant result, then you will need to tick one of the homogeneity corrections, normally the Welch test, and report those findings.)

Testing differences between groups – Non-parametric tests

The Mann-Whitney test

The Mann-Whitney is an alternative to the independent *t*-test, and it is used when your data is ordinal and non-parametric. This test works on ranking the data rather than testing the actual score and scoring each rank (so the lowest score would be ranked '1', the next lowest '2' and so on), ignoring the group to which each participant belonged. The principle of the test is that if the groups were equal, then the sum of the ranks should also be the same. If there are differences between the groups, the Mann-Whitney will identify them through the difference in rank scores. To undertake a Mann-Whitney test, follow the initial steps for an independent *t*-test outlined previously, but tick "Mann-Whitney" instead of "Student".

The Wilcoxon signed-rank test

This test is similar to the Mann-Whitney test. However, it examines differences where the two sets of scores are from the same participants (effectively it is a non-parametric alternative to a one-sample *t*-test, and it can be found under the "One sample t-test" menu in JASP).

The Kruskal-Wallis test

This is a non-parametric alternative to the ANOVA test, and it can be used to identify differences between three or more independent groups. This can be found under the "ANOVA" menu, described earlier. Enter the variables as you would for an ANOVA, scroll down to the Non-Parametric menu, tick "Nonparametrics" and move the Fixed Factor (independent variable) across.

KEY TERM

TYPE I AND TYPE II ERRORS

When selecting a particular level of significance at which to reject the null hypothesis, be aware that there is a possibility of two types of error, basically when the answer you get doesn't reflect the true result. Some controversy over different COVID-19 tests is a useful illustration of this. Although most test results were accurate, we heard a lot about "false positives" and "false negatives", or what we refer to as "type I" and "type II" errors.

Type I error. This occurs when you reject the null hypothesis when it is, in reality, true. Thus, you would suggest a relationship where, in reality, none exists. Hence, for a COVID-19 test, this would be where a test result suggested the individual had COVID-19, when in reality they were COVID-19 free.

Type II error. This occurs when you accept the null hypothesis when it is false. Thus, you would suggest no relationship, where a relationship does actually exist. An individual would thus test negative for COVID-19 despite having the virus.

The likelihood of making a type I or II error depends on the level of significance that you choose. Thus, if you choose to operate at the 0.1 level of significance, then you are more likely to make a type I error. If you choose a level of significance of 0.01, then a type II error becomes more likely. Always be aware of the possibilities for these errors and discuss them if necessary (for example a *p*-value close to 0.05).

CASE STUDY

COMMON MISTAKES IN STUDENT RESEARCH PROJECTS

BY DR DANIEL LOCK, BOURNEMOUTH UNIVERSITY, UK

When teaching students about levels of measurement in quantitative research, it is unlikely that the audience will be interested or excited. Yet, in terms of producing robust research instrumentation, and conducting sound analyses, understanding of different levels of measurement is foundational to comprehending when tests can and cannot be used. For example, it is commonplace for students to conduct inferential tests (e.g. ANOVA) using unsuitable variables (e.g. ANOVA is premised on a categorical independent variable with two or more levels and a continuous or scale-dependent variable). Where a student conducts an ANOVA using a dichotomous dependent variable (e.g. Yes = 1, No = 0), the output is invalid because the test variable is non-parametric and one of the main test assumptions is violated.

The issues created by a poor understanding of different levels of measurement often results in students conducting weak analysis. In terms of achieving high grades, this is hugely problematic and stems from a misunderstanding about sophistication. Typically, student projects are graded not on the degree of sophistication in data analysis (many students use sophisticated analyses incorrectly) but on the extent to which the tests used were an appropriate means to test the hypotheses. It is for this reason that using the flowchart in this book (see Figure 13.8) and making time to become familiar with different kinds of variables and levels of measurement is crucial for *analysis and study design*. Then, the hypotheses designed will be tested using variables that are captured at an appropriate level of measurement for the analysis required.

Reporting the findings

You should always provide detail about the results beyond simply saying that the results were significant or non-significant. It's good practice to follow APA guidelines. Consider first whether you need to report the findings within the text or to tabulate the findings (preferable for anything other than simple results).

- For a correlation, you would generally report the correlation coefficient and the probability. If you have undertaken a one-tailed test, you should also state this, so you may report that 'There was a significant positive relationship between the number of times a sponsor's logo was seen by television viewers, and subsequent recall of that brand ($r = 0.47$, $p < 0.01$)'. It is also good practice to report the effect size (see Field 2017) for tests wherever possible.
- Paired and independent t-tests should be reported by stating the test statistic, the degrees of freedom, the probability value and the effect size if possible.
- To report an ANOVA, report the F-ratio, the degrees of freedom and the probability. For example, 'Analysis of variance demonstrated that there was a significant gender effect in the findings ($F(4, 245) = 3.93$, $p = 0.03$)'.

- For Wilcoxon signed-rank tests, Mann-Whitney and Kruskal-Wallis tests, report the test statistic, the degrees of freedom if appropriate (normally for Kruskal-Wallis) and the probability. Thus, you may report that 'A Kruskal-Wallis test demonstrated clear differences between pre-match meals and subsequent performance ($H(3) = 5.76$, $p = 0.04$)'.
- For Chi-square, the test statistic should be reported, the degrees of freedom and the probability value, e.g. 'Those born in March were more likely to play cricket as their main sport ($\chi^2(1) = 29.89$, $p = 0.04$)'. You may also want to report an effect size.

This is a very simple guide to the different statistical tests that you may use. I have not included every test, and it may be that there are other tests that will be more appropriate. If your research involves statistical analysis, we strongly recommend that you read a specialist text so that you gain a fuller understanding of the principles underlying each test.

A final word on statistics

As a final note, I should stress that undertaking statistical analysis and producing significant results is not, in itself, the key part of your research. The important part is in being able to interpret your findings, that is being able to understand what they actually mean. Thus, if you have carried out a paired-samples t-test, then what does a significant result actually suggest? The interpretation is just as important as undertaking the correct test. Statistics are simply a tool to be used to assist you in your analysis. The second thing to remember is that non-significant results are just as interesting as significant results. It is fairly common for students to get a non-significant result and think that this is somehow 'wrong' or inferior to a significant result. This isn't the case and will, in many cases, give you just as much of interest to examine when you discuss your findings.

Mistakes sometimes made in quantitative analysis

- Choosing an incorrect statistical test, often through applying parametric tests to non-parametric data (especially ordinal data).
- Designing the questionnaire so that the data is in the incorrect format for the appropriate statistical test; thus the format of the response may provide you with ordinal data when you require interval data.
- Misinterpreting a p-value, or deciding upon an inappropriate level of significance, and making a type I or type II error.
- Testing as many variables as possible to pick up any significant results without any theoretical rationale for selecting those variables.
- Deciding upon a level of significance after undertaking the analysis.

Summary

- There are a number of ways in which you can analyse quantitative data. Descriptive statistics allow you to organise and summarise your data. Inferential statistics allow you to draw inferences regarding the association or difference between two or more variables. A number of computer packages exist to help you carry out descriptive or inferential statistics. JASP has been outlined here, but others, such as SPSS for Windows, are also worth considering.

- Inferential tests will provide you with a 'p-value'. The p-value indicates the likelihood that any association or difference (depending upon the test) was down to chance or not. A p-value of 0.05 indicates that in 95 cases out of a 100 you could be confident that there was an actual difference or association, rather than a chance difference or association.

- The importance of statistical analysis lies not in the analysis itself – although that has to be done correctly. Instead, it is the correct interpretation of the results that you obtain!

- You should try to gain some experience using JASP. Using some of the sample data files available with the package, try to undertake some descriptive and inferential analysis. Don't be too concerned with the subject matter of the data. Instead, it is more important that you begin to understand the principles of the package. Try to produce some tables and graphical output for some data you have created, or from an existing data set. Again, don't worry too much about what the data is saying, but simply try to gain confidence in using the programme.

ABOUT YOUR RESEARCH PROJECT

If you are undertaking quantitative analysis, can you answer the following:

- What is the purpose of your analysis; that is, what exactly do you want to find out?
- What statistical test will provide you with the result that you need?
- Have you gotten the right data for this test (for example, in terms of ordinal or interval data for certain tests, parametric data where such data are required and so on)?

Have you assessed the likelihood of making a type I or a type II error?

Further reading

I can fully recommend Field's (Field, A. (2017) *Discovering Statistics Using SPSS*, London: Sage) for anyone undertaking quantitative analysis, even if you aren't using SPSS. It's also worth having a look at the following, again, even if you use JASP rather than SPSS, as they cover the key principles of statistical analysis:

Acton, C. and Miller, R. (2009) *SPSS for Social Scientists* (2nd edition), Basingstoke: Palgrave Macmillan.

Ntoumanis, M. (2009) *A Step-by-Step Guide to SPSS for Sport and Exercise Studies* (2nd edition), London: Routledge.

Spiegelhalter, D. (2019) *The Art of Statistics: Learning from Data*, London: Pelican.

Vincent, W. (2005) *Statistics in Kinesiology*, Champaign, IL: Human Kinetics.

Chapter 14
Analysing data II:
Qualitative
data analysis

Analysing data II: Qualitative data analysis

This chapter will:

- Introduce the basic principles of qualitative data analysis.
- Introduce the concepts of 'codes' and 'themes'.
- Describe the different types of coding that form the framework for qualitative analysis.
- Describe the ways by which you can graphically represent your qualitative analysis.
- Discuss some ways by which you can maximise the trustworthiness of your interpretations.

Introduction

Analysing qualitative data can prove to be much less straightforward – at least initially – than the seemingly more 'logical' and 'objective' analysis of quantitative data. This is partially due to the lack of a commonly accepted method of qualitative analysis and also because, as you may have noted from your own reading, many researchers reporting qualitative research do not always make it clear how the analysis has taken place. Thus, there is often an air of mystery about qualitative analysis, especially when compared with the seemingly more straightforward and objective approaches to quantitative data analysis, which follow tried and tested procedures. Essentially, the aim of both qualitative and quantitative data analysis is the same, that is to make sense of your data so that evidence can be obtained to answer your research question. Although quantitative and qualitative data are different

DOI: 10.4324/9781003195467-14

Table 14.1 Similarities and differences between quantitative and qualitative analysis

Similarities	Differences
Analysis for both involves inference – that is, they both reach a conclusion based on evidence.	Quantitative analysis is highly standardised and varies little between projects; qualitative analysis has many more possible approaches.
Both involve a systematic process.	Quantitative analysis takes place at the end of data collection; qualitative analysis takes place during data collection.
Both involve comparison, either internally or with related evidence from elsewhere.	Quantitative analysis tends to test hypotheses through the manipulation of numbers representing 'facts'.
Both strive to avoid errors, false conclusions, and misleading inferences and description; both seek valid explanations.	Qualitative analysis blends empirical evidence and abstract concepts in the form of words to explain or illustrate a theory or interpretation.
	Qualitative analysis is less abstract and does not assume that real life can be measured by numbers.

Source: Adapted from Neuman (2000).

in their nature, as Table 14.1 shows, the principles of analysis of each are, however, not entirely different.

Stages of qualitative analysis

As I have noted, there is no single accepted method of analysing qualitative data. This section will provide a brief overview of one method of analysis. However, if you are analysing qualitative data, it is worth having a look at texts such Silverman (2020) for more detail on the various methods of analysis available to you. The key, as always, is to ensure that your analysis is appropriate to achieve your research objectives.

Your data collection will invariably result in pages and pages of transcripts, field notes and so on. This needs to be focused, organised and interpreted. To do this, you will need to undertake the following steps:

1   Data familiarisation. Read your transcripts/field notes all of the way through at least two or three times. You may also want to listen to them again if appropriate. Essentially the idea is for you to firstly get to know your data 'inside out', and secondly, to begin the analytical process. As well as writing down your initial thoughts and ideas about your analysis, you do also need to be aware at this stage about how such early

analysis might impact upon the rest of the process, for example by lead-ing you in a specific direction too early, or by overlooking alternative theories or explanations. Such reflexivity is important in maximising the quality of your analysis, so keep an open mind at this stage. Write down all your initial ideas at this stage, not just those that seem strongest.

2   Data reduction. At this stage, try to discard all irrelevant information, but do ensure that you have access to it later if required, as unexpected findings may need you to re-examine some data previously considered unnecessary. The amount of data you discard will depend upon how focused your data collection has been; if in doubt, do not discard.

3   Data organisation. You will have to organise your data firstly through coding and subsequently through developing broader themes to make sense of the data itself. These issues are covered later.

4   Data display. To draw conclusions from the mass of data, Miles and Huber-man (1994) suggest that a good display of data, in the form of tables, charts, networks and other graphical formats, is essential. Again, this is a continual process, rather than just one to be carried out at the end of the data collec-tion. See Figures 14.1 and 14.2 to see how this can be done.

5   Conclusion drawing/verification. Your analysis should allow you to begin to develop conclusions regarding your study. These initial conclu-sions can then be verified, that is their validity examined through refer-ence to your existing field notes, further data collection or even critical discussion with your colleagues.

Figure 14.1 A framework for the thematic analysis of qualitative data

Developing codes and themes

Coding is the organisation of your raw data into 'conceptual categories'. As Miles and Huberman (1994, p. 56) note: 'Codes are tags or labels for assigning units of meaning to the descriptive or inferential information compiled during a study. Codes are usually attached to "chunks" of varying size – words, phrases, sentences or whole paragraphs.' Each code is effectively a category or 'bin' into which a piece of data is placed, with the choice of bin reflecting the broader meaning of the data (see Table 14.2 for an example).

Table 14.2 An example of generating codes

Raw data	Data coded into similar themes	First-order themes generated	General dimension
After COVID-19, I decided I was going to make more of an effort to get healthy. I really want to join the gym, but it's just too expensive really, and getting there can be difficult. I also worry that I'll stand out if I go, as it seems a different type of people go there. I guess I'm just too lazy to make the change overall, and I don't quite have the confidence to do it yet. I think it might be easier if I had someone to go with, as I think doing it on your own is more difficult.	After COVID-19, I decided I was going to make more of an effort to get healthy. I really want to join the gym, but it's just too expensive really, and getting there can be difficult. I also worry that I'll stand out if I go, as it seems a different type of people go there. I guess I'm just too lazy to make the change overall, and I don't quite have the confidence to do it yet. I think it might be easier if I had someone to go with, as I think doing it on your own is more difficult.	**Intrapersonal barriers** • I guess I'm just too lazy to make the change overall • I don't quite have the confidence to do it yet **Interpersonal barriers** • I do worry that I'll stand out if I go • I think doing it on your own is more difficult **Structural barriers** • but it's just too expensive really • getting there can be difficult	Constraints to gym membership

Thus, for example, a piece of data that refers to an individual not wanting to take part in an activity because they feel they don't have the required skills might be coded as 'lack of confidence'. A statement from a participant about the rising costs at their gym might be coded as 'pricing concerns' and so on. Any further data with the same meaning would also be coded in the same way (i.e. put in the same 'bin'). Some codes will consist of a lot of data from a broad range of participants; other codes might have fewer data from only a few participants. Remember, though, that it's the qualitative meaning and importance of the data, rather than the quantitative significance of the data within a code, that is important.

Coding is the first stage to providing some form of logical structure to the data. Codes should be valid; that is, they should accurately reflect what is being researched, they should be mutually exclusive (in that codes should be distinct, with no overlap) and they should be exhaustive (that is, all relevant data should fit into a code of some description). Once you have coded your data, you can look for emerging themes. A theme is, essentially, a conceptual label for a group of linked codes, and it is more abstract in nature. Thus, codes such as 'fear of failure', 'lack of confidence' and 'lack of interest' might all be grouped together under a theme of 'intrapersonal barriers to participation'. In this case it would be a 'first-order theme', as it has emerged from your codes. First-order themes may then be grouped together in the same way if they are conceptually linked; for example, first-order themes of 'intrapersonal barriers to participation' and 'structural barriers to participation' may be grouped together as a second-order theme of 'general barriers to participation'. Themes may emerge from your conceptual framework if you have developed one prior to data collection, or inductively, through your own interpretation of the data. Whichever you choose, it is your job to convince the reader of the suitability of your themes. Themes should be insightful and provide the reader with an idea of the underlying social processes, rather than simple one-word descriptions. Thus, if you are researching the experiences of athletes with a disability and find data regarding the impacts of injury, then rather than naming your theme 'injury', ensure that is called 'reaction to injury'.

CODES AND THEMES IN PRACTICE: THE NATURE OF TEAM COMEDIANS IN SPORT TEAM

As well as formal roles within a sport team (such as team captain), there are also a number of other informal roles that may exist – for example *social conveners*, who organise social aspects for the team, or informal leaders, who provide guidance and leadership without having a formal role. Another informal role is that of *team comedian*, a member of the team who uses humour, often with both positive and negative impacts upon the social interactions and relations within the team. Kim *et al.* (2020) identified four objectives in their study of team comedians, these being: (1) to understand their behaviour, (2) to identify how they emerged, (3) to ascertain their impact and (4) to identify how they were 'managed' by other team members. After undertaking a mix of focus groups and interviews, the authors began a process of thematic analysis. The general dimensions were deductively created and linked to their objectives (behaviours, emergence, outcomes and management). Under each, a number of inductively generated second-order themes were generated (for example, under the general dimension of 'outcomes', the themes of 'team outcomes' and 'outcomes for the comedian' were identified). Under each of these themes, a number of first-order themes were generated (for example, under 'team outcomes', sub-themes included 'increased enjoyment', 'reduced tension and stress', 'team integration' and 'distraction'.)

The following is a suggested process for developing your themes from your data:

1   The data is carefully read, all statements relating to the research question are identified, and each is assigned a code, or category. These codes are then noted, and each relevant statement is organised under its appropriate theme, either manually or on computer, along with any notes or memos (see later text) that the researcher wishes to add of their own. This is referred to as open coding.

2   Using the themes developed in stage 1, the researcher rereads the qualitative data and searches for further statements that may fit into any of the codes and subsequently become part of a theme. Alternatively, further themes may also be developed in this stage. This is referred to as axial coding.

3   Once the first two stages have been completed, the researcher should become more analytical and look for patterns and explanation in the themes. Questions should be asked such as:

   ● Can I relate certain themes (your 'first-order themes') together under more general themes (second-order themes')?
   ● Can I organise themes sequentially (for example, does code A happen before code B)?
   ● Can I identify any causal relationships (does theme A cause theme B)?

4   The fourth stage is that of selective coding. This involves reading through the raw data for cases that illustrate your analysis or explain the themes developed. You should also look for data that are contradictory, as well as confirmatory, as it is important not to be selective. You must avoid what is referred to as 'confirmation bias', or the tendency

to seek out and report data that support your own ideas about the key findings of the study.

While you are coding your data and developing your themes, you should also be prepared to write memos on an ongoing basis. These are the ideas that occur to you while you are coding your data, for example concerning explanation, theorising or other ideas about the data. They can be extremely helpful to you in trying to make sense of the data at a later date. You can write them directly on the transcripts or keep a record of them elsewhere. Try to make your memos as detailed as you can, as this will help you with later analysis.

Using your codes and themes, your data may then be presented graphically as suggested by Biddle *et al.* (2001), where you demonstrate to the reader how the codes you generate have been clustered into themes. A simple example of how this may appear is provided by Roberts *et al.* (2001), who were interested in how comfortable golfers felt with their clubs. Their analysis is shown in Figure 14.2. Such a display is helpful for the reader to see the relationship between codes and themes, and one should always be presented within the study.

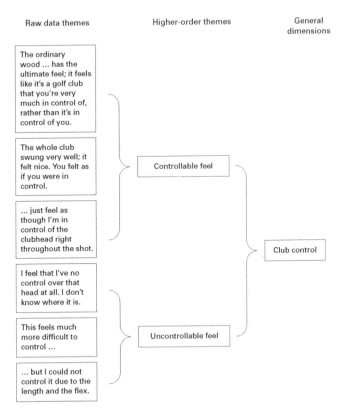

Figure 14.2 A qualitative analysis of golfers' perceptions

As you will notice, there is no indication of any numerical analysis, and at no stage are numbers assigned to any category. As Krane *et al.* (1997, p. 214) suggest:

> Placing a frequency count after a category of experiences is tantamount to saying how important it is; thus value is derived by number. In many cases, rare experiences are no less meaningful, useful, or important than common ones. In some cases, the rare experience may be the most enlightening one.

The layout and complexity of your thematic analysis will vary from project to project. Some data will result in a minimal number of codes, and they will look similar to that of Roberts *et al.* presented in this chapter. Other projects will result in many more first- and second-order themes. The important element is to let the data drive your analysis, and if the data suggests a level of complexity, then you should be guided by that.

CASE STUDY

THEMATIC ANALYSIS IN PRACTICE: CHINESE FOOTBALL FANDOM RESEARCH

BY DR KAIXIAO JIANG, LIVERPOOL HOPE UNIVERSITY

My research (Jiang and Bairner 2020) explored how Chinese people developed their fandom for local football clubs, specifically those of Beijing Guoan and Shanghai Shenhua football clubs, and how fandom contributed to these teams' local symbolic status. The thematic analysis was based on the deductive path that required the identified themes to be embedded with two specific research questions: (1) How did Chinese football fans develop fandom for their local football clubs? and (2) How did their fandom contribute to the clubs becoming local symbols?

This research also emphasised *data familiarisation* as the essential step of thematic analysis. Through coding, both authors commented on every piece of data with the social context. This approach allowed them to identify the detailed similarities and differences across the dataset that integrated information of their cases and developed the knowledge of Chinese football fandom, thus contributing to the study's originality in the subject.

Hence, our study demonstrated that undertaking thematic analysis requires a clear and appropriate data analysis path, inductive or deductive, to address research questions and avoid unfounded discussion. Moreover, improving researchers' understandings of data details through extensive familiarisation may result in a more comprehensive interpretation of the research phenomenon.

Presenting your analysis

When you write up your analysis, you will generally find it better to combine your results and discussion into one chapter or section. Assuming that you have both first- and second-order themes, then I would strongly recommend that you briefly summarise second-order themes one at a time and then present each first-order theme that makes up that second-order theme in more detail. Begin by summarising your key findings for that first-order theme. Then present your evidence in the form of quotes from your participants, including any data that contradict such conclusions. Finally, provide a conclusion for each first-order theme. Using quotes can enrich your report and bring your findings to life, often making the report much more readable. Although it essential to provide the reader with an idea of the voices of participants, you should resist the temptation to over-use them. As a rule of thumb, you should use direct quotes or observations:

- When they describe a phenomenon particularly well.
- To show cases or instances that are unusual.
- To show data that is unexpected.

You should also avoid including quotes without making clear reference to how such quotes refer to your analysis; so avoid having isolated quotes, and never finish a section with a quote.

Once you have discussed each of the themes, then it is important to revisit the data as a whole. You should try and bring everything together to discuss what everything means when taken together and how this relates back to, and makes sense of, your research question. Essentially this is where you answer the question 'What does it all mean?'. As with any analysis, don't let the reader have to make sense of it themselves. You are there to do this, and this is often a good way to conclude the discussion.

Computer analysis and qualitative data

Unlike quantitative analysis, where the use of software such as JASP or SPSS for Windows is simply a given, the use of qualitative analysis software such as NVivo generates a little more controversy. In reality, there are strong arguments on both sides (as comprehensively summarized by Bryman 2016), and it's just not possible to make an overall recommendation one way or the other without taking into account the nature of the research, the type and volume of data, and the characteristics and preferences of the researcher. Using software is certainly more efficient, and it can save time in the long term, as well as enable you to carry out certain types of analysis much more quickly than manual analysis. It could however, as has been argued, mean that you lose a 'feel' for the data, or that it encourages a mechanistic approach to analysis. It's also just as possible to undertake poor qualitative analysis using software as it is using manual methods. Finally the time saved using software might well be cancelled out by the time spent learning the package. Overall, it's your decision. What counts are the outcomes from the analysis, not the process. Provided the analysis is rigorous, systematic and draws out the key insights from the data, then your analysis will be successful, whether it is carried out on NVivo, Word or pen and paper. To help you make your decision, have a look at something like Lewins and Silver (2007), which provides some useful background information.

USING NVIVO TO ANALYSE QUALITATIVE DATA

NVIVO is a programme that can be used to qualitatively analyse text, images and videos. It can import your data from Word and Excel, as well as allow you to transcribe your data directly into the programme. In addition, through the NCapture plug-in, it can capture data from various social media sources such as Facebook and Twitter. It enables you to undertake all of the aspects of qualitative analysis that we talk about in this chapter in terms of organising your data, and it provides perhaps a more structured approach to analysis than manual analysis. There are also features that may save you significant amounts of time, for example being able to analyse sub-groups (such as comparing male and female responses) easily, as well as being able to create memos, where ongoing ideas can be stored. Finally, it is relatively straightforward to learn, especially with the online resources freely available. Using NVivo in itself won't necessarily improve your analysis, but it may help you with certain aspects, for example saving time that may then allow greater focus on developing your insights from the data. The choice to use such software is subject to a number of different considerations and will vary depending upon factors such as the nature of the research, the data collected and the preferences of the researcher.

Ensuring the trustworthiness of your data analysis

Whereas the analysis of quantitative data is, on the outside at least, relatively objective and transparent, qualitative data analysis is open to considerably more interpretation and debate, especially with regard to the validity of the interpretation. There are a number of techniques that can be used to validate the interpretations, and Holloway and Wheeler (2009) summarise the means by which you can try to ensure the trustworthiness of your data. These include the following.

Member checking – One particular method of note is to ask those being investigated to judge the analysis and interpretation themselves, by providing them with a summary of the analysis and asking them to critically comment upon the adequacy of the findings. While this is not a requirement of all qualitative analysis, it can be a useful exercise for the qualitative researcher to undertake. The issue arises, however, of what happens when subjects disagree with the analysis. In such instances, it is important to identify the source of disagreement and to assess whether such disagreement is indeed valid (it may be, for example, that participants have misunderstood some of the analysis, or they approach the analysis with a different agenda to the researcher). Thus, even agreement or disagreement with the analysis can be problematic. Despite this, however, member validation can be an important tool to the qualitative researcher. An alternative may be peer review, whereby a fellow researcher takes the place of the member and seeks inconsistencies, bias or possible errors in interpretation.

Searching for negative cases and alternative explanations – Interpretation should not focus on identifying only cases to support the researcher's ideas or explanations, but it should also identify and explain cases that contradict.

Triangulation – Triangulation was introduced in Chapter 7 and is useful as a means to demonstrate trustworthiness in the analysis.

ENSURING TRUSTWORTHINESS OF DATA – PARENTS' PERCEPTIONS OF PHYSICAL ACTIVITY FOR CHILDREN WITH VISUAL IMPAIRMENTS

Perkins *et al.* (2013) were interested in how the perceptions of parents with visually impaired children impacted upon the participation of those children in physical activity. To do this, they interviewed 11 parents and produced a number of first-order themes, such as 'living a healthy lifestyle' and 'building confidence'. In addition, they grouped such themes into second-order themes, such as 'holistic benefits of physical activity'. To enhance the quality of their analysis, they undertook a number of activities, including:

- Member checking, which involved sending the transcripts back to the participants to ensure that the interviews were an accurate account of the participant's perceptions.
- Data analysis, by multiple researchers, first independently of one another and subsequently together until a consensus on the themes was reached.
- A search for negative cases by looking for responses that were counter to or did not align well with their themes.
- Consultation with an external reviewer who reviewed the themes to ensure that they reflected the purpose of the study and corresponded with the research questions.

The audit trail – To ensure reliability (in the qualitative sense, see Chapter 6) all research should have an audit trail by which others are able to judge the process through which the research has been conducted and the key decisions that have informed the research process. This should include rich (or 'thick') descriptions of the setting and participants, the context within which data were collected and a clear description of the rationale for any decisions made regarding the data collection or analysis.

Reflexivity – Reflexivity means that researchers critically reflect on their own role within the whole of the data-collection process and demonstrate an awareness of this, and how it may have influenced findings, to the reader.

In addition, you should also ensure that your written account of the research:

- Is contextually complete. Your account makes full reference to the context within which the group exists through rich description of the setting, identification of any idiosyncratic features and so on.
- Tells a 'good story' to the reader.
- Provides 'verisimilitude'. It provides the reader with a sense of almost 'being there' and gives them a feeling of understanding of the culture.

A good qualitative analysis places the emphasis clearly upon the data, and it is vital that it is not hidden away but takes primacy within your analysis. This should be apparent in your presentation of the data, and the error of not reporting enough data is more common than that of reporting too much.

Summary

- Although qualitative and quantitative data are different in nature, the analysis of both involves inference, systematic analysis and comparison. Both try to seek valid conclusions and avoid errors.
- There are a number of ways of approaching qualitative analysis.
- Analysing qualitative data should be an ongoing process throughout, as well as after the collection of data.
- There are three key stages to qualitative data analysis: Data reduction, data display and conclusion drawing/verification.
- Data reduction takes place through the process of coding. Coding involves assigning units of meaning to data chunks and can be open, axial or selective. These codes can then be displayed or organised to allow the drawing of conclusions.
- Your analysis can be done either manually or by computer. There are advantages and disadvantages to each, but the final analysis should be the same whichever method you adopt.
- There are a number of means by which you can maximise the trustworthiness of your data, these being member validation, searching for negative cases and alternative explanations, triangulation, having an audit trail and reflexivity.

Activity

1 Carry out and transcribe a short interview with someone you know who is keen on sport. Question them on their experiences of playing and/or watching sport. Now try to code the interview, first using open, and then axial, coding.
2 Can you draw any conclusions from your coding?
3 Now undertake selective coding to explain, support or refute your conclusions.
4 Ask a colleague to undertake the same process in terms of open and axial coding. How reliable are the results?
5 Try to produce a graphical display of your findings.

ABOUT YOUR RESEARCH PROJECT

If your research project involves the analysis of qualitative data, you need to consider the following questions:

■ How will you maximise the trustworthiness of your data? Have you considered strategies such as member validation?
■ In your write-up of the research, have you made clear to the reader the processes by which your data was analysed? Have you a clear audit trail? Have you demonstrated reflexivity?
■ Will you consider the use of software to analyse the data? What are the benefits and/or limitations of doing so?

Further reading

I would fully recommend Silverman here (Silverman, D. (2020) *Interpreting Qualitative Data*, London: Sage). This is extremely comprehensive and covers they key areas extremely well. Other sources that are also worth consulting are:

Denzin, N. and Lincoln, Y. (eds) (1994) *Handbook of Qualitative Research*, London: Sage.

Denzin, N. and Lincoln, Y. (eds) (1998) *Collecting and Interpreting Qualitative Materials*, London: Sage.

Jackson, K. and Bazeley, P. (2019) *Qualitative Data Analysis with NVivo*, London: Sage.

Lewins, A. and Silver, C. (2007) *Using Software in Qualitative Research: A Step-by-Step Guide*, London: Sage.

Miles, M. and Huberman, A. (1994) *Qualitative Data Analysis*, Thousand Oaks, CA: Sage.

Chapter 15
Writing the research report

Writing the research report

This chapter will:

- Introduce the process of writing up your research.
- Outline the structure of a typical research report.
- Identify some of the areas where you should be assessing the quality of your written report.
- Describe some of the issues related to oral and poster presentations of your research.
- Suggest some alternative means by which you can disseminate the findings of your research.

Introduction

An important part of your research is being able to communicate what you have done through presenting it, whether in the form of a written report, dissertation, journal article, presentation or through publicising your research on social media. It does not matter how good your data collection and analysis have been if the report is poorly written – you must ensure that you do not let yourself down in the final write-up. This chapter will guide you through the process of writing up and high-light some of the problems that you may face, so that you can present a final report that will do the many hours spent undertaking the research justice.

DOI: 10.4324/9781003195467-15

Writing the research report

Writing the research report is a difficult and time-consuming task, and it will generally take much longer than you think. The six main pieces of advice to bear in mind in terms of your overall strategy for approaching the process are:

1   Begin writing up the report as soon as you can. Do not leave it until you have finished your data collection. Many sections, for example the literature review and the methodology, can be drafted during or even before data collection. To help you with this, prepare an outline plan. At the bare minimum, this should be a list of chapter headings. Ideally you should be able to have more detail and include likely subheadings as well. The more detailed your initial outline, the easier you will find the process of writing up the first draft of the report.

2   Write down ideas as soon as you get them, rather than leaving them to the writing-up stage. As I noted at the end of Chapter 1, you should be keeping a research diary in which you can safely note any ideas. Not all of your ideas will be useful, but it is certain that some of them will be! Don't imagine that you will be able to remember these ideas at a later date.

3   Be aware of the nature of the report and the intended audience. If it is for an assessed piece of coursework, then ensure you have read and understood the criteria laid down by your institution in terms of content, presentation, length and so on. Familiarise yourself with the layout and technical requirements, for example maximum word length and required formatting such as double spacing or specific referencing style, so that you have an idea of the final product before you start. Look at the relative weightings of each section to see which elements assume greater importance. If you are writing for a journal, ensure that your research fits within the scope of that journal's objectives as well as its editorial requirements. If you are producing a report or piece of consultancy, ensure that you are clear about the requirements of your audience. If any examples of past reports are available, read as many as you can. Try to identify what was good/bad about them, and ensure that you bear these evaluations in mind when compiling your own report. If there are specific marking criteria, then make sure you clearly understand them before you start writing.

4   You will need to rewrite your report a number of times. You should allow for this when planning your research timetable so that you do not become discouraged when the first draft is not perfect. Writing is like training – the more you do, the better you will get. Critically evaluate your draft work, either through reading it yourself or – preferably – getting somebody else to read it with a critical eye. Ask this 'critical friend' to comment upon the content (although remember they will

almost certainly – at this stage – be less knowledgeable than you about the subject matter) as well as the flow of the work, clarity of argument, layout and presentation, and the overall 'feel'. Once you are happy, you can undertake the final editing and proofreading. When you have gotten this far, the temptation is to skip over the final proofreading. Do carefully read over to check spelling and grammar, and get someone else to do the same (once you have read your own work several times, it becomes very difficult to take in what you have read). Don't rely on the spell-checker that comes with your word processing package. It is a useful tool, but it will not pick out every mistake, for example when you type *there* instead of *their*.

5   Have a clear schedule of when certain sections are to be completed, and ensure you monitor your progress against this schedule.

6   Make sure before you begin writing up that you have an adequate strategy for backing up your work, whether on memory sticks or using online/cloud storage, and that you make backups of your work at every available opportunity. Whatever you do, don't assume that whatever you save on a hard drive will be safe! You should keep your backups in a separate location. It is no good keeping them with your laptop on whose hard drive your work is saved – if the laptop does go missing, then you have lost all of your work.

When writing the report, do not feel that you have to complete one chapter or section before starting another. It can be a good idea to be working on several sections simultaneously, so that if you do – as is likely – get 'writer's block', then you can carry on writing. Often, it then becomes easier to go back to the problematic section. Nor should you attempt to write the report in the same order as it is to be presented. Early sections, such as the abstract and the introduction, for example, are better left until towards the end of the writing process. There is no set way to go about the process of writing a report, and it is often a case of personal preference. It can be useful, however, to ensure that you have all the sections (literature review, methodology and so on) on a single file, as this will encourage you to see the written report as one coherent flowing document, rather than as a series of sections.

Structuring the written report

It is possible to structure a report in different ways, depending upon the nature of the research. You may find that your approach lends itself to a different layout from the one suggested here, for example if you have undertaken a qualitative piece of research, in which case you may wish to combine your results and discussion into a more integrated section. If you consider that a different approach is necessary, then discuss this with your tutor or research supervisor. A commonly used structure for an undergraduate dissertation is as follows:

1 Abstract.
2 Acknowledgements.
3 Table of contents.
4 List of tables and figures.
5 Introduction.
6 Literature review.
7 Research methodology.
8 Results.
9 Discussion.
10 Conclusions and recommendations.
11 References and/or bibliography.
12 Appendices.

1 Abstract

This is, essentially, a summary of the research. It describes the topic under examination and outlines the research question or hypothesis, objectives and methods of the study. It should also give a brief résumé of the main conclusions and recommendations. The abstract is a brief section and should be within the word limits set down by your institution, journal, etc., often between 150 and 250 words (slightly longer for a postgraduate thesis). It is often the basis upon which others will assess the usefulness of the research, so you should ensure that you include all relevant details. The abstract should include:

- The aim of the research.
- The background to the research, and the focus of past literature.
- A brief outline of the methodology you adopted.
- Your key findings/conclusions.
- What is distinctive about your study and how it adds to or extends existing knowledge.

2 Acknowledgements

Your report should thank various people who have helped in the research. You might include specific individuals who have given information, offered insightful clues or have been especially supportive. If funding has been provided, then acknowledgement should be made here. Gratitude may also be expressed to groups of people, such as those who formed the sample group. It is best to avoid tendencies towards the extremes of either flippancy or sycophancy. Sometimes, for example in a journal article, acknowledgements may be placed after the main body of the report.

3 Table of contents

The contents page gives the reader the first view of how the report is structured and how you have attempted to develop the topic. It should list sequentially the chapters and the major subdivisions of chapters, each identified by a heading and located by a page number. Contents are not always required; for example, you won't need them if you submit your work as a journal article.

4 List of tables and figures

Throughout the written report you may want to present material in tabulated (tables) or diagrammatic (figures) form. For example, if you have undertaken any quantitative analysis, you will need to report the analysis in the form of tables. The location of this material needs to be listed, with separate lists for figures and tables.

5 Introduction

The introduction is there to help the reader see that this is a study that needs doing and is worth reading. In many ways, it is there to market the rest of the report to the reader. It should describe the subject under investigation, the purpose of the research and why you are doing the research – essentially what you are doing, why you are doing it and how you are doing it. In the introduction you should provide some academic justification for the choice of topic, if possible, as well as any particular personal or practical justification. You should include a summary of how you are going to treat the chosen topic and, importantly, set out and explain (especially if your terminology requires clarification) your research question or hypothesis and your subsidiary questions or objectives, including defining any key terms or concepts. Finally, it may be useful to show your intentions by briefly running through your intended chapters or sections. What you must not neglect, or hide away, is what Creswell (1994) refers to as your purpose statement. The purpose statement is the statement that establishes the direction of the research and highlights the objectives that are hopefully to be met. You can often start this with: 'The purpose of this study is to. . . '. For a quantitative purpose statement, Creswell suggests including the following:

- The theory or model that is to be used in the study.
- The specific research design (cross-sectional, experimental, etc.).

- The variables to be tested and their relationship with each other (begin with the independent variable, followed by the dependent variable).
- The unit of analysis, or the sample that you are investigating.

For a qualitative study, Creswell suggests the following:

- Use words such as *develop*, *understand*, and so on that convey the emergent sense of the research, rather than words such as *test* or *measure*.
- Clearly state and define the central concept or idea being researched.
- Describe the research design and method of data collection to be used, for example an ethnographic design, involving participant observation, etc.
- Identify the unit of analysis, such as the setting, organisation, group and so on.

6 Literature review

After an introductory chapter, most reports will include one or more chapters where you draw upon and consider theories, arguments and findings from the literature that obviously relate in some way to your question or hypothesis (see Chapter 5). As suggested earlier, the literature review should not just be a list of all of the literature you have discovered; rather it should be a critical appraisal of existing work, and you should be explicit as to how your study is related to, or has emerged from gaps in, the literature (more common with quantitative studies) or the context and rationale for the study (more common for qualitative studies). A common weakness in literature reviews is to list or summarise existing literature then conclude with a number of research objectives that are unrelated to the literature. You should ensure that there is a strong link between your written literature review and your research objectives.

7 Research methodology

The literature review should 'set the scene' in terms of how your research relates to, and emerges from, existing knowledge and understanding. The methodology should outline how your objectives are to be achieved. Although the methodology may be one of the shorter sections, it is crucial to the entire project. You must address the area of research methods, including a justification of the methodology chosen and an explanation of how the data was gathered. Generally the methodology section or chapter will consist of a number of sections:

- An outline of your underlying methodological assumptions. You may wish to justify your epistemological stance, for example, or your use of qualitative rather than quantitative data. You don't, however, need to provide lots of basic description about the nature of positivist approaches or the characteristics of qualitative data in general. Instead, you should draw out the key points as they apply to your research project

- Your research design. Explain your choice of research design, making it clear what data is to be collected and at what times.
- Methods. You should describe your choice of method, such as an online questionnaire, and outline some of the design issues. What questions were included and why? If you have adopted an existing questionnaire or interview schedule, then explain why you have done this, perhaps referring to issues of reliability and validity. You may also – depending upon the nature of the report – include details about the piloting or pre-testing procedure.
- Sample. You should include details of your sample or participants, how you achieved the sample and any limitations of your sampling method.
- Procedures. Describe how the research was carried out, for example whether questionnaires were emailed or handed to participants, what instructions were given and so on.
- Methods of analysis. You should briefly outline your methods of analysis, for example a description of the statistical tests to be used and a justification of their appropriateness.
- An overview of the ethical issues that emerged and how these issues were addressed.
- You may also consider including an evaluation of the methodology, highlighting the strengths and weaknesses, and making any limitations clear to the reader.

Qualitative methodologies should always include a section about reflexivity, that is the role of the researcher, their characteristics, experience and values, and how this will have impacted upon all aspects of the data collection and analysis.

The methodology section or chapter needs to include a lot of detail in a relatively short space (often about 1,500–2,000 words in a 10,000-word undergraduate project). One rule of thumb that you can use to check whether you have included enough detail is whether another researcher, through reading only your methodology and equipped with copies of your data collection instruments, could undertake the same research and gain similar results. You should also justify your key decisions throughout. Rather than just presenting generic justifications (such as 'online question-naires were adopted because of their ability to reach a geographically dis-persed sample'), you should explain why you have made the methodological choices specifically for your study.

8 Results

Do not simply report every finding here – report only those results that are relevant to your study. In terms of the presentation of results, think about how to put your findings over as clearly as possible. You may want to look at past research reports to see how they have presented their results. The purpose of the data analysis is to develop a series of logical and convincing answers to the research question(s) that have emerged from the literature review. You should not, therefore, present data that does not relate to your research, even if you think it would be 'interesting'. Be careful in your graphical treatment of data – it is very tempting to include as many charts and graphs as possible, and to try to make them extremely impressive in terms of colour, layout and so on. In practice, it is often the case that the chart with minimal detail is often the clearest to understand. You should only consider the use of colour if it clarifies a particular chart, a situation that is actually rare (and in many instances, such as when you submit to an academic journal, you will be restricted to black and white line drawings anyway).

9 Discussion

The purpose of this chapter or section is to discuss the implications of your results in light of your research objectives. Remember when you are writing this section that it is all about what the results mean, rather than what they say. Berg and Latin (2008) identify four components of a typical discussion:

- A restatement of the results. Keep this as brief as possible, and avoid repeating material from the results chapter.
- Relating the results to theory, either deductively, in comparing your findings to your underlying theoretical framework, or more inductively, by developing your own theoretical framework.
- Assessing the limitations of the study (I would go further and suggest that the strengths of the study could be discussed as well).
- Discussion of the implications of the findings. This can be both the 'academic' implications (such as the implications for the theory or models you might have chosen to underpin your study) or the practical implications, for example who might be impacted by the findings of the study, and how?

A common error at this stage is simply to discuss your own findings without any reference to existing knowledge. Do remember, however, that you are building on such existing knowledge, so refer back to what has been discussed in your literature review. Do your results find support in the literature? Were they predicted by the literature? If they did and were, then how does your research add to the literature? If your findings differed from your expectations, then are there any possible reasons why? Does the particular theory or model you've used still hold true in light of your research? If not, to what extent is this a limitation of the theory or model, or a possible limitation of your research? If the theory or model seems flawed, then how can it be refined to explain your findings? When discussing such issues, it is important to ensure that the discussion is grounded on your own observations, analysis and reading of the literature. By doing this, your arguments are more likely to be well-constructed and convincing.

10 Conclusions and recommendations

Your discussion of findings/literature should lead to a final conclusion chapter or section. Your conclusion is very important and often receives inadequate attention. Importantly, it should stem from the findings/discussion and lead to consistent, feasible recommendations if applicable. All the matters you wish to discuss and develop in the concluding section should be related to and follow logically from what's gone before. The conclusion should include a summary of your main arguments, drawing together the various themes and issues so that they can be brought to bear on the defined objectives or subsidiary questions of the study. The original research question or hypothesis should be revisited at this stage, and the dialogue would explain the extent to which this has been addressed within the context of the study. Strengths and limitations of your project and what, in hindsight, you might have done differently should be included.

When you have completed the first draft of your introductory chapter and your conclusion, try to read them together. Ideally, reading the introduction followed by the conclusion should make sense without reading anything in between – remember, the introduction should set the scene to the research question, and the conclusion will provide the answers! Depending upon the nature of your project, recommendations often follow the conclusion, but not in all cases. Recommendations based on the research itself are more likely to be included where your project is of a practical nature (e.g. in terms of the potential application of your findings to industry or education). Recommendations for further research are generally an excellent way to finish off the main body of the research, and I would strongly advise you to include one or two suggestions for how future researchers could extend the work that you have done.

11 References and/or bibliography

Some confusion exists over the difference between 'references' and 'bibliography' and whether it is a requirement to include both lists. In reality, the terms are often used interchangeably – the minimum requirement is normally for a list of references, which contains all items cited in the text in alphabetical order of author. If you want to use both a list of references

(references cited in your own text) and a bibliography (items not necessarily cited, but deemed relevant to the research), then this may be in order. Including the latter can be advantageous, as a bibliography can demonstrate the width of literature that you have accessed, which may not always be clear from doing a reference list alone. You should check the requirements of your own institution if there is any doubt. Whatever you do, it is critical that you reference any work that you are citing accurately, giving a detailed description of the source from which you obtained the information. You must acknowledge sources and clearly differentiate between ideas or words that are your own and those that originate from others.

12 Appendices

You should include in the appendices all information that gives any additional support to the arguments you are constructing. It is important, however, that you put all the crucial information you wish to be read in the main text, rather than hiding it away in an appendix. All appendices that you do include should be referred to in the text. You may also want to include copies of correspondence, details of organisations, people you have contacted, details of interviewees, etc. Your research instruments, such as copies of questionnaires or interview schedules, should also be included in an appendix.

THE PURPOSES OF THE MAIN SECTIONS OF YOUR WRITTEN REPORT

- Abstract – what is the study about, how did you do it and what you found.
- Introduction – what you are doing, why you are doing it and how you are doing it.
- Literature review – what is known about the subject of your research, what isn't known and how your research relates to the existing literature.
- Methodology – how you collected the data to answer that question and why you used that method.
- Results – what the data say.
- Discussion – what the data mean, and how the data relate back to the literature you discuss earlier in the report.
- Conclusion – what the answer to your research question was.

Language and writing style

The issue of language and style can often be overlooked in a research report. What you should be aiming for is to present a well-written, readable report that will actually interest your readers. There are four very general styles that can be identified:

1 The 'dry' and objective style. This is characterised by reporting everything in a totally objective manner, with no sense of humour or enthusiasm for the research. This style is difficult to read, especially in an extended report, and makes it quite difficult for the reader to actually complete the report! Try to avoid this style if at all possible.

2 The informal style. Here, the researcher feels that they have to chat to the reader. The language used is informal, as if the writer were explaining the research to their friends over lunch. Again try to avoid this style!

3 The 'long-winded' style. Also referred to as 'verbosity', this sometimes happens when writers try to imitate some of the more complex pieces of literature that they have come across in their reading, or, alternatively, to impress the reader with their use of complex academic language. This type of report uses technical jargon when perfectly acceptable words in plain English exist, in an effort to impress. Such reports can be difficult to read, and it may be harder for the reader to accurately assess what the researcher is actually saying! Holt (1989, p. 357) identifies an example of this style when he refers to a paper that suggests that 'Massification as the negation of publics designates that moral inter-subjectivity as a process of need expression and sublimation is replaced by corporatized, desublimating modes'. Remember – write to express, rather than to impress!

4 The 'elegant' style. This is the style towards which you should strive. It lies somewhere between the dry and informal, and it allows the information to be presented in a manner that is readable and interesting. Technical terms can be used where appropriate, but sparingly. This style often conveys the researcher's own sense of enthusiasm and makes for an interesting yet 'academic' read.

You also need to be confident in your writing. Remember that by this stage, you should have some degree of expertise both in the subject matter and research methodology. This expertise should come out in your writing. Avoid being overconfident and making grand or unsupported claims, but think about how your writing style can convince the reader that you have credibility as a researcher. Bryman (2016) refers to this as being *persuasive*, and this comes from both what you write and how you write it. A final, yet crucial, point is to ensure that however you write the report, you must ensure that you avoid language that could be construed as sexist, racist or disablist (avoiding, as just one example of this, referring to 'the World Cup' instead of 'the Women's World Cup').

Assessing your own research report

Before your report is read or assessed by others, such as your examiners, it is important that you critically evaluate its content beforehand. This can sometimes be a time-consuming task, and you should allow yourself as much time as you can for this stage, especially if it is likely that you will find significant errors, or if you think that a significant rewrite is required. There are a number of specific questions that you should ask yourself with regard to the content of your report. These are as follows.

Setting the scene

- Does your abstract give a clear idea of what is in the report? Has it clearly described the background to the study, what is distinctive about what you are doing, the methodology adopted, the main conclusions that have emerged and how your study adds to knowledge?
- Is your table of contents well-structured, and does it give an accurate picture of what's included? Have you included a list of tables and a list of figures if appropriate?
- Have you introduced your research adequately? Is it totally clear to the reader what the aim of the research is and why it is important? Do you have a clearly constructed and suitable research question or hypothesis that leads to a set of clear and related subsidiary questions or objectives?
- Are you happy that you have 'set the scene' for the reader? What is the rationale behind your research report? Have you clearly identified this? Why should the reader read your piece of work? Is it saying something worthwhile?

Your use of the literature

- Do you have a logically structured review of literature, either using a funnel approach with a broad outline of the key concepts (focusing towards more specific literature as the review progresses) or a thematic approach that deals with key concepts in turn?
- Is your issue or focus underpinned by theory? Is it clear which theory or model you have adopted?
- How up-to-date are your references? Have you included the most up-to-date work in your area? Have you also included the older, 'classic' sources?
- Have you used a variety of sources or are you over-reliant upon certain authors? Have you included or acknowledged competing theories or viewpoints, or simply selected literature that supports your hypothesis? Have you explored all possible sources?

- Have you assessed the quality of your non peer-reviewed sources?
- Is it clear to the reader how your research relates to what has been done before or how it builds upon existing knowledge?
- In your literature review do you merely identify and describe, with no real critical edge? Have you been analytical enough?

Your methodology

- Have you clearly explained your broad ontological and epistemological assumptions? Does the methodology reflect these assumptions throughout?
- Do you clearly identify and explain your choice of research design?
- Have you explained the rationale behind your chosen means of collecting information? If it is an existing instrument, whose is it? Why did you choose it? Is it clear to the reader why your methods were the most appropriate ones for your research question?
- Have you made it clear who the subjects are and to what population these subjects belong? Is it clear how they were selected?
- Did you undertake any piloting of your data-collection instruments? If so, what was the outcome? Have you reported any piloting in your write-up?
- Have you been explicit in outlining how data were analysed?
- Have you evaluated the methodology? Can you identify what was strong and what was weaker?
- Are you making assumptions? You know what you did in terms of research methods, but would the reader? Have you expressed yourself clearly and given adequate details? Would someone else be able to replicate your study on the basis of the information you've given?
- Have you justified your key decisions?

Discussion and conclusions

- Are your findings clearly presented? Have you included tables for your descriptive and inferential analysis of quantitative data?
- If you have included graphs, charts and so on, are these appropriate? Do they add anything?
- Is the content of each chart clear? Is it clear how each chart relates to your research objectives?
- How have you analysed your findings? If you have undertaken quantitative analysis, which statistical tests have you used? Are you sure these are the correct tests? Have you interpreted the results correctly? For qualitative analysis, have you demonstrated that you have analysed your data in a systematic manner?

- In your discussion, do you adequately revisit the literature and relate your findings to the literature, or do you simply discuss what you found?
- Are your arguments coherent, logical and sound? Are they consistent with the evidence that you have collected?
- Have your conclusions clearly emerged from the evidence collected and discussed? Have you acknowledged unexpected evidence, or evidence that contradicts your chosen theory or model?
- Do you return to your research question or hypothesis?
- Do you evaluate the research? Have you identified the strengths and the limitations of the project?
- Are any recommendations you make based upon your findings? Are they feasible and practical? Have you identified recommendations for further research?

General presentation of the report

- Is your content well-planned and logically structured?
- Is the work well-presented? Have you used an appropriate font and followed the guidelines of your institution in terms of margins, double spacing and so on?
- Have you made appropriate use of supportive materials to enhance presentation (i.e. graphs, tables, illustrations)?
- Have you conducted a thorough read-through to eliminate careless spelling and typographical errors, poor grammar and poor sentence construction?
- Are you writing in the most appropriate tense? Is your writing too informal?
- How well do you communicate your ideas? Does what you write make sense?
- Do you link your various chapters and make use of signposting to help the reader?
- Have you set out your references and/or bibliography with the required detail and in the recommended format?
- Have you acknowledged all sources used and made it clear whether it's your views that are being expressed or the views of others?
- Have you made appropriate use of appendices? Are there any unnecessary appendices?
- Have you ensured that your report is as stimulating and as interesting as possible? Have you conveyed your enthusiasm to the reader throughout the project?

DISSEMINATING YOUR FINDINGS USING PICTURES

JAYNE CAUDWELL, BOURNEMOUTH UNIVERSITY

Disseminating the findings of your research usually involves writing a report or a dissertation. This process can include images. Providing pictures can capture and convey the results of your study in a simple and effective way. Drawings that are done by your research participants or by an illustrator can be included in academic outputs and in industry reports.

In a project that was funded by the British Academy and the Leisure Studies Association, research participants drew pictures to show how swimming made them feel. The research participants belonged to a trans group, which offered a safe social space for young people that identified as transgender and non-binary. In addition to their drawings, a professional illustrator made drawings during the focus group research. Some of these images appear in an open-access journal (Caudwell 2020). During the focus group research the participants talked about feeling unsure about using changing rooms. Figure 15.1 depicts the discussion.

Figure 15.1 Illustration courtesy of Jayne Caudwell

In another research project funded by Sport England and Energise Me, the aim was to find out how the physical activity workforce can enable and increase LGBT+ physical activity participation. Again, professional illustrators were hired to visually document the focus group research. The images produced were later used in a report for practitioners and industry (www.energiseme. org/wp-content/uploads/2020/09/Pride-in-Our-Workforce.pdf).

Figures 15.2, 15.3 and 15.4 demonstrate three themes that emerged from the focus group research with people employed in the physical activity workforce. The drawings show their ideas surrounding what might cause barriers to LGBT+ physical activity participation.

Figure 15.2 Illustration courtesy of Jayne Caudwell

Figure 15.3 Illustration courtesy of Jayne Caudwell

Figure 15.4 Illustration courtesy of Jayne Caudwell

Defending your research

It may be the case that you are called upon to defend your research orally, generally through what is referred to as a *viva voce* (or just *viva*). This is still rare at undergraduate level, although it is a requirement of higher degrees such as a doctorate. Alternatively, you may be asked to give a short presentation about your research (this is often a useful way to answer questions where there are doubts about the authenticity of some aspect of the research).

The viva voce

The difficulty with preparing for an examination of this nature is that it is simply not possible to predict with total accuracy the questions that will be asked! The best advice is that you simply have to know your research inside and out. You should be able to anticipate some of the questions, for example on the main findings of the research and so on, and prepare for them. If you are asked a question that you can't answer straight away, then stop and carefully consider your answer rather than rush into a response. Write down the question if necessary, and ask the examiner for clarification of what they mean if you are not sure. If you really cannot answer the question, then don't panic! The examiners are not expecting a perfect response to every question anyway. You should put such questions to the back of your mind and concentrate upon the rest of the viva – remember, one question that you cannot answer will not lead to a failed exam!

COMMON VIVA QUESTIONS

The following are some of the questions that do appear regularly at viva examinations. It is by no means an exhaustive list, and you should always expect the unexpected or unusual questions as well!

- How did you come to research this topic?
- Why is this topic worth exploring?
- How has the research contributed to knowledge in this area?
- What were the important research decisions that you made?
- On what basis did you make these decisions?
- How did you choose which theory to focus upon?
- How did you come to decide upon a particular methodological approach?
- What were the key ethical issues related to the research, and how did you address these?
- What are the most interesting findings from the research? the most unexpected?
- What would you have done differently if you had repeated the research?
- What have you learnt personally from doing the research?

Presenting your research

An alternative to the viva is to present your research in front of a small audience. Not everyone in the audience may have read your work, and you may well be addressing differing levels of expertise. Presentations of this nature are often short and need to be well-rehearsed. When preparing a presentation, think about the following points:

- Have a clear structure. This should consist of three main elements: (1) the introduction, (2) the main body of the presentation and (3) the conclusion.

- Have as few slides as possible. Almost every presentation is improved by the presenter talking more and reading off the slides less. For a 20-minute presentation, 10 slides would be an absolute maximum (ideally have less). Ensure you have a run-through beforehand to check your timing, especially if you are presenting at an institution that will simply cut you off without warning at the end of your allocated time slot! Even if you are not cut off, over-running can show a lack of respect to any following speakers, so it is imperative to keep to time.
- Don't include too much detail on your slides, and don't include any more text than is absolutely necessary. Stick to the key points, and ensure you can't simply read the slides out loud. Sticking to the essentials will help prevent this and help you maintain eye contact with your audience.
- Make the presentation clear and easy to read. Firstly, ensure that you have a sufficiently large and easily readable font. Fonts such as Arial are better for presentations than fonts such as Times New Roman. If in doubt about the font size, then err on the side of caution and use a minimum font size of 24 points. Secondly, try to avoid complex models or diagrams. Use handouts for such material if they are to be included. Finally, use a background that is clear and uncluttered, and ensure sufficient contrast between the background and the text.

You may wish to adopt the following structure if you are called upon to present your research, assuming a 20-minute presentation:

- Slide 1 – Introduction, main aims and objectives of the research.
- Slides 2/3 – A brief outline of your theoretical approach.
- Slide 4 – The key features about your methodology.
- Slides 5/6 – Your important/significant results.
- Slides 7/8 – Key points for discussion.
- Slide 9 – The conclusion.

You will find that using less than 10 slides, with only one or two points on each slide, will be more than adequate, provided you are able to talk about your own research freely.

Presenting a research poster

A poster summarises your research project on a single large sheet of paper (typically A0). It also has other functions, perhaps most importantly to attract people to read about your research in the first place and also to stimulate subsequent discussion between you, as the presenter, and the audience who may, in many cases, have limited knowledge of the subject matter. Thus, your poster has to demonstrate a balance between content and attractiveness.

Designing your poster

First, identify the main message that you want the poster to put over. Then identify the essential elements that will need to be included for this message, for example background, methodology, key findings and so on. Some institutions have set requirements of the layout and what should be included, so if this is the case you should ensure you follow these. Otherwise, you will need to put together an initial draft design of your own. The guidelines you need to follow are:

- Keep the poster simple. Put across your message in as few words as possible, while providing all relevant detail. Your audience will not want to read long blocks of text, so think about how to communicate in as concise a way as possible.
- Keep your results as clear as possible. Present data in graphical format, rather than text or in tables. Ensure that the labelling of graphs is large enough that the results are clear when read in isolation from the rest of the poster.
- Avoid the temptation to use too many colours. Try to use three to four at most, and avoid overly bright colours. Keep backgrounds light and text dark. Make sure there is enough contrast between content and background.
- Fonts such as Arial and Verdana are good for posters. Avoid obscure or unusual fonts. You will be trying to attract an audience from some distance, so make sure your font is large enough. A font size of approximately 100 points should be used for the title, 30–36 for headings and 20–24 for text.
- Use bullet points/tables to aid clarity.
- Leave a minimum 3 cm white border around the poster to frame your work.
- Use blank space to make the poster more attractive.
- Consider the use of a QR code on the poster that people viewing your poster can use to access certain information, such as reference lists, a biography of the researcher and so on.

As well as thinking about what will make the poster attractive, also consider what will put off people coming to view your poster. Things such as too much dense text, unclear results and a message that is difficult to identify from a brief glance will all impact negatively upon interest in your research.

Other ways of reporting your research

Given all of the time and effort that you will have put into the research, it's important to think about how your findings could be communicated beyond the limited audience involved in assessing your written report or presentation. If you feel that you've made even a modest contribution to knowledge, understanding or practice, then it's important to disseminate it. There are a number of ways you could consider doing this:

1   If you feel like the work has real merit and makes a significant contribution, then you could always discuss with your supervisor the possibility of writing it up and submitting it to a peer-reviewed journal. There is a growing volume of research being published in such journals that has emerged from student research, so it's worth considering this if the work is of sufficient standard. Professor Heather Gibson, a highly experienced journal editor, has provided a number of key tips about publishing for the first time.

CASE STUDY

KEY ADVICE FOR PUBLISHING YOUR WORK
BY PROF. HEATHER GIBSON, UNIVERSITY OF FLORIDA

When you have a piece of work that you think is worthy of publication, it is hard to know where to start. Here are a few pointers to help you navigate the process:

1   If you have not submitted a paper for publication before, ask an advisor, mentor or colleague who is familiar with the publishing process to read through your work. They can tell you if your work is publishable, and they may also suggest a potential journal.
2   Refine your paper for your target journal. Look at the mission statement for the journal, recent issues where you can see the types of studies it publishes and the writing style. It is important that you write for a journal rather than trying to match your paper to a journal post hoc. Read through the author guidelines for the journal, and format your paper accordingly.
3   If you receive a 'revise and resubmit' notice, do not get upset by the reviewer's comments. Take a big breath and work through the comments. Often your revised paper will be much stronger than your original submission due to the insights and advice you received from the reviewers.

2   If the work doesn't quite have the merit for a fully peer-reviewed journal, then many universities will run their own in-house journals for publishing good student research. These journals will still go through a peer-review process, but it is likely to be less demanding. Ask your supervisor if your institution does have such a journal; it is often an excellent opportunity.

3   You can always present your work at a student conference such as the British Conference for Undergraduate Research (BCUR). This conference allows students from all disciplines to present papers, posters and workshops to other undergraduate researchers, and there is generally a good presentation from students studying sport-related topics.

4   Use social media. Report the key findings (remember any ethical issues related to aspects such as confidentiality and anonymity) through your Twitter, Instagram or LinkedIn account. This can often be an excellent way to attract interest in your research. You can also download a video summary of your research to a site such as YouTube. If you use social media to communicate your findings, remember your audience will differ from those who would normally assess your research. Don't present things in an overly academic way, but don't oversimplify or dumb it down.

5   If you carried out the research for an organisation or sporting body of some sort, think about how they are going to disseminate the findings. You should also find out if they are going to implement any changes as a result of your research, this way you can assess any impact of what you have done.

Summary

1   Writing the report is the culmination of a lot of time and energy spent doing the research, so make sure that you do yourself justice!

2   Writing the report will almost certainly take longer than you think.

3   You will generally have to go through the process of writing and rewriting a number of times until you are happy with the result.

4   There is normally no single acceptable structure for your research report. A typical undergraduate dissertation may follow the order of abstract, acknowledgements, table of contents, list of tables and figures, introduction, literature review, methodology, results, discussion, conclusion and recommendations, references and/or bibliography and appendices.

5   Take care with your writing style. Avoid the extremes of informality, dryness or jargon.

6   While you are writing the report, be self-critical and read your work with an eye to continually improving its content.

7   Consider other ways of presenting your research, and do so in a way that is both informative and interesting.

You should obtain, if appropriate, a copy of the marking criteria used by your institution. Carefully and critically assess your own performance against the criteria. Identify the areas where you feel that you fulfil the criteria and also those areas that you are not sure about. Identify what you see to be the strengths and the weaknesses of the research. Now is the time to look at the weaknesses – are they remediable? If the weaknesses are things such as a lack of literature, poor structure and so on, you should address these and redo the activity. Get a colleague to read your research report. What do they think? Often they will be able to spot things that you will have missed – once you have read a section more than a few times, it becomes extremely difficult to take in everything you are reading.

Further reading

One thing that you must read is any documentation associated with your project (handbook, guidance and marking criteria, for example). This will help you in terms of structuring the final report. It's also worth a read of the following:

Weyers, J. and MacMillan, K. (2009) *How to Write Dissertations and Research Projects*, Upper Saddle River, NJ: Prentice Hall.

Chapter 16
Practical issues

Practical issues

This chapter will:

- Outline the different types of research that you may undertake as a student.
- Describe some of the initial considerations that you should make about your research project.
- Outline some of the issues that you may need to consider when trying to gain collaboration for your research.
- Discuss the role of your tutor or supervisor in your research project.

Introduction

This chapter is designed for those undertaking research as part of a taught degree, for example a final-year dissertation at undergraduate level. If this is the case, then this is possibly the first significant piece of research that you will have to do. This chapter will highlight some of the specific issues that you may want to consider before starting your research and throughout the research process.

The types of student research

Student research takes on a number of forms, each with its own requirements, depending both upon the nature of the course and the institution within which the research is being conducted. This section can only give a broad overview of the issues, and you should ensure that you read your own institution's regulations carefully before you start the research.

DOI: 10.4324/9781003195467-16

Student research can be broadly separated into two forms. First, the research may be the culmination of a period of taught study, generally at undergraduate or master's level. The research produced for the purpose of these degrees is referred to as a dissertation. The dissertation gives students the opportunity to conduct an in-depth study of a particular topic, synthesising various course elements, yet pursuing one area of interest in depth. The dissertation allows students scope for expression of skills, knowledge and abilities, and it offers the chance to develop – in an original and creative way – areas of particular interest. The dissertation also performs the important integrative function of bringing together different elements from the course, testing the ability and discipline of the student in producing a detailed piece of work through a sustained period of independent study.

Other types of award are based entirely upon the production of a research report – in this instance a thesis – and an accompanying defence of the research with two or more examiners who are expert within the field (the viva voce). These awards are normally at master's level (MRes/MPhil) or doctoral level (PhD or DPhil). The objectives of these programmes are naturally considerably more advanced, with the criteria generally requiring the student to have satisfactorily completed a research training programme and to have investigated and evaluated or critically studied an appropriate topic over normally a minimum of one year (MRes), two years (MPhil) or three years (PhD/DPhil).

The research project – at whatever level – is an important part of any programme of study, as it allows you to both develop and demonstrate a number of key transferable skills. The transferable skills that you could expect to develop and demonstrate as part of a research project are as follows:

- To demonstrate familiarity with the core knowledge base of a particular field of sport-related study.
- To be able to evaluate that core knowledge base, its strengths, weaknesses and omissions.
- To be able to create a suitable methodology to achieve a series of research objectives.
- To be able to describe, analyse and interpret data from such a methodology using appropriate techniques.
- To be able to draw appropriate conclusions from evidence.
- To produce a complex piece of work that demonstrates a grasp of vocabulary of the subject and deploys a range of skills of written expression appropriate to the subject.
- To be able to decide on action plans and implement them effectively.
- To manage time effectively in order to achieve intended goals.
- To use appropriate IT resources independently.
- To deliver a paper or presentation that succeeds in communicating a series of points effectively.
- To produce creative and realistic solutions to complex problems.

Thus, by undertaking a piece of research, you are likely to show a potential employer that you possess a wide range of desirable skills that you may not develop to the same extent elsewhere during your academic career. Potential employers are likely to look at any research project you have undertaken – especially a dissertation or thesis – much more closely than taught modules, and you should bear this in mind when you commence your research programme.

Initial considerations

Whatever programme of study you are on, you will almost certainly have to present a proposal for your research project at an early stage, in the form of either a written or verbal presentation, which may in itself be assessed or non-assessed. Even for a non-assessed piece of work, it is important to be as detailed and as thorough as possible, as it is at this stage that you should highlight any potential problems. You should remember that your research will be restricted in terms of time and resources, and poor planning can lead to difficulties later. At this stage, you may want to consider the criteria in Table 16.1 and assess your intended project against such criteria.

Table 16.1 Criteria for consideration at the planning stages

Research topic
- Is it focused enough? Avoid making it too broad.
- Is it realistic? Will you get the cooperation you need?
- Is it related to your programme of study?

Background
- Is there a well-defined theoretical background?
- What particular theories or models are you going to use?
- Have you defined your concepts?
- How will you measure these concepts?
- Have you mentioned at least one or two key authors?

Research design
- What design will you use?
- What type of data will you collect?
- What methods do you anticipate using?
- Can you justify your methodology?

Sampling
- Who will be your sample?
- What is your desired sample size?
- How will you choose them?
- Have you gotten confirmed access to your sample?

General
- Have you gotten the collaboration/access you need?
- Do you have the appropriate skills to carry out such research?

What characterises a good piece of student research?

Identifying what makes a piece of research 'good' or 'bad' is an important skill to develop. First, it is important for you to be able to assess the work of others. Second, you will also have to assess your own research. Finally, it is important to know how others will be assessing your work. It is important to know upon what criteria you are to be assessed before you start your research. Although there are some general areas upon which your research will be judged, which I will outline later, there may also be specific requirements of your institution, organisation, etc., and you should familiarise yourself with these at the earliest possible stage. Generally speaking, there will be five areas upon which you will be assessed:

1   Your understanding of existing knowledge, the use of existing ideas and the development of your own research question from relevant literature, based upon logical argument and rational thought.
2   The use of an appropriate methodology to collect valid and reliable data with which to answer that question.
3   The critical analysis and interpretation of your data.
4   The development of sound conclusions.
5   The associated transferable skills.

Read any marking criteria as soon as you can. What are the areas being assessed? What are the relative weightings of each, and which elements are given the highest importance? From the marking criteria you should be able to identify what examiners are seeking in terms of an 'excellent' piece of work. Try to identify what makes the difference between a good and an excellent piece of work. By knowing this before you start, you can focus on achieving excellence throughout the research process.

Originality and generalisability

There may also be the requirement with certain research projects (for example at master's or doctoral level) to make a 'contribution to human knowledge' through the development of new theories, methods, etc. At undergraduate level, there is not the need to make such a contribution, and the extent of 'originality' required is minimal (although you should aim to make your project 'original' in some way, for example in one of the ways suggested in Chapter 4). It is also a good idea in most cases to ensure that your project has some relevance beyond the context within which it was carried out, for example in terms of your findings being representative beyond your sample or setting.

The research timescale

You also need to consider the timescale for your research. From my experience, students often underestimate the time required to undertake a piece of research, and it is important to be realistic rather than optimistic. Take for example the following activities:

- Locating relevant literature using an online database. This can be an ongoing and seemingly endless task. You may need to spend an entire day locating literature on one specific area of the project. You may then have to order this (for example from the British Library), which could mean up to a fortnight before you even get a look at the key literature.

- Reading a single journal article. To read such an article could take you anywhere from an hour upwards, especially at the beginning of the research, when you are still developing your own understanding of the subject, and you may find yourself struggling with an article for three hours or more.

- Designing an initial questionnaire/interview schedule. A good questionnaire or interview will take a substantial period of time to develop, even once you have developed an understanding of the concepts that you are researching.

- Piloting an initial questionnaire. This may take several weeks – remember that it is up to your respondents to get the questionnaire back to you, which they may need to be reminded of several times!

- Undertaking a postal survey. Even using a pre-designed questionnaire, you will need to post the questionnaires to your sample (taking several days). They will then need to complete the questionnaires (up to two weeks, for those who remember) and return them to you (several more days). You will then have to repeat the process for those who didn't return the questionnaires in the first round (another two to three weeks). Even an online survey will involve a period of time where you allow respondents to complete the questionnaire, which will be a minimum of two weeks.

- Writing up an interview. Even if you are a good typist, you should allow yourself about four to five hours to transcribe a one-hour interview, often more, especially if the recording is not clear or if there is background noise.

- Entering the results from 100 questionnaires into a statistical analysis package. Obviously this is dependent upon the length and complexity of the questionnaire, but you may need to allow yourself several days to do this.

These are just some of the activities you may find yourself undertaking as part of a research project. You need to timetable as many of the activities that you think you will be undertaking as soon as possible and ensure that your objectives are feasible within the time available to you.

Gaining collaboration and access

Developing a focused, feasible research proposal is, unfortunately, only part of the story. As part of your research, it is very likely that you will have to negotiate access to a sport-related body, whether it is a sport team, a school, sport organisation, local authority and so on. Securing good relations at an early stage can be extremely beneficial to you and can make the whole research process seem a lot easier, so it is worth considering three questions:

1   What organisation/school/team, etc. do I need to gain access to?
2   How likely are they to provide access?
3   What is the best way to gain access?

The issue of access is important, and one that you should think about sooner rather than later (it is no good completing your literature review, designing your questionnaire and so on, only to find out that you have no way of accessing your intended sample!). The two pieces of advice I can give are:

1   Be realistic. You may think that professional sport teams would be only too willing to distribute your questionnaires among their players and/or supporters. In reality, professional teams, governing bodies, etc. are often inundated with requests from students (often with requests such as 'Please, could you suggest an area for my dissertation?'!), and your chances of a positive response are minimal in most cases. If you do require assistance, then consider regional or local – rather than national – bodies. They are much more likely to be interested in your research, and they may be more willing to provide assistance.

2   Try to gain the cooperation of whichever body you choose at the earliest appropriate stage. This does not mean that you should approach them as soon as you have a rough idea of your research question. They are much more likely to be impressed if you can provide the following information:

   ● What is the rationale behind the research? Why is it important?
   ● What is the expertise of the researcher to undertake such a research project?
   ● What are the benefits for the particular body if they provide you access?
   ● What is the anticipated methodology? What data would you need to collect, and from whom?
   ● What is the timescale of the research?
   ● Will the organisation have the opportunity to view the research report before it is submitted?

- Will a copy be available to the organisation after the research is completed?
- How will confidentiality be ensured if the research involves sensitive information?

The first step is generally to telephone or email the organisation to identify the appropriate person to contact. If you are using a personal acquaintance (for example you may know someone who works for a particular organisation), then you should also find out whether they are the best person to deal with, or if there is someone else in the organisation that you should be in contact with. (There is no harm at this stage in approaching several different organisations to maximise your chances of access. Do ensure that if you receive an offer of help that you have to decline, then you should respond in writing explaining your reasons and thanking them for the offer.)

Your next stage, even if verbal agreement has been given, is to write to the appropriate individual within the organisation. Include the information about the project mentioned above. Put as much detail as you can into this letter. Following this, you should wait until you receive a response in writing before assuming that cooperation is assured! Finally, you should confirm your acceptance in writing and make arrangements for the next stage, which will often be a face-to-face meeting with the organisation.

The role of your tutor

So far, it may seem the case that you are on your own, that coming up with a suitable proposal is your task and that you are left to sink or swim. Thankfully this is not normally the case! Normally you will be allocated a tutor (also referred to as a supervisor) who will provide guidance throughout the research. The student-tutor relationship can be crucial to the success of the project in many cases. It is important to strike the right balance – a final-year dissertation, for example, is designed to test the student's ability to carry out a piece of in-depth research independently, yet you are not expected to undertake the task without any help or assistance at all. Different institutions have differing guidelines.

Frequently asked questions on dissertation tutors and their role

Q. What will my tutor do?
A. Your tutor will help you complete the research by providing guidance on key areas of the research. Your tutor will tell you whether you are on the right track or if anything is wrong. It is not the tutor's role, however, to give you a topic to research, to suggest the detailed methodology, to interpret the results for you or to keep in contact with you.

Q. *How often should I see my tutor?*
A. That is up to you and your tutor. Past experience has shown that no or minimal contact correlates with failed work. You should be aiming to see your tutor at least once every two weeks, sometimes more regularly, especially during key stages of the research. If there is a problem, then you must make alternative arrangements with your tutor. You should always have an agenda for your meeting – do not turn up without a clear idea of what you want to discuss.

Q. *What sort of things will I discuss with my tutor?*
A. The function of meetings will differ, depending upon the stage that you are at. Once you have decided upon your research question, it is often a good idea to produce written work on a regular basis, which can form the focus of the meeting. Do not expect the meeting to consist of your tutor giving you advice or telling you what to do. It is up to you to discuss and debate your project with them, and to lead the meetings. You must have an objective for each meeting with your tutor. You should discuss progress and attempt to resolve any issues that might detract from your ability to work towards maximum performance. Examples of these issues are:

- Recommendation of suitable references.
- Amendment of project objectives.
- Advice on carrying out research.
- Advice on suitability of research instruments, e.g. questionnaire/interview schedule.
- Advice on planning/scheduling your work, setting deadlines.
- Debate about theoretical issues.
- Making personal contacts.

Q. *Can I bring in work for my tutor to check on the day of my appointment, or should I hand it in prior to the meeting?*
A. Usually you will have a relatively short time allocated to you, thus you should not expect your tutor to give you feedback on the spot. Often it is a good idea to give work to your tutor in plenty of time. To do this, you will need to be well prepared!

Q. *Is the tutor responsible for getting me to complete the research?*
A. No. While the tutor acts as adviser and facilitator, the onus is clearly on you to be responsible for your own progress, to keep in contact with your tutor and to come to an agreement on frequency of attendance. Ideally, you should see your tutor at regular intervals. While it is difficult to come up with an optimum amount of contact, as suggested before, past experience has shown that no or minimal contact correlates with failed project work. Equally, the tutor does not expect you to be camped on their doorstep, nor to do the work for you!

Q. The skills being tested as part of the project include communication skills. Will my tutor check my spelling and grammar in my draft?
A. No. They will not have time to check for grammatical errors. It is up to you to have this done, through the use of spelling/grammar checkers in your word processing package and through using someone who is skilled in the use of English. You should not rely on spellcheckers, as they will not always pick out incorrect usage of words, e.g. there/their.

Q. Will my tutor mark individual chapters for me before I hand in the final submission?
A. No. While tutors may be prepared to look at drafts or rough sections of your work, do not expect any pre-marking. You should also be aware that even if you have completed a number of individual chapters, each of a good standard, that is no guarantee of a good grade. It is how the chapters link together as a holistic piece of work that is important. Thus, you may have a detailed and well-written methodology chapter, but if your chosen methodology is not appropriate to the research objectives developed from your review of literature, then the worth of the chapter is significantly reduced. Remember that all work that you hand to your tutor should be word-processed.

Q. Will my tutor tell me what to do if I have a problem with my project?
A. Your tutor will help you solve the problem, but do not expect them to solve the problem for you. Problem-solving is part of your work. Your tutor may suggest materials to read, refer you to someone else who may be able to give advice or give you some ideas on how to solve the problem. You should, whatever happens, make the most of your tutor – remember, they are there to help you! Conflict can, and does, happen, however, between tutor and student, often as a result of differing expectations. Phillips and Pugh (1994) provide a useful list that is informative for both students and tutors. They suggest that tutors expect students to:

- Be more independent than the student expects.
- Produce regular written work.
- Seek help from others, not just the tutor.
- Organise and attend meetings regularly at their own initiative.
- Follow advice given in those meetings.
- Report progress honestly.
- Be enthusiastic!

For their part, students expect their tutors to:

- Actively supervise them.
- Have a good knowledge of the subject area.

- Be friendly, open and supportive.
- Read and understand written work provided by the student.
- Be constructive in their criticisms.
- Recommend appropriate reading.

Thus, the student-tutor relationship is clearly a two-way process, and you should approach it as such. However, you need to remember that overall responsibility for the completion of the research project lies with the student!

Common faults in student research

It is a good idea at this stage to alert you to some of the most common faults that are found in research projects so that you may be aware of them before you commence, rather than reading about them when your research is almost complete! Although by no means an exhaustive list, these are the sorts of issues that you should consider and hopefully avoid!

- Poor time management. Often the time required to complete a piece of research is underestimated. Although the written research report may often be relatively short, the time required for the entire research process is disproportionate. It is simply not possible to leave a research project until the last minute and complete it successfully.
- The research question is too broad. If the topic is too broad, then it is difficult to cover it in sufficient depth. You must be focused and realistic in terms of what you can achieve. Often students are concerned that a focused question is unlikely to be able to provide them with the 10,000 or so words required by their institution. In reality, this is rarely a problem!
- The research is too descriptive. Often there is insufficient theoretical content to allow you to analyse and explain your findings. What theories are you using to inform your research? If you are unsure, then it is likely that your research will be descriptive rather than analytical.
- Not acknowledging the research process. There should be clear links between each section, and the research should follow a logical process, as highlighted in Chapter 2. The final written report should not read as a collection of unrelated chapters but as an integrated piece of work.
- Coming to conclusions that are not based upon the evidence. Remember that research adds to knowledge through considering evidence gathered with the purpose of answering your research question.
- Limited sources. Good research shows evidence of wider reading. Do not simply use sport-related books as your main source of information. You should also be using texts from your theoretical discipline (e.g. sociology or marketing) and also a wide range of journal articles.

- Lack of objectivity. The research can be based too much on personal opinion, anecdotal evidence and a lack of detachment. Often, the conclusions may not be based upon the evidence that is presented; rather they are selected to highlight a particular opinion of the author.
- Poor presentation. This is often a problem with rushed reports! The research report has to be acceptable in terms of spelling, grammar, punctuation, layout and overall appearance. If the report is being undertaken for a particular body or institution, ensure that you have adhered to its particular requirements (e.g. word limits, referencing format and so on).

Undertaking research in a pandemic

At the time of writing, we are still experiencing the impacts of COVID-19 upon our day-to-day activities, including research. It is appropriate, therefore, to explore some of the considerations that face us as researchers during times where previously taken-for-granted elements such as face-to-face contact and the ability to travel freely no longer apply. The COVID-19 pandemic did have a number of negative impacts upon researchers, but it also demonstrated that good, quality research can still take place within any restrictions that are laid down. The key questions that need to be asked are: (1) Do I collect data, and if so how can I do this given the constraints I face? and (2) Do I focus on already existing data?

In terms of the first question, research designs become much more difficult – for example experimental and ethnographic designs become increasingly hard. Others, such as cross-sectional and autoethnographic are much more feasible. In terms of the methods you might consider, some remain largely unaltered by a pandemic. An online survey, for example, can still be carried out (both quantitative and qualitative, as we outlined in Chapter 8). Analysis of online communities, such as when you undertake a netnographic study (Chapter 12), is an option (provided that the community under exploration has not been impacted by the pandemic). With other methods, there are a number of options available to adapt them to the context. Interviews, for example, can be done online through Zoom, Skype or WhatsApp (although this excludes participants without access to Wi-Fi or the necessary software). The key is, as a researcher, to assess the impact of this, for example it may well be that it is more difficult to develop rapport or trust with participants.

Deborah Lupton (2021) has compiled an excellent resource that outlines a wide range of other methods available to the researcher in a pandemic. These include the use of reflexive diaries, participants using wearable cameras and a technique called "Duoethnography", where students can investigate a phenomenon based on their own experiences by interviewing each other. Another alternative is to explore the wealth of data that already exists. We can analyse any text (for example, we can analyse social media, newspaper reports, television programmes and books to name just some). Instead of surveying fans' attitudes towards the proposed European Football League in soccer, for example, we could explore the Manchester City FC fan forum. One day after the league was announced, there were over 8,000 posts about it, a wealth of data easily accessible. The data generated on such a forum could even be argued to be much more authentic than, for example, that gained by interviewing fans, as it captures their feelings in a more 'natural' context.

Continuing your research career

Undertaking your research project might well inspire you to continue to do more research, for example by undertaking a research degree such as an MRes (typically 12 to 18 months), an MPhil (two to three years) or a PhD (a minimum of three years). These opportunities range from fully funded projects where the research topics are often already developed to self-funded programmes where you will have much more opportunity to develop your own research topic. There are a number of places where you can see what is on offer (for example, *www.jobs.ac.uk/search/phds* or *www.findaphd.com*). If you are thinking about this, then there are some key questions to consider:

- Why do you want to do further research? Is it to help your career aspirations, for example? If so, you need to be realistic about those prospects – there are more people graduating with sport-related PhDs than there are full-time academic posts for newly qualified PhD graduates. If it's because you enjoyed being a student and want to continue for another three years, then remember being a research student is very different from being an undergraduate student.
- You may have enjoyed a nine-month research project – would you still enjoy, and be motivated to complete, a project that may take three or four years?
- If you are able to develop your own research proposal, then what would you want to research? Simply replicating an undergraduate project won't be enough, so how will you identify an area that's worthy of postgraduate research?
- Where would you like to study? Don't become obsessed with league tables and reputations. Instead, you should undertake your research where there are people who are enthusiastic and expert about your subject. Also consider the broader support that is offered and the environment within which you will undertake the research (for example, desk space, additional training and so on). Your supervisor(s) will be crucial in terms of your overall experience, so make sure you spend some time finding out more about them – for example how many successful research degrees have they supervised?

Summary

- You can undertake research as a student for a number of purposes. A research project may be carried out to complete your study at undergraduate level and for most master's degrees. Alternatively, the research may form the basis of the entire degree, such as for some master's and most doctoral degrees.
- As a student, there are a number of key issues that you must consider about your research. Is it feasible given your timescale? Do you have the necessary resources to complete the research?
- One key issue is that of gaining collaboration. This is an important task and must be carried out carefully and thoughtfully. You need to be realistic in terms of your chosen partners.
- Use your tutor or supervisor appropriately. They are not there to do the research for you – but they can ensure that you are on the right track and give useful advice.

ABOUT YOUR RESEARCH PROJECT

Once you have been allocated your tutor or supervisor, you should ensure that you clarify each other's expectations at an early stage. What do you want from your tutor? What does your tutor expect from you? Doing this at an early stage can help prevent misunderstandings later on! If possible, write down each other's expectations for reference throughout the project.

Further reading

Dawson, C. (2019) *Introduction to Research Methods 5th Edition: A Practical Guide for Anyone Undertaking a Research Project*, Oxford: How To Books Ltd.

Phillips, E. and Pugh, D. (1994) *How to Get a PhD*, Buckinghamshire: Open University Press. (Although this book is aimed at PhD students, there is a lot of valuable information of use to the undergraduate researcher, especially at the beginning of a research project.)

Bibliography

Acton, C. and Miller, R. (2009) *SPSS for Social Scientists* (2nd edition), Basingstoke: Palgrave Macmillan.

Anderson, L. (2006) 'Analytical autoethnography', *Journal of Contemporary Ethnography* 35 (4), 373–95.

Andrews, D., Nonnecke, B. and Preece, J. (2003) 'Electronic survey methodology: A case study in reaching hard to involve Internet users', *International Journal of Human – Computer Interaction* 16 (2), 185–210.

Armour, K. and MacDonald, D. (2011) *Research Methods in Physical Education and Youth Sport*, London: Routledge.

Atkinson, P. and Hammersley, M. (1994) 'Ethnography and participant observation', in Denzin, N. and Lincoln, Y. (eds), *Handbook of Qualitative Research*, London: Sage, pp. 248–61.

Australian Bureau of Statistics. (2001) *The Impact of the Olympics on Participation in Australia: Trickle Down Effect, Discouragement Effect or no Effect?* Draft paper, Adelaide: Australian Bureau of Statistics (ABS).

Azzarito, L. (2012) 'Photography as a pedagogical tool for shedding light on "bodies-at-risk" in physical culture', *Visual Studies* 27 (3), 295–309.

Azzarito, L. and Kirk, D. (2013) *Pedagogies, Physical Culture and Visual Methods*, London: Routledge.

Baert, P. (2005) *Philosophy of the Social Sciences: Towards Pragmatism*, Cambridge: Polity Press.

Baker, T. (1994) *Doing Social Research*, New York: McGraw-Hill.

Banks, M. (2018) *Using Visual Data in Qualitative Research*, London: Sage.

Baranov, D. (2013) *Conceptual Foundations of Social Research Methods*, London: Routledge.

Barbour, K. (2018) 'Embodied ways of knowing: Revisiting feminist epistemology', in Mansfield, L., Caudwell, J., Wheaton, B. and Watson, B. (eds), *The Palgrave Handbook of Feminism and Sport, Leisure and Physical Education*, London: Palgrave Macmillan, pp. 209–26.

Barker, J., McCarthy, P., Jones, M. and Moran, A. (2011) *Single Case Research Methods in Sport and Exercise Psychology*, London: Routledge.

Beal, B. (2018) 'Feminist ethnographies in sport and leisure', in Mansfield, L., Caudwell, J., Wheaton, B. and Watson, B. (eds), *The Palgrave Handbook of Feminism and Sport, Leisure and Physical Education*, London: Palgrave Macmillan, pp. 227–42.

Berg, K. and Latin, R. (2008) *Essentials of Research Methods in Health, Physical Education, Exercise Science and Recreation* (3rd edition), Baltimore, MD: Lippincott, Williams and Wilkins.

Bergmann, I. (2020) 'Naturalness and the legitimacy of thoroughbred racing: A photo-elicitation study with industry and animal advocacy informants', *Animals*, 19 (9), 1–34.

Besnier, N., Brownell, S. and Carter, T. (2018) *The Anthropology of Sport: Bodies, Borders, Biopolitics*, Oakland: University of California Press.

Biddle, S., Markland, D., Gilbourne, D., Chatzisarantis, N. and Sparkes, A. (2001) 'Research methods in sport and exercise psychology: Quantitative and qualitative issues', *Journal of Sport Sciences* 19 (10), 777–809.

Biermeier-Hanson, B., Wynne, K., Thrasher, G. and Lyons, J. (2021) 'Modeling the joint effect of leader and follower authenticity on work and non-work outcomes', *The Journal of Psychology* 155 (2), 140–64.

Brackenridge, C. (1999) 'Managing myself', *International Review for the Sociology of Sport* 34 (4), 399–410.

Braun, V., Clarke, V., Boulton, E., Davey, L. and McEvoy, C. (2020) 'The online survey as a qualitative research tool', *International Journal of Social Research Methodology*, advance online publication, doi:10.1080/13645 579.2020.180555 (accessed 14 May 2021).

Bray, S., Martin, K. and Widemeyer, W. (2000) 'The relationship between evaluative concerns and sport competition state anxiety among youth skiers', *Journal of Sport Sciences* 18 (5), 353–61.

Brewer, J. (2000) *Ethnography*, Buckingham: Open University Press.

Brinkmann, S. and Kvale, S. (2014) *Interviews: Learning the Craft of Qualitative Research Interviewing*, London: Sage.

Brown, N. and Billings, A. (2013) 'Sports fans as crisis communicators on social media websites', *Public Relations Review* 39 (1), 74–81.

Brownell, S. (2006) 'Sport ethnography; A personal account', in Hobbs, D. and Wright, R. (eds), *The Sage Handbook of Field Research*, London: Sage, pp. 243–54.

Brustad, R. (2002) 'A critical analysis of knowledge construction in sport psychology', in Horn, T. (ed.) *Advances in Sport Psychology* (2nd edition), Champaign, IL: Human Kinetics, pp. 21–38.

Bryman, A. (2016) *Social Research Methods*, Oxford: Oxford University Press.

Brymer, E. and Schweitzer, R. (2013) 'The search for freedom in extreme sports: A phenomenological exploration', *Psychology of Sport and Exercise* 14 (6), 865–73.

Buckley, C. (2007) 'Doing your undergraduate dissertation using qualitative research: Tutor reflections', *Journal of Qualitative Research in Sports Studies* 1 (1), 89–93.

Butterworth, A. and Turner, D. (2014) 'Becoming a performance analyst: Autoethnographic reflections on agency, and facilitated transformational growth', *Reflective Practice: International and Multidisciplinary Perspectives* 15 (5), 552–62.

Carless, D. and Douglas, K. (2007) 'Narrative, identity and mental health: How men with serious mental illness re-story their lives through sport and exercise', *Psychology of Sport and Exercise* 9 (5), 576–94.

Caudwell, J. (2002) 'Women's experiences of sexuality within football contexts: A particular and located footballing epistemology', *Football Studies* 5 (1), 24–45.

Caudwell, J. (2020) 'Transgender and non-binary swimming in the UK: Indoor public pool spaces and un/safety', *Frontiers in Sociology* 5 (64), 1–12.

Chelladurai, P. (1990) 'Leadership in sports: A review', *International Journal of Sport Psychology* 21 (4), 328–54.

Chelladurai, P. and Saleh, S. (1980) 'Dimensions of leader behaviour in sports: Development of a leadership scale', *Journal of Sport Psychology* 2, 34–45.

Chen, C. (2021) '(Un)making the international student a settler of colour: A decolonising autoethnography', *Qualitative Research in Sport, Exercise and Health* 13 (5), 743–62.

Chen, N., Ji, S. and Funk, D. (2014) 'An extended study on destination image decay of sport tourists over time', *Journal of Destination Marketing and Management* 2 (4), 241–52.

Chen, Y., While, A. and Hicks, A. (2015) 'Physical activity among older people living alone in Shanghai, China', *Health Education Journal* 74 (2), 156–67.

Clarke, G. and Humberstone, B. (1997) *Researching Women and Sport*, London: Macmillan.

Clarke, M., Riley, M., Wilkie, E. and Wood, R. (1998) *Researching and Writing Dissertations in Hospitality and Tourism*, London: Thomson Business Press.

Coakley, J. (2009) *Sport in Society: Issues and Controversies* (10th edition), Boston, MA: McGraw-Hill.

Coakley, J. and Dunning, E. (eds) (2000) *Handbook of Sports Studies*, London: Sage.

Crawford, D., Jackson, E. and Godbey, G. (1991) 'A hierarchical model of leisure constraints', *Leisure Sciences*, 13 (4), 309–20.

Creswell, J. (1994) *Research Design: Qualitative and Quantitative Approaches*, Thousand Oaks, CA: Sage.

Creswell, J. and Creswell, J. (2018) *Research Design: Qualitative, Quantitative, and Mixed Methods Approaches*, Thousand Oaks, CA: Sage

Cronin, O., Jordan, J., Quigley, F. and Molloy, M. (2013) 'Prepared for sudden cardiac arrest? A cross-sectional study of automated external defibrillators in amateur sport', *British Journal of Sports Medicine* 47 (18), 1171–4.

Crotty, M. (1998) *The Foundations of Social Research*, London: Sage

Darnell, S. and Dao, M. (2017) 'Considering sport for development and peace through the capabilities approach', *Third World Thematics: A TWQ Journal* 2 (1), 23–36.

Dean, R. and Whyte, W. (1978) 'How do you know if the informant is telling the truth?', in Bynner, J. and Stribley, K. (eds), *Social Research: Principles and Procedures*, Harlow: Longman, pp. 179–88.

De Moragas, M. and Botela, M. (1995) *The Keys to Success: The Social, Sporting, Economic and Communications Impact of Barcelona'92*, Barcelona: Centre d'Estudis Olímpics i de l'Esport, Universitat Autònoma de Barcelona.

Denison, E., Faulkner, N., Jeanes, R. and Toole, D. (2020) 'Relationships between attitudes and norms with homophobic language use in male team sports', *Journal of Science and Medicine in Sport*, advanced online publication, doi:10.1016/j.jsams.2020.10.018 (accessed 28 March 2021).

Denscombe, M. (2002) *Ground Rules for Good Research: A Ten-point Guide for Social Researchers*, Buckingham: Open University Press.

Denzin, N. (1989) *Interpretive Biography*, London: Sage.

Denzin, N. and Lincoln, Y. (eds) (1994) *Handbook of Qualitative Research*, London: Sage.

Denzin, N. and Lincoln, Y. (eds) (1998) *Collecting and Interpreting Qualitative Materials*, London: Sage.

De Vaus, D. (2001) *Research Design in Social Research*, London: Sage.

Dey, I. (1993) *Qualitative Data Analysis*, London: Routledge.

Dijksterhuis, A. and van Knippenberg, A. (1998) 'The relation between perception and behavior, or how to win a game of Trivial Pursuit', *Journal of Personality and Social Psychology* 74 (4), 865–77.

Dingwall, R. (1997) 'Accounts, interviews and observations', in Miller, G. and Dingwall, R. (eds), *Context and Method in Qualitative Research*, London: Sage, pp. 51–65.

Dismore, H. and Bailey, R. (2005) '"If only": Outdoor and adventurous activities and generalised academic development', *Journal of Adventure Education and Outdoor Learning*, 5 (1), 9–19.

Dixon, A., Henry, T. and Martinez, J. (2013) 'Assessing the economic impact of sport tourists' expenditures related to a university's baseball season attendance', *Journal of Issues in Intercollegiate Athletics*, 6, 96–113.

Doherty, A. (2013) '"It takes a village:" Interdisciplinary research for sport management', *Journal of Sport Management* 27 (1), 1–10.

Dunn, J. (2003) *Locke: A Very Short Introduction*, Oxford: Oxford University Press.

Eagly, A. and Johnson, B. (1990) 'Gender and leadership style: A meta-analysis', *Psychological Bulletin* 108 (2), 233–56.

Edwards, A. and Skinner, M. (2009) *Qualitative Research in Sport Management*, Oxford: Butterworth-Heinemann.

Efron, S. and Ravid, R. (2018) *Writing the Literature Review: A Practical Guide*, New York: Guilford.

Ehrlén, V. and Villi, M. (2020) '"I shared the joy": Sport-related social support and communality on Instagram', *Visual Studies* 35 (2–3), 260–72.

Ehsani, M., Amiri, M. and Hossini, R. (2012) 'The relationship between leadership styles of coaches with coaching efficacy among elite Iranian judokas', *International Journal of Sport Studies*, 2 (8), 399–405.

Eichler, M. (1988) *Nonsexist Research Methods*, London: Routledge.

Eisner, E. W. (1998 [1991]) *The Enlightened Eye: Qualitative Inquiry and the Enhancement of Educational Practice*, New York: Macmillan.

Eysenbach, G. and Till, J. (2001) 'Ethical issues in qualitative research on Internet communities', *British Medical Journal* 323 (7321), 103–5.

Field, A. (2017) *Discovering Statistics Using SPSS*, London: Sage.

Finley, S. (2005) 'Art-based inquiry: Performing revolutionary pedagogy', in Denzin, N. K. and Lincoln, Y. S. (eds), *Handbook of Qualitative Research* (3rd edition), London: Sage, pp. 681–94.

Fishwick, L. and Leach, K. (1998) 'Game, set and match: Gender bias in television coverage of Wimbledon 1994', in Scraton, S. and Watson, R. (eds), *Sport, Leisure Identities and Gendered Spaces*, Eastbourne: Leisure Studies Association, pp. 31–44.

Fontana, A. and Frey, J. (1998) 'Interviewing: The art of science', in Denzin, N. and Lincoln, Y. (eds), *Collecting and Interpreting Qualitative Materials*, Thousand Oaks, CA: Sage, pp. 47–78.

Frankfort-Nachimas, C. and Nachimas, D. (1996) *Research Methods in the Social Sciences* (5th edition), London: Arnold.

Fuller, R., Percy, V., Bruening, J. and Cotrufo, R. (2013) 'Positive youth development: Minority male participation in a sport-based afterschool program in an urban environment', *Research Quarterly for Exercise and Sport* 84 (4), 469–82.

Funk, D. and James, J. (2006) 'Consumer loyalty: The meaning of attachment in the development of sport team allegiance', *Journal of Sport Management* 20 (2), 189–217.

Gall, M., Borg, W. and Gall, J. (1996) *Educational Research: An Introduction* (6th edition), White Plains, NY: Longman.

Gallmeier, C. (1988) 'Methodological issues in qualitative sport research: Participant observation among hockey players', *Sociological Spectrum* 8 (3), 213–35.

Gilhespy, I. (2006) 'The status of visual data in research methods textbooks for sport and leisure programmes', *Journal of Hospitality, Leisure, Sport and Tourism Education* 5 (2), 71–6.

Gill, F. and Johnson, P. (1997) *Research Methods for Managers* (2nd edition), London: Paul Chapman.

Giulianotti, R. (1995) 'Participant observation and research into football hooliganism: Reflections on the problems of entrée and everyday risks', *Sociology of Sport* 12 (1), 1–20.

Goss-Sampson, M. (2020) *Statistical analysis in JASP: A guide for students*, available at https://static.jasp-stats.org/Statistical%20Analysis%20in%20JASP%20-%20A%20Students%20Guide%20v2.pdf (accessed 1 February 2021).

Greene, J., Caracelli, V. and Graham, W. (1989) 'Toward a conceptual framework for mixed-method evaluation designs', *Educational Evaluation and Policy Analysis* 11 (3), 255–74.

Grills, S. (1998) 'An invitation to the field: Fieldwork and the pragmatists' lesson', in Grills, S. (ed.), *Doing Ethnographic Research: Fieldwork Settings*, Thousand Oaks, CA: Sage, pp. 3–18.

Gross, T. (2021) 'Bodies as arenas of experimentation: Experiencing novel ways of running', *Journal of Contemporary Ethnography*, advanced online publication, doi:10.1177/0891241621996789 (accessed 16 May 2021).

Gruneau, R. (1989) 'Making spectacle: A case study in television sports production', in Wenner, L. (ed.) *Media, Sports and Society*, Newbury Park, CA: Sage, pp. 134–54.

Guicciardi, M. and Pazzona, R. (2020) 'The rebooting in sports and physical activities after COVID-19 Italian lockdown: An exploratory study', *Frontiers in Psychology*, available at www.frontiersin.org/articles/10.3389/fpsyg.2020.607233/full (accessed 10 June 2021).

Guillemin, M. and Drew, S. (2010) 'Questions of process in participant-generated visual methodologies', *Visual Studies* 25 (2), 175–88.

Gwartz, E. and Spence, K. (2020) 'Conscious capitalism and sport: Exploring higher purpose in a professional sport organization', *Sport Management Review* 23 (4), 750–63.

Hallmann, K., Feiler, S., Muller, S. and Breuer, C. (2012) 'The interrelationship between sport activities and the perceived winter sport experience' *Journal of Sport and Tourism* 17 (2), 145–63.

Hammersley, M. and Atkinson, P. (2007) *Ethnography: Principles in Practice*, London: Routledge.

Hannabus, S. (1996) 'Research interviews', *New Library World* 97 (1129), 22–30.

Hanni, S., Vedung, F., Tegner, Y., Marklund, N. and Johansson, J. (2020) 'Soccer-related concussions among Swedish elite soccer players: A descriptive study of 1030 players', *Frontiers in Neurology*, available at www.ncbi.nlm.nih.gov/pmc/articles/PMC7538773/ (accessed 10 June 2021).

Harley, E., Stepan, L. and Scher, I. (2020) 'An observational study of skier compliance with posted "slow" signs and ski patrollers', *Journal of Science and Medicine in Sport*, advanced online publication, doi:10.1016/j.jsams.2020.12.008 (accessed 11 May 2021).

Hart, C. (2009) *Doing a Literature Review: Releasing the Social Science Research Imagination*, London: Sage.

Hindson, A., Gidlow, B. and Peebles, C. (1994) 'The "trickle-down" effect of top-level sport: Myth or reality? A case study of the Olympics', *Australian Journal of Leisure and Recreation*, 4 (1), 16–24.

Hing, N., Vitartas, P., Lamont, M. and Fink, E. (2014) 'Adolescent exposure to gambling promotions during televised sport: An exploratory study of links with gambling intentions', *International Gambling Studies* 14 (3), 374–93.

Hoeber, L. and Shaw, S. (2017) 'Contemporary qualitative research methods in sport management', *Sport Management Review* 20 (1), 4–7.

Hogan, K. and Norton, K. (2000) 'The "price" of Olympic gold', *Journal of Science and Medicine in Sport* 3 (2), 203–18.

Holloway, I. and Wheeler, S. (2009) *Qualitative Research in Nursing and Healthcare*, Oxford: Blackwell.

Holt, N., Scherer, J. and Kock, J. (2013) 'An ethnographic study of issues surrounding the provision of sport opportunities to young men from a western Canadian inner-city', *Psychology of Sport and Exercise* 14 (4), 538–48.

Holt, N. and Sparkes, A. (2001) 'An ethnographic study of cohesiveness in a college team over a season', *The Sport Psychologist* 15 (3), 237–59.

Holt, R. (1989) *Sport and the British*, Oxford: Blackwell.

Hooley, T., Marriott, J. and Wellens, J. (2012) *What is Online Research?* London: Bloomsbury.

Hoon Lee, Y., Woo, B. and Kim, Y. (2018) 'Transformational leadership and organizational citizenship behavior: Mediating role of affective commitment', *International Journal of Sports Science & Coaching* 13 (3), 373–82.

Hoskyn, K., Dickson, G. and Sotiriadou, P. (2018) 'Leveraging medium-sized sport events to attract club participants', *Marketing Intelligence & Planning* 36 (2), 199–212.

Houlihan, B. (2007) *Sport and Society: A Student Introduction* (2nd edition), London: Sage.

Howells, K., Bowen, J. and McMartin, C. (2019) 'The adoption of the daily mile as an active mile initiative: The children's and teachers' voices', *Physical Education Matters*, Autumn 2019, 37–39.

Hussain, U. and Cunningham, G. (2020) 'These are "our" sports': Kabaddi and kho-kho women athletes from the Islamic republic of Pakistan', *International Review for the Sociology of Sport*, advanced online publication, doi:10.1177/101269 0220968111 (accessed 21 March 2021).

Hussey, J. and Hussey, R. (1997) *Business Research*, Basingstoke: Macmillan.

Hutchins, B. and Rowe, D. (2012) *Sport Beyond Television*, Abingdon: Routledge.

Hylton, K. (2009) '*Race' and Sport*, London: Routledge.

Ikramullah, A., Koutrou, N. and Pappous, S. (2018) 'Sportivate: A case study of sports policy implementation and impact on the sustainability of community physical activity programmes', *The International Journal of Sport and Society* 9 (3), 1–20.

Ingham, A. and Donnelly, P. (1992) 'Whose knowledge counts?', in Yiannakis, A. and Greendorfer, S. (eds), *Applied Sociology of Sport*, Champaign, IL: Human Kinetics, pp. 247–55.

Jackson, K. and Bazeley, P. (2019) *Qualitative Data Analysis with NVivo*, London: Sage.

Jakobsen, J., Solberg, H., Halvorsen, T. and Jakobsen, T. (2013) 'Fool's gold: Major sport events and foreign direct investment', *International Journal of Sport Policy and Politics* 5 (3), 363–80.

Jankowicz, A. (1995) *Business Research Projects* (2nd edition), London: Chapman-Hall.

Jankowicz, A. (2000) *Business Research Projects* (3rd edition), London: Thomson.

Jarvie, G. (2012) *Sport, Culture and Society*, London: Routledge.

Jayaratne, T. (1993) 'Quantitative methodology and feminist research', in Hammersley, M. (ed.) *Social Research: Philosophy, Politics and Practice*, London: Sage, pp. 109–23.

Jiang, K. and Bairner, A. (2020) 'Chinese football fandom and civic identities: A study of the fans of Shanghai Shenhua and Beijing Guoan', *Sport in Society* 23 (12), 2078–98.

Jones, C. (2014) 'Sports ethics: Drunken role models: Rescuing our sporting exemplars', in Neil, R., Hanton, S., Fleming, S. and Wilson, K. (eds), *The Research Process in Sport, Exercise and Health: Case Studies of Active Researchers*, London: Routledge, pp. 5–20.

Jones, I., Brown, L. and Holloway, I. (2013) *Qualitative Research in Sport and Physical Activity*, London: Sage.

Jowett, S. and Frost, T. (2007) 'Race/ethnicity in the all-male coach – athlete relationship: Black footballers' narratives', *International Journal of Sport and Exercise Psychology* 5 (3), 255–69.

Kavanagh, E., Jones, I. and Sheppard-Marks, L. (2016) 'Towards typologies of virtual maltreatment: Sport, digital cultures & dark leisure', *Leisure Studies* 35 (6), 783–96.

Keegan, R., Harwood, C., Spray, C. and Lavallee, D. (2014) 'A qualitative investigation of the motivational climate in elite sport', *Psychology of Sport and Exercise* 15 (1), 97–107.

Kellehear, A. (1993) *The Unobtrusive Researcher*, St Leonards, NSW: Allen & Unwin.

Keogh, J., Power, N., Wooller, L., Lucas, P. and Whatman, C. (2014) 'Physical and psychosocial function in residential aged care elders: Effect of Nintendo Wii sports games', *Journal of Aging and Physical Activity* 22 (2), 235–44.

Kerrigan, F., Larsen, G., Hanratty, S. and Korta, K. (2014) 'Gimme shelter': Experiencing pleasurable escape through the musicalisation of running', *Marketing Theory* 14 (2), 147–66.

Khasnis, U., Chapman, P., Toering, T. and Collins, D. (2021) 'Focus on the people: Key stakeholders' perceptions of elite sport in India and its potential for development', *Managing Sport and Leisure*, advanced online publication, doi:10.1080/2 3750472.2021.1877568 (accessed 1 June 2021).

Kim, J., Godfrey, M. and Eys, M. (2020) 'A double-edged sword: The nature of team comedians in sport teams', *Journal of Applied Sport Psychology*, advanced online publication, doi:10.1080/10413200.2020.1759158 (accessed 16 October 2021).

Kim, J. and Taggart, A. (2004) 'Teachers' perception of the culture of physical education: Investigating the silences at Hana primary school', *Issues in Educational Research*, available at www.iier.org.au/iier14/kim.html (accessed 9 September 2009).

Kim, Y. and Lee, J. (2019) 'Common mistakes in statistical and methodological practices of sport management research', *Measurement in Physical Education and Exercise Science* 23 (4), 314–24.

King, N. and Horrocks, C. (2010) *Interviews in Qualitative Research*, London: Sage.

Knott, B. (2014) '*The strategic contribution of sport mega events to nation branding: The case of South Africa and the 2010 FIFA World Cup*', unpublished PhD thesis, School of Tourism, Bournemouth University.

Knowles, A., Niven, A. and Fawkner, S. (2014) 'Once upon a time I used to be active: Adopting a narrative approach to understanding physical activity behavior in adolescent girls', *Qualitative Research in Sport, Exercise and Health* 6 (1), 62–76.

Kozinets, R. (2010) *Netnography: Doing Ethnographic Research Online*, Los Angeles, CA: Sage.

Krane, V. Anderson, M. and Stean, W. (1997) 'Issues of qualitative research methods and presentation', *Journal of Sport and Exercise Psychology* 19 (2), 213–18.

Kvale, S. (1996) *Interviews: An Introduction to Qualitative Research Interviewing*, Thousand Oaks, CA: Sage.

Kvale, S. (2007) *Doing Interviews*, London: Sage.

Lee, R. and Fielding, N. (1996) 'Qualitative data analysis: Representations of technology: A comment on Coffey, Holbrook and Atkinson', *Sociological Research Online* 1 (4), available at www.socresonline.org.uk/1/4/lf.html (accessed 9 September 2009).

Leedy, P. (1985) *Practical Research: Planning and Design*, New York: Macmillan.

Lewins, A. and Silver, C. (2007) *Using Software in Qualitative Research: A Step-by-Step Guide*, London: Sage.

Li, B., Scott, O., Naraine, M. and Ruihley, B. (2021) 'Tell me a story: Exploring elite female athletes' self-presentation via an analysis of Instagram stories', *Journal of Interactive Advertising*, advanced online publication, doi:10.1080/15252019.2020.1837038 (accessed 12 June 2021).

Lincoln, Y. and Guba, E. (1985) *Naturalistic Inquiry*, Newbury Park, CA: Sage.

Lizzo, R. and Liechty, T. (2020) 'The *Hogwarts Running Club* and sense of community: A netnography of a virtual community', *Leisure Sciences*, advanced online publication, doi:10.1080/01490400.2020.1755751 (accessed 8 May 2021).

Lloyd, B., Matthews, S., Livingston, M., Jayasekara, H. and Smith, K. (2013) 'Alcohol intoxication in the context of major public holidays, sporting and social events: A time-series analysis in Melbourne, Australia, 2000–2009', *Addiction* 108 (4), 701–9.

Lonsdale, C., Hodge, K. and Rose, E. (2006) 'Pixel vs paper: Comparing online and traditional survey methods in sport psychology', *Journal of Sport and Exercise Psychology* 28 (1), 10–108.

Lucas, S. (2000) 'Nike's commercial solution', *International Review for the Sociology of Sport* 35 (2), 149–64.

Luna, P., Rodríguez-Donaire, A., Rodrigo-Ruiz, D. and Cejudo, J. (2020) 'Subjective well-being and psychosocial adjustment: Examining the effects of an intervention based on the Sport Education Model on children', *Sustainability* 12 (11), 1–15.

Lupton, D. (ed) (2021) *Doing fieldwork in a pandemic (crowd-sourced document)*, revised version, available at https://docs.google.com/document/d/1clGjGABB2h-2qbduTgfqribHmog9B6P0NvMgVuiHZCl8/edit (accessed 2 March 2021).

MacClancy, J. (1996) 'Nationalism at play', in MacClancy, J. (ed.) *Sport, Identity and Ethnicity*, Oxford: Berg, pp. 1–19.

Madrigal, R. (1995) 'Cognitive and affective determinants of fan satisfaction with sporting event attendance', *Journal of Leisure Research* 27 (3), 205–27.

Malhotra, A. (2021) 'The postpandemic future of work', *Journal of Management* 47 (5), 1091–102.

Mansfield, L., Caudwell, J., Wheaton, B. and Watson, B. (eds) (2018) *The Palgrave Handbook of Feminism and Sport, Leisure and Physical Education*, London: Palgrave Macmillan.

Marshall, P., Walker, D. and Russo, N. (2010) 'Mediating the Olympics', *Convergence* 16 (3), 263–78.

Martinent, G., Campo, M. and Ferran, C. (2012) 'A descriptive study of emotional process during competition: Nature, frequency, direction, duration and co-occurrence of discrete emotions', *Psychology of Sport and Exercise* 13 (2), 142–51.

Matlin, M. and Gawron, V. (1979) 'Individual differences in Pollyannaism', *Journal of Personality Assessment* 43 (4), 411–12.

McGannon, K. and Pomerleau-Fontaine, L. (2020) 'Extreme sport, identity, and well-being: A case study and narrative approach to elite skyrunning', *Case Studies in Sport and Exercise Psychology* 4 (S1), S1:8–S1:16.

McGuire-Adams, T. (2020) 'Paradigm shifting: Centering Indigenous research methodologies, an Anishinaabe perspective', *Qualitative Research in Sport, Exercise and Health* 12 (1), 34–47.

McNamee, M., Olivier, S. and Wainwright, P. (2007) *Research Ethics in Exercise, Health and Sports Sciences*, London: Routledge.

Mhanna, R., Blake, A. and Jones, I. (2019) 'Spreading tourists around host countries of mega sport events: A strategy to overcome overtourism in host cities', *Worldwide Hospitality and Tourism Themes* 11 (5), 611–26.

Miles, M. and Huberman, A. (1994) *Qualitative Data Analysis*, Thousand Oaks, CA: Sage.

Mills, C. and Hoeber, L. (2013) 'Using photo-elicitation to examine artefacts in a sport club: Logistical considerations and strategies throughout the research process', *Qualitative Research in Sport, Exercise and Health* 5 (1), 1–20.

Mitchell, R., Agle, B. and Wood, D. (1997), 'Theory of stakeholder identification and salience: Defining the principle of who and what really counts', *Academy of Management Review* 22 (4), 853–86.

M'mbaha, J. and Chepyator-Thomson, R. (2019) 'Factors influencing career paths and progress of Kenyan women in sport leadership', *Qualitative Research in Sport, Exercise and Health* 11 (3), 316–33.

Moyo, L., Swart, K. and Hattingh, C. (2020) 'Repeat visitation to a host destination post a sport mega-event: South Africa and the 2010 FIFA World Cup legacy', *African Journal of Hospitality, Tourism and Leisure* 9 (3), 57–72

Muslim, M., Bakar, Z. and Omar, Z. (2021) 'Using qualitative research in identifying and developing young talents in elite amateur golf in Malaysia', *Jurnal Penyelidikan Sains Sosial* 4 (10), 117–26.

Nakray, K., Alston, M. and Whittenbury, K. (2015) *Social Science Research Ethics for a Globalizing World – Interdisciplinary and Cross-Cultural Perspectives*, New York: Routledge.

Nau, D. (1995) 'Mixing methodologies: Can bimodal research be a viable postpositivist tool?', *The Qualitative Report* 2 (3), available at www.nova.edu/ssss/QR/QR2-3/nau.html (accessed 9 May 2014).

Neil, R., Hanton, S., Fleming, S. and Wilson, K. (2014) *The Research Process in Sport, Exercise and Health: Case Studies of Active Researchers*, London: Routledge.

Neuendorf, K. (2001) *The Content Analysis Guidebook*, London: Sage.

Neuman, W. (2000) *Social Research Methods: Qualitative and Quantitative Approaches* (4th edition), Boston, MA: Allyn and Bacon.

Nixon, H. and Frey, J. (1996) *A Sociology of Sport*, Belmont, CA: Wadsworth.

Ntoumanis, M. (2009) *A Step-by-Step Guide to SPSS for Sport and Exercise Studies* (2nd edition), London: Routledge.

O'Donoghue, P. (2012) *Statistics for Sport and Exercise Studies: An Introduction*, London: Routledge.

Oman, S. (2020) 'Leisure pursuits: Uncovering the "selective tradition" in culture and well-being evidence for policy', *Leisure Studies* 39 (1), 11–25.

Oppenheim, A. (1992) *Questionnaire Design, Interviewing and Attitude Measurement*, London: Pinter.

Osmond, G. and Phillips, M. (2019) 'Yarning about sport: Indigenous research methodologies and transformative historical narratives', *The International Journal of the History of Sport* 36 (13–14), 1271–88.

Owusu-Sekyere, F., Rhind, D. and Hills, L. (2021) 'Safeguarding culture: Towards a new approach to preventing child maltreatment in sport', *Sport Management Review*, advanced online publication, doi:10.1080/14413523.2021.1930951 (accessed 17 June 2021).

Palmer, C. (2000) 'Spin doctors and sportsbrokers: Researching elites in contemporary sport – A research note on the *Tour de France*', *International Review for the Sociology of Sport* 35 (3), 364–77.

Papathomas, A. and Lavallee, D. (2013) 'Self starvation and the performance narrative in competitive sport', *Psychology of Sport and Exercise* 15 (6), 688–95.

Perkins, K., Columna, L., Lieberman, L. and Bailey, J. (2013) 'Parents' perceptions of physical activity for their children with visual impairments', *Journal of Visual Impairment & Blindness* 107 (2), 131–42.

Peshkin, A. (1988) 'In search of subjectivity: One's own', *Educational Researcher* 17 (7), 17–21.

Phillips, E. and Pugh, D. (1994) *How to get a PhD*, Buckingham: Open University Press.

Pink, S. and Morgan, J. (2013) 'Short-term ethnography: Intense routes to knowing', *Symbolic Interaction* 36 (3), 351–61.

Podlog, L., Wadey, R., Stark, A., Lochbaum, M., Hannon, J. and Newton, M. (2013) 'An adolescent perspective on injury recovery and the return to sport', *Psychology of Sport and Exercise* 14 (4), 437–46.

Pol, L. and Pak, S. (1994) 'The use of a two-stage survey design for gathering data from people who attend sporting events', *Sport Marketing Quarterly* 3 (3), 9–12.

Poynter, R. (2010) *The Handbook of Online and Social Media Research*, Chichester: Wiley.

Richard, R., Burlot, F., Duquesne, V. and Joncheray, H. (2021) '"I had a dream: It was to play the games": Sports socialisation processes of French Paralympic athletes', *European Journal for Sport and Society*, advanced online publication, doi: 10.1080/16138171.2021.1878438 (accessed 17 May 2021).

Richards, J. (2015) 'Which player do you fancy then? Locating the female ethnographer in the field of the sociology of sport', *Soccer & Society* 16 (2–3), 393–404.

Ridley, D. (2012) *The Literature Review: A Step-by-Step Guide for Students*, London: Sage.

Riemer, H. and Chelladurai, P. (1998) 'Development of the athlete satisfaction questionnaire (ASQ)', *Journal of Sport and Exercise Psychology* 20 (2), 127–56.

Riff, D., Lacy, S., Fico, F, and Watson, B. (2019) *Analyzing Media Messages: Using Quantitative Content Analysis in Research*, New York: Routledge.

Roberts, J., Jones, R., Harwood, C., Mitchell, S. and Rothberg, S. (2001) 'Human perceptions of sports equipment under playing conditions', *Journal of Sport Sciences* 19 (7), 485–97.

Rosenthal, R. and Jacobsen, L. (1968) *Pygmalion in the Classroom*, New York: Rinehart and Winston.

Rovio, E., Arvinen-Barrow, M., Weigand, D., Eskola, J. and Lintunen, T. (2012) 'Using team building methods with an ice hockey team: An action research case study', *Sport Psychologist* 26 (4), 584–603.

Sands, R. (2002) *Sport Ethnography*, Champaign, IL: Human Kinetics.

Saunders, M., Lewis, P. and Thornhill, A. (2000) *Research Methods for Business Students* (2nd edition), Harlow: Prentice Hall.

Scelles, N., Durand, C., Bonnal, L., Goyeau, D. and Andreff, W. (2013) 'Competitive balance versus competitive intensity before a match: Is one of these two concepts more relevant in explaining attendance? The case of the French football Ligue 1 over the period 2008–2011', *Applied Economics* 45 (29), 4184–92.

Schreier, M. (2012) *Qualitative Content Analysis in Practice*, London: Sage.

Seidman, I. (1991) *Interviewing as Qualitative Research*, New York: Teachers College Press.

Silk, M. (2005) 'Sporting ethnography: Philosophy, methodology and reflection', in Andrews, D., Mason, D. and Silk, M. (eds), *Qualitative Methods in Sports Studies*, Oxford: Berg, pp. 65–103.

Silverman, D. (2006) *Interpreting Qualitative Data* (3rd edition), London: Sage.

Silverman, D. (2020) *Interpreting Qualitative Data* (5th edition), London: Sage.

Siuda, P. (2021) 'Sports gamers practices as a form of subversiveness – the example of the FIFA ultimate team', *Critical Studies in Media Communication* 38 (1), 75–89.

Smith, A., Stavros, C., Westberg, K., Wilson, B. and Boyle, C. (2014) 'Alcohol-related player behavioral transgressions: Incidences, fan media responses, and a harm-reduction alternative', *International Review for the Sociology of Sport* 49 (3–4), 400–16.

Smith, A. and Stewart, B. (2001) 'Beyond number crunching: Applying qualitative techniques in sport marketing research', *The Qualitative Report* 6 (2), available at www.nova.edu/ssss/QR/QR6-2/smith.html (accessed 9 May 2014).

Smith, M., Arnold, R. and Thelwell, R. (2018) '"There's no place to hide": Exploring the stressors encountered by elite cricket captains', *Journal of Applied Sport Psychology*' 30 (2), 150–70.

Smith-Tran, A. (2021) '"Finally something for us": Black girls run! and racialized space-making in recreational running', *Journal of Sport and Social Issues* 45 (3), 235–50.

South, J., Woodall, J., Southby, K, Jones, R., Yates, G., Kinsella, K. and May, E. (2020) 'Volunteerism, social context and health impacts: A qualitative study of Glasgow Commonwealth Games event volunteers', *Cities & Health*, advanced online publication, doi:10.1080/23748834.2020.1791424 (accessed 28 March 2021).

Spaaij, R. and Thiel, A. (2017) 'Big data: Critical questions for sport and society', *European Journal for Sport and Society* 14 (1), 1–4.

Sparkes, A. (2000) 'Illness, premature career-termination, and the loss of self', in Jones, R. and Armour, K. (eds), *Sociology of Sport: Theory and Practice*, Harlow: Longman, pp. 13–28.

Sparkes, A. (2002) *Telling Tales in Sport and Physical Activity*, Champaign, IL: Human Kinetics.

Sparkes, A. (2009) 'Ethnography and the senses: Challenges and possibilities', *Qualitative Research in Sport and Exercise* 1 (1), 21–35.

Sport England (2002) *What We Do – Evaluating the Regional Economic Impact of Sport (2002–03)*, London: Sport England.

Stein, A., Mitgutsch, K. and Consalvo, M. (2013) 'Who are the sport gamers? A large scale study of sports video game players', *Convergence* 19 (3), 345–63.

Stewart, L., Oates, J. and O'Halloran, P. (2020) '"My voice is my identity": The role of voice for trans women's participation in sport', *Journal of Voice* 34 (1), 78–87.

Stone, B. (2009) 'Running man', *Qualitative Research in Sport and Exercise* 1 (1), 67–71.

Su, Y., Baker, B., Doyle, J. and Yan, M. (2020) 'Fan Engagement in 15 Seconds: Athletes' Relationship Marketing During a Pandemic via TikTok', *International Journal of Sport Communication*, 13 (3), 436–46.

Sugden, J. (1996) *Boxing and Society*, Manchester: Manchester University Press.

Sugden, J. (2021) 'Sport and ethno-racial formation: Imagined distance in Fiji', *Sport in Society* 24 (6), 847–66.

Suler, J. (2004) 'The online disinhibition effect', *CyberPsychology and Behavior* 7 (June), 321–26

Sust, F. (1995) 'The sports legacy of the Barcelona Games', in De Moragas, M. and Botela, M. (eds), *The Keys to Success: The Social, Sporting, Economic and Communications Impact of Barcelona'92*, Barcelona: Centre d'Estudis Olímpics i de l'Esport, Universitat Autònoma de Barcelona, pp. 261–65.

Swart, K. and Maralack, D. (2020) 'COVID-19 and the cancellation of the 2020 Two Oceans Marathon, Cape Town, South Africa', *Sport in Society* 23 (11), 1736–52.

Tainsky, S. and Babiak, K. (2011) 'Professional athletes and charitable foundations: An exploratory investigation', *International Journal of Sport Management and Marketing* 9 (3/4), 133–53.

Taylor, S., Eklund, R. and Arthur, C. (2021) 'Fear of failure in sport, exercise, and physical activity: A scoping review', *International Review of Sport and Exercise Psychology*, advanced online publication, doi:10.1080/1750984X.2021.1901299 (accessed 10 June 2021).

Thomas, J. and Nelson, J. (2010) *Research Methods in Physical Activity* (6th edition), Champaign, IL: Human Kinetics.

Truno, E. (1995) 'Barcelona: City of sport', in De Moragas, M. and Botela, M. (eds), *The Keys to Success: The Social, Sporting, Economic and Communications Impact of Barcelona'92*, Barcelona: Centre d'Estudis Olimpics i de l'Esport, Universitat Autonoma de Barcelona, pp. 43–56.

Turner, J. (2013) 'A longitudinal content analysis of gender and ethnicity portrayals on ESPN's SportsCenter from 1999 to 2009', *Communication & Sport* 1 (1), 1–27.

Turnnidge, J., Côté, J., Hollenstein, T. and Deakin, J. (2014) 'A direct observation of the dynamic content and structure of coach – athlete interactions in a model sport program', *Journal of Applied Sport Psychology* 26 (2), 225–40.

UK Sport (1999) *Major Events, The Economics: A Guide*, London: UK Sport.

Van der Roest, J., Spaaij, R. and van Bottenburg, M. (2013) 'Mixed methods in emerging academic subdisciplines: The case of sport management', *Journal of Mixed Methods Research* 9 (1), 70–90.

Van der Veken, K., Lauwerier, E. and Willems, S. (2020) 'How community sport programs may improve the health of vulnerable population groups: A program theory', *International Journal for Equity in Health*, 19 (1), 1–12.

Veal, A. (2006) *Research Methods for Leisure and Tourism: A Practical Guide* (3rd edition), Harlow: Prentice Hall.

Veal, A. and Darcy, S. (2014) *Research Methods in Sport Studies and Sport Management: A Practical Guide*, London: Routledge.

Veal, A., Toohey, K. and Frawley, S. (2012) 'The sport participation legacy of the Sydney 2000 Olympic Games and other international sporting events hosted in Australia', *Journal of Policy Research in Tourism, Leisure and Events* 4 (2), 155–84.

Veal, A., Toohey, K. and Frawley, S. (2019) 'Sport participation, international sports events and the "trickle-down effect"', *Journal of Policy Research in Tourism, Leisure and Events* 11 (sup1), s3–s7.

Vincent, W. (2005) *Statistics in Kinesiology* (3rd edition), Champaign, IL: Human Kinetics.

Voldby, C. and Klein-Døssing, R. (2020) '"I thought we were supposed to learn how to become better coaches": Developing coach education through action research', *Educational Action Research* 28 (3), 534–53.

Walliman, N. (2001) *Doing Your Research Project*, London: Sage.

Walseth, K. (2007) 'Sport and belonging', *International Review for the Sociology of Sport* 41 (3/4), 447–64.

Wann, D. (1997) *Sports Psychology*, Upper Saddle River, NJ: Prentice Hall.

Waring, M., Warburton, P. and Coy, M. (2007) 'Observation of children's physical activity levels in primary school: Is the school an ideal setting for meeting government activity targets?', *European Physical Activity Review* 13 (1), 25–40.

Watson, B. (2018) 'Thinking intersectionally and why difference (still) matters in feminist leisure and sport research', in Mansfield, L., Caudwell, J., Wheaton, B. and Watson, B. (eds), *The Palgrave Handbook of Feminism and Sport, Leisure and Physical Education*, London: Palgrave Macmillan, pp. 313–34.

Watson, B. and Scraton, S. (2001) 'Confronting whiteness? Researching the leisure lives of South Asian mothers', *Journal of Gender Studies* 10 (3), 265–75.

Weiss, R. (1995) *Learning from Strangers: The Art and Method of Qualitative Interview Studies*, New York: Simon and Schuster.

Weyers, J. and MacMillan, K. (2009) *How to Write Dissertations and Research Projects*, Upper Saddle River, NJ: Prentice Hall.

Worsley, P. (1992) *The New Introducing Sociology*, London: Penguin.

Wright, K. (2005) 'Researching internet-based populations: Advantages and disadvantages of online survey research, online questionnaire authoring software packages, and web survey services', *Journal of Computer-Mediated Communication* 10 (3), article 11, available at http://onlinelibrary.wiley.com/doi/10.1111/j.1083-6101.2005.tb00259.x/full (accessed 13 May 2009).

Yamada, M., Kimura, Y., Ishivama, D., Otobe, Y., Suzuki, M., Koyama, S., Kikuchi, T., Kusumi, H. and Arai, H. (2020) 'Effect of the COVID-19 epidemic on physical activity in community-dwelling older adults in Japan: A cross-sectional online survey', *The Journal of Nutrition, Health & Aging* 24 (9), 948–50.

Yin, R. (1994) *Case Study Research: Design and Methods* (2nd edition), London: Sage.

Yin, R. (2008) *Case Study Research: Design and Methods* (4th edition), London: Sage.

Yoo, E. (2021) '"I can't just post anything I want": Self-management of South Korean sports stars on social media', *International Review for the Sociology of Sport*, advanced online publication, doi:10.1177/10126902211014122 (accessed 22 June 2021).

Index

Page numbers in *italics* indicate a figure and page numbers in **bold** indicate a table on the corresponding page.